T0385470

Black
Scholarship
in a
White
Academy

Black Scholarship in a White Academy

PERSEVERANCE IN THE FACE OF INJUSTICE

Edited by
ROBERT T. PALMER,
ALONZO M. FLOWERS III,
and SOSANYA JONES

JOHNS HOPKINS UNIVERSITY PRESS | *Baltimore*

© 2023 Johns Hopkins University Press
All rights reserved. Published 2023
Printed in the United States of America on acid-free paper

2 4 6 8 9 7 5 3 1

Johns Hopkins University Press
2715 North Charles Street
Baltimore, Maryland 21218
www.press.jhu.edu

Cataloging-in-Publication Data is available from the Library of Congress.
A catalog record for this book is available from the British Library.

ISBN: 978-1-4214-4746-9 (hardcover)
ISBN: 978-1-4214-4747-6 (ebook)

*Special discounts are available for bulk purchases of this book. For more information,
please contact Special Sales at specialsales@jh.edu.*

To all critical scholars seeking to make change.
And to all the Black scholars whose voices remain muted
by the systematic policies and procedures within the academy that
continue to support anti-Blackness and resist social change.
Through critical reflection, counternarratives, and
open dialogue, our stories will elevate change.

CONTENTS

ACKNOWLEDGMENTS

ROBERT T. PALMER
I am grateful to Alonzo M. Flowers III for inspiring the idea for this book and to Sosanya Jones for working with Alonzo and me to bring it to fruition. I would also like to dedicate this book to the many faculty colleagues and mentors who have poured their wisdom into me and given unselfishly of themselves to help me grow and develop professionally.

ALONZO M. FLOWERS III
This work would not have been possible without the collaboration among the editorial team (Rob, Katrina, and Nicole) at the *Journal of African American Males in Higher Education*. I am especially indebted to Drs. Palmer and Jones for their commitment to this work and their dedication to social justice and change. Finally, nobody has been more important to me in the pursuit of educational change than the members of my family. I wish to thank my loving and supportive husband, Ricky; our two wonderful children, Michael and Jonathan; and our amazing pups, Bailey and Bella-Rose, all of whom provide me with unending inspiration and hope.

SOSANYA JONES
To the freedom fighters who suffered in silence while standing in the gap to serve as teachers, mentors, guardian angels, providers, confidants, and friends: thank you.

Black
Scholarship
in a
White
Academy

Framing the Context

Situating Black Tenure-Track Faculty in the Academy
and Unpacking the Theoretical Anchor
of Anti-Blackness

ROBERT T. PALMER, ALONZO M. FLOWERS III, SOSANYA JONES,
NICOLE JOHNSON, AND KATRINA STRULOEFF

The idea for this book originated with the experience of Paul Harris, who was seeking promotion from assistant professor to a tenured position as associate professor at the University of Virginia (UVA). While Harris produced thoughtful and effective research in the field of counselor education and received positive reviews from his department chair, he was denied tenure because of concerns about the publication of some of his scholarship in certain journals (Zahneis, 2020). Specifically, Harris sought to publish his research in journals directed at Black and Brown educators, administrators, and practitioners. One such peer-reviewed journal was the *Journal of African American Males in Education* (*JAAME*). Though the journal accepted only 23% of submissions, some external reviewers questioned the scholarly legitimacy of *JAAME* and argued that Harris's publications in this journal were equivalent to self-publishing (Hudson, 2021). Due to overwhelming support for Harris's application from the scholarly community, including many prominent Black and Brown scholars, UVA reversed its decision and promoted Harris to a tenured position as associate professor in the counselor education program (Hudson,

2021; Zahneis, 2020). Harris left UVA in 2021 for a tenured position at Penn State. Though Harris's story may sound exceptional, his experience is typical of many Black faculty in higher education, particularly at predominantly White institutions (PWIs). While his story received national attention, countless Black scholars have had experiences similar to Harris's that did not generate wide publicity.

According to data from the American Association of University Professors, Black faculty account for only 6% of full-time faculty at US postsecondary institutions, whereas White faculty made up 76.2% (Colby & Fowler, 2020). This disparity should be a matter of deep concern: although the racial and ethnic diversity of students at US colleges and universities has grown significantly over the last two decades, the composition of postsecondary institutions' faculty remains predominantly skewed toward White scholars. One of the salient factors that has contributed to the underrepresentation of Black faculty in the academy is racism. The qualifications and expertise of Black faculty are often questioned, and they are forced to tout their scholarly credentials and professional experience just to be seen as credible among their colleagues as well as within the classroom by their White students. Black faculty are often viewed as "diversity gurus" and are overburdened with service work related to diversity, equity, and inclusion. While many Black faculty willingly engage in this type of service work, the expectation that they should and will do it impinges on time they could devote to scholarship, which is vital to securing tenure and promotion at most universities (Bellas & Toutkoushian, 1999; Griffin et al., 2013).

Many Black professors have reported feeling invisible to their White colleagues and lacking critical institutional support to help navigate the unwritten rules of the tenure and promotion process (Williams & Williams, 2006; Zambrana et al., 2015). Indeed, the experience of many Black faculty at PWIs is dominated by racial microaggressions, systemic racism, and racial toxicity. This leads to isolation, mental health challenges stemming from racial battle fatigue, and the exodus of Black junior faculty (Dade et al., 2015; Haynes et al., 2020; Palmer, 2019; Smith, 2004). While many colleges and universities publicly profess to value a diverse faculty, few institutions have implemented policies and procedures to augment the retention and success of Black faculty (Gasman, 2016). Moreover, despite not making a concerted effort to improve the institutional climate to help facilitate the success of Black faculty, administrators at many PWIs cite a leaky pipeline to explain the dearth of Black faculty at their institutions (Carey et al., 2018; Liera, 2019; Sensoy & DiAngelo, 2017). This problem pervades the academy, which is still mainly White and normalizes White hegemony. As illustrated in Harris's experience with the tenure process at UVA, the research of Black scholars is more likely to be questioned, scrutinized, impugned, and deemed inconsequential, especially when their research focuses on the Black and Brown community (Croom, 2017; Settles et al., 2020; Zambrana, 2017). This contributes to an uneven playing field in the academy and makes it even more difficult for Black scholars to achieve success in their academic careers.

Nikole Hannah-Jones's 1619 Project is indicative of this racial divide. The 1619 Project, which reexamined the legacy of slavery in the United States and documented the contributions of Black Americans to the nation's founding, was vigorously attacked by conservatives; President Donald J. Trump even signed an executive order (thereafter rescinded by President Joe Biden) to establish the 1776 Commission, with the goal of promoting a "patriotic education" (Clifton, 2021). While Hannah-Jones received accolades for the 1619 Project, including a Pulitzer Prize, conservatives questioned the accuracy of some of the information in the project and argued that it was divisive and anti-American (Silverstein, 2021). In 2021, Hannah-Jones was invited to join the Hussman School of Journalism and Media at the University of North Carolina as the Knight Chair in Race and Investigative Journalism (Robertson, 2021). Other scholars who held the chair received tenure. Because of lobbying by conservative groups who objected to the 1619 Project, Hannah-Jones was offered the position without tenure. This disparate treatment led to a backlash by faculty at the University of North Carolina and caused great concern in the higher education community and beyond (Robertson, 2021). This public outcry, coupled with Hannah-Jones's threat of legal action, resulted in the university reversing its decision and offering her tenure. Ultimately, Hannah-Jones accepted an offer to join Howard University as a tenured professor.

As demonstrated by Harris's and Hannah-Jones's encounters with the tenure process, the experiences that Black faculty and scholars have with racism—be it subtle or blatant—are all too common in society in general and in higher education specifically. One need look no further than the recent attacks on critical race theory (CRT) by conservative pundits. Because many Black and minoritized scholars use CRT as an analytical tool to critique racism and White supremacy, it has come under siege. This anti-CRT movement is guided by ill-informed notions intended to delegitimize CRT. As a consequence, some state and local educational agencies have banned CRT from the public K–12 system, even though it is generally taught at the graduate school level. This same anti-CRT sentiment has even led to the introduction of a bill in the Texas legislature that would abolish tenure altogether (Flaherty, 2022). This has provoked concern and fear among some Black faculty whose research uses CRT, especially those in tenure-track positions at colleges and universities located in predominantly conservative states, as Larry J. Walker documents in chapter 10 in this volume.

The experiences of Black tenure-track faculty with racist toxicity and subjugation in postsecondary education are a central theme of this book. While many books, journal articles, and reports have examined the plight of Black tenure-track faculty through various theoretical prisms, this book considers the experiences of Black faculty in a White academy through an anti-Blackness epistemological lens. Originating in the perception of Black inferiority (James & Turner, 2017), anti-Blackness is a theoretical framework that illuminates society's disregard for Black people and failure to recognize Black humanity (Dumas, 2016; Sexton, 2018). Anti-Blackness has its roots in an "intellectual project" referred to as Afro-pessimism (Dumas, 2016, p. 13). Afro-pessimism maintains that "Black people exist in a structurally antagonistic relationship with humanity" (p. 13). In this sense, the social recognition that humanizes others systemically excludes the humanization of Black people.

Afro-pessimist scholars argue that Black people are positioned as slaves in a cultural and societal context and denied "human agency, desire, and freedom" (Dumas, 2016, p. 13). This does not imply that Black people are currently enslaved by law, but that slavery is indicative of the "ontological position of Black people" (p. 13). It is this depiction of Black people as nonhuman that has served as the impetus for centuries of anti-Black violence. Though slavery was abolished by constitutional amendment in 1865, the notion of Blacks as slaves has engendered and facilitated the everyday suffering of Black people (Dumas, 2016; Sexton, 2018). The perceptions and assumptions about Blackness are related to the daily experiences of Black people and may contribute to such systemic issues as poverty, limited access to education, and barriers to social mobility. Indeed, anti-Black attitudes are expressed through discrimination, stereotyping, and bias against Black people (Dumas & ross, 2016).

By using anti-Blackness as a framework, this book seeks to provide insight into how White hegemonic structures and policies within the academy have systemically undervalued Black faculty and Black scholarship. As Black faculty struggle to dismantle systemic oppression within and outside the academy, this book will present ways they can challenge racial microaggressions and other forms of discrimination and oppression at their institutions and within the academy overall. We hope that this book will offer a validating source for Black faculty to engage in critical reflection about strategies for resisting and overcoming the various systems of racial oppression within the academy. The chapters that follow are intended to help Black professors achieve success in White spaces dominated by anti-Black politics, related especially to scholarship on Black and Brown communities.

Overview of Chapters

This book is divided into three parts and consists of eleven chapters that are framed by this introduction and a conclusion. Part I uses the perspective of anti-Blackness to examine the ways in which Black scholarship is undermined and undervalued in various scholarly higher education outlets. The chapters also provide recommendations to help address these challenges.

In chapter 1, Chad E. Kee provide insights into the lived experiences of Black scholars and the ways in which Black scholarship is devalued in higher education. Specifically, he draws from anti-Blackness theory in higher education to conceptualize the experiences of Black faculty by conducting an extensive review of the literature on Black scholars and Black scholarship in US higher education. His chapter also discusses the ways that Black bodies and the Black experience are dehumanized and devalued, fueling the perception of Black scholars as "less than"—lacking credentials and marginalized as outsiders in the higher education community. This chapter concludes with a list of recommendations for higher education leaders and policy makers, higher education training programs, and Black scholars to counter the White hegemonic practices that permeate higher education.

In chapter 2, Erik M. Hines, Donna Y. Ford, James L. Moore III, Edward C. Fletcher Jr., and Brian L. Wright push back against the vertical view that ranks the research and scholarship of Black scholars below that of White scholars. The authors argue that this binary racist and discriminatory practice perpetuated in predominantly White institutions serves to discredit the lived experiences of Black scholars and the approaches they use to measure, understand, and articulate perspectives that significantly influence the educational contexts and communities of color in general, and Black communities in particular. In their critique of the status quo, they challenge what Donna Ford has termed "#scholarSHIT" that permeates far too many mainstream publications. #ScholarSHIT, in the guise of "scholarship," undermines Black epistemologies, ignoring, undervaluing, delegitimizing, and rendering invisible the necessity of Black scholarship and its impact on the ways of being and knowing of Black and Brown people within and outside the academy. This chapter interrogates these racial injustices and addresses strategies for countering the marginalization of our scholarship. It also discusses the importance of publishing in journals devoted to scholarship on Black and Latinx populations, as these are invaluable academic and professional outlets that must be given higher regard in the academy overall, as well as in promotion and tenure decisions.

In chapter 3, Terrell L. Strayhorn addresses the consistent and persistent devaluation of Black scholars and Black scholarship by White editors, reviewers, and evaluators, especially those affiliated with the most highly regarded, highly ranked journals in education and psychology. He tackles this issue using an anti-Blackness lens that provides language and perspective for engaging in a race- and socially conscious critique of the peer-review process, the reviewer-author-reader dynamic, and specific examples of problematic feedback from unenlightened reviewers—in the guise of "Reviewer #2." Strayhorn's critical analysis reveals how vacant criticisms get privileged in a White academy in ways that undermine Black scholars' research aims, undervalue their contributions, and devalue them and their work, thereby perpetuating the status quo. The chapter includes strong recommendations and strategies to help discourage the systematic relegation of Black scholars and Black scholarship in the academy.

In chapter 4, H. Bernard Hall describes the challenges facing scholars who specialize in hip-hop pedagogy in White hegemonic spaces such as teacher education and higher education more broadly. Topics include higher education's genuine and voyeuristic interests in hip-hop pedagogy; hip-hop pedagogy and anti-(ultra-)Blackness in teacher education; and the dilemmas that come with hip-hop pedagogy's "mainstreaming." This chapter concludes with a discussion of implications for research and practice.

While the chapters in part II discuss Black scholarship through an anti-Blackness lens, they focus on the racialized experiences of Black faculty in higher education. In chapter 5, Martinque K. Jones, Isis H. Settles, NiCole T. Buchanan, and Kristie Dotson focus on how institutions of higher education have been working toward increasing faculty diversity, yet progress has been limited, particularly for Black faculty. They indicate that this may be due, in part, to a revolving door of Black faculty, who are successfully hired but not retained and promoted in their academic positions. In this chapter, the authors theorize that epistemic exclusion is a factor that may help to explain these negative outcomes. The chapter details the theory of epistemic exclusion, framing it within Black feminist theory and CRT, and then describes the results of empirical research on this topic. The chapter concludes with recommendations for disciplinary gatekeepers, institutions, and faculty for addressing epistemic exclusion.

In chapter 6, Blanca Elizabeth Vega explores how to cultivate more Black spaces for the development of Black scholarship. She theorizes that the unavailability of Black spaces in higher education contributes to epistemic exclusion. Using a BlackCrit lens, the author argues that to counter epistemic exclusion, Black spaces that foster the development of Black scholarship—such as writing groups, Black student organizations, and Black studies programs or departments—must be cultivated, supported, and funded by the institution in order to demonstrate that racial care must be cultivated and supported. This chapter concludes with recommendations for campus administrators.

In chapter 7, Sheron Fraser-Burgess provides a narrative reflection on confronting racial microaggressions in higher education. Fraser-Burgess sheds light on how Black female academics' internal dialogue can challenge White normative gaze and enable ways of resisting regimes of delegitimization. Ingeniously framing her argument as a five-act play recounting a Black female faculty member's reflection on her experience of an extended series of interpersonal interactions with White colleagues at a predominantly White institution of higher education, Fraser-Burgess argues that womanist thinking offers philosophical resources that can buffer the onslaught of subjugation.

In chapter 8, Beverly-Jean M. Daniel examines ways in which academic institutions and their leaders reinforce, condone, and legitimize racialized violence against Black faculty, through the failure to attend to issues of incivility. Drawing primarily from CRT and anti-Black racism theory, this chapter discusses the experiences of Black Canadian faculty members and racism in Canadian society. The chapter also explores the racialized dynamics of the interactions that students have with Black faculty and the impacts of such interactions, and it argues that the institutional failure to address the racial incivility of students who target Black faculty is indicative of the persistence of anti-Black racism within Canadian institutions. This chapter concludes by expanding the theory of anti-Black racism and developing a model aimed at eliminating anti-Black racism that moves beyond its identification and discusses strategies and interventions to address racism aimed at Black faculty members.

Consistent with the theme of the book, the chapters in part III discuss Black scholarship from an anti-Blackness perspective; however, they focus on facilitating the success of Black faculty in the academy. In chapter 9, Fred A. Bonner II, Stella L. Smith, and aretha f. marbley use three critical frameworks to provide scholarly personal narratives that reflect on their past and contemporary experiences, foregrounding their scholarship as Black scholars and scholar-practitioners in the White academy. This chapter concludes with recommendations for institutional practice to help promote the success of Black faculty in postsecondary education.

In chapter 10, Larry J. Walker utilizes autoethnographic vignettes to describe the lived experiences of a Black male tenure-track faculty member teaching in a conservative state. Central to the author's chapter is how his research epistemology uses CRT, which has been vigorously attacked and banned in his state at the K–12 level. The author argues that the negative perception and stigma currently associated with CRT have provoked concerns about his tenure and promotion within the university state system. In a broader sense, this chapter uses extant literature on anti-Blackness and CRT to examine the politics of teaching in a red state. This chapter concludes with implications for other Black faculty who may be facing similar challenges or grappling with the same concerns at their colleges and universities.

In chapter 11, Antonio L. Ellis discusses how anti-Blackness intersects with disability among African American males who stutter while pursuing tenured professorships at colleges and universities. The author concludes his chapter with implications for research on this salient topic and for those navigating the tenure-track process.

In the concluding chapter, Alonzo M. Flowers III, Sosanya Jones, Robert T. Palmer, Katrina Struloeff, and Nicole Johnson recenter the chapters' thematic trends on the theory of anti-Blackness. This chapter also offers recommendations to stakeholders on ways to better support Black faculty members and discusses possibilities for future research.

REFERENCES

Bellas, M. L., & Toutkoushian, R. K. (1999). Faculty time allocations and research productivity: Gender, race, and family effects. *Review of Higher Education, 22*(4), 367–390.

Carey, J. M., Carman, K. R., Clayton, K. P., Horiuchi, Y., Htun, M., & Ortiz, B. (2018). Who wants to hire a more diverse faculty? A conjoint analysis of faculty and student preferences for gender and racial/ethnic diversity. *Politics, Groups, and Identities.* Advance online publication. https://doi.org/10.1080/21565503.2018.1491866.

Clifton, D. (2021). How the Trump administration's "1776 Report" warps the history of racism and slavery. NBC News, January 20, 2021. https://www.nbcnews.com/news/nbcblk/how-trump-administration-s-1776-report-warps-history-racism-slavery-n1254926.

Colby, G, & Fowler, C. (2020). Data snapshot: IPEDS data on full-time women and faculty of color. American Association of University Professors. https://www.aaup.org/news/data-snapshot-full-time-women-faculty-and-faculty-color.

Croom, N. N. (2017). Promotion beyond tenure: Unpacking racism and sexism in the experiences of Black womyn professors. *Review of Higher Education, 40*(4), 557–583.

Dade, K., Tartakov, C., Hargrave, C., & Leigh, P. (2015). Assessing the impact of racism on Black faculty in White academe: A collective case study of African American female faculty. *Western Journal of Black Studies, 39*(2), 134–146.

Dumas, M. J. (2016). Against the dark: Antiblackness in education policy and discourse. *Theory into Practice, 55*(1), 11–19.

Dumas, M. J., & ross, k. m. (2016). "Be real Black for me": Imagining BlackCrit in education. *Urban Education, 51*(4), 415–442.

Espinosa, L. L., Turk, J. M., Taylor, M., & Chessman, H. M. (2019). *Race and ethnicity in higher education: A status report.* American Council on Education. https://vtechworks.lib.vt.edu/handle/10919/89187.

Flaherty, C. (2022). "A new low" in attacks on academic freedom. *Inside Higher Ed,* February 21, 2022. https://www.insidehighered.com/news/2022/02/21/texas-lt-govs-pledge-end-tenure-over-crt-new-low.

Frey, W. H. (2018). A demographic bridge to America's diverse future. Brookings Scholar Lecture Series, February 14, 2018. https://digitalscholarship.unlv.edu/brookings_lectures_events/126/.

Gasman, M. (2016). An Ivy League professor on why colleges don't hire more faculty of color: "We don't want them." *Washington Post,* September 26, 2016. https://www.washingtonpost.com/news/grade-point/wp/2016/09/26/an-ivy-league-professor-on-why-colleges-dont-hire-more-faculty-of-color-we-dont-want-them/.

Griffin, K. A., Bennett, J. C., & Harris, J. (2013). Marginalizing merit? Gender differences in Black faculty D/discourses on tenure, advancement, and professional success. *Review of Higher Education, 36*(4), 489–512.

Haynes, C., Taylor, L., Mobley Jr., S. D., & Haywood, J. (2020). Existing and resisting: The pedagogical realities of Black, critical men and women faculty. *Journal of Higher Education.* Advance online publication. https://doi.org/10.1080/00221546.2020.1731263.

Hudson, W. (2021). After fighting to gain tenure, Dr. Paul Harris leaves UVA on his own terms. *Diverse Issues in Higher Education,* May 11, 2021. https://www.diverseeducation.com/tenure/article/15109207/after-fighting-to-gain-tenure-dr-paul-harris-leaves-uva-on-his-own-terms.

James, C. E., & Turner, T. (2017). *Towards race equity in education: The schooling of Black students in the Greater Toronto Area.* York University.

Lee, J. A. (2010). Students' perceptions of and satisfaction with faculty diversity. *College Student Journal, 44*(2), 400–413.

Lichter, D. T. (2013). Integration or fragmentation? Racial diversity and the American future. *Demography, 50*(2), 359–391.

Liera, R. (2019). Moving beyond a culture of niceness in faculty hiring to advance racial equity. *American Educational Research Journal, 57*(5), 1554–1994. https://doi.org/10.3102/0002831219888624.

National Center for Educational Statistics. (2018). Race/ethnicity of college faculty: Fast facts. https://nces.ed.gov/fastfacts/display.asp?id=61.

Palmer, R. T. (2019). Teaching while Black: My experience as a faculty member at a predominantly White institution. In N. D. Hartlep & D. Ball (Eds.), *Racial battle fatigue in higher education: Racialized lessons learned at different institutions of higher learning* (pp. 30–42). Routledge.

Robertson, K. (2021). Nikole Hannah-Jones denied tenure at the University of North Carolina. *New York Times,* May 19, 2021. https://www.nytimes.com/2021/05/19/business/media/nikole-hannah-jones-unc.html.

Sensoy, Ö., & DiAngelo, R. (2017). "We are all for diversity, but . . .": How faculty hiring committees reproduce Whiteness and practical suggestions for how they can change. *Harvard Educational Review, 87*(4), 557–580.

Settles, I. H., Jones, M. K., Buchanan, N. T., & Dotson, K. (2020). Epistemic exclusion: Scholar(ly) devaluation that marginalizes faculty of color. *Journal of Diversity in Higher Education.* Advance online publication. https://doi.org/10.1037/dhe0000174.

Sexton, J. (2018). Unbearable Blackness. In *Black men, Black feminism* (pp. 75–105). Palgrave Pivot.

Silverstein, J. (2021). The 1619 Project and the long battle over US history. *New York Times Magazine,* November 9, 2021. https://www.nytimes.com/2021/11/09/magazine/1619-project-us-history.html.

Smith, W. A. (2004). Black faculty coping with racial battle fatigue: The campus racial climate in a post-civil rights era. In D. Cleveland (Ed.), *A long way to go: Conversations about race by African American faculty and graduate students* (pp. 171–190). Peter Lang.

Turner, C. S. V., González, J. C., & Wood, J. L. (2008). Faculty of color in academe: What 20 years of literature tells us. *Journal of Diversity in Higher Education, 1*(3), 139–168.

Williams, B. N., & Williams, S. M. (2006). Perceptions of African American male junior faculty on promotion and tenure: Implications for community building and social capital. *Teachers College Record, 108*(2), 287–315. https://doi.org/10.1111/j.1467-9620.2006.00649.x.

Zahneis, M. (2020). Reversing course, UVa recommends tenure for a Black scholar who had been denied. *Chronicle of Higher Education*, July 25, 2020. https://www.chronicle.com/article/reversing-course-uva-recommends-tenure-for-a-black-scholar-who-had-been-denied.

Zambrana, R. E., Harvey Wingfield, A., Lapeyrouse, L. M., Dávila, B. A., Hoagland, T. L., & Valdez, R. B. (2017). Blatant, subtle, and insidious: URM faculty perceptions of discriminatory practices in predominantly White institutions. *Sociological Inquiry, 87*(2), 207–232.

Zambrana, R. E., Ray, R., Espino, M. M., Castro, C., Douthirt Cohen, B., & Eliason, J. (2015). "Don't leave us behind": The importance of mentoring for underrepresented minority faculty. *American Educational Research Journal, 52*(1), 40–72.

PART I

An In-Depth Examination of
Anti-Blackness in the Evaluation
of Higher Education Scholarship

1

White Hegemonic Practices That Undervalue Black Scholarship within Higher Education through the Lens of Anti-Blackness Theory

CHAD E. KEE

I have situated this literature review at the intersection of anti-Blackness theory, White hegemony, and Black scholarship. I have applied anti-Blackness theory as the central focus of the literature review and used it to frame the discussion. Bledsoe and Wright (2019) refer to observations and experiences grounded in anti-Blackness as "expressions," a term I will use throughout this chapter. I present expressions of anti-Blackness theory to demonstrate ways in which anti-Blackness is observed, witnessed, and experienced within higher education. In searching for literature to explore anti-Blackness theory, I focused greater attention on the literature published within the past twenty years (2002–2022) to identify trends, patterns, and ways in which the discussion has evolved. I also included studies related to White hegemony and Black scholarship that I perceived as most relevant and strongly aligned with discussions of anti-Blackness, without limitations on publication date.

This review adds to the literature on Black scholarship by providing insights into the historical and present-day social movements that influence the adoption or devaluation of Black scholarship in higher education. It focuses on ways in which Black scholarship is devalued through White hegemonic practices. White hegemony can be understood as the practice by which White dominant cultural norms are adopted as the standard or as common sense (Hughes, 2013). The chapter provides a high-level review of the literature on Black scholarship and is organized by concepts adapted from anti-Blackness theory. I then uncover the impact of anti-Blackness and White hegemony on the promotion and inclusion of Black scholarship within higher education. Finally, I present a list of recommendations to dismantle and disrupt anti-Blackness practices within higher education that have normalized the devaluation of Black scholarship.

I placed Black scholarship at the center of the chapter, focusing on how Black scholars experience higher education and ways in which Black scholarship is devalued. To do so, I searched the following databases: Web of Knowledge, Education Full Text, JSTOR, and Google Scholar. I selected these databases to ensure access to peer-reviewed scholarly journals. I used the following search terms and phrases: "Black scholars," "Black scholarship," "Black scholarship in higher education," "African American scholars in higher education," and "minority scholars in higher education."

Most of the literature reviewed was qualitative in nature, with some exceptions that focused on quantitative measures such as salary comparisons and tenure and rank across racial groups. Also, given that Black scholars are identified as "faculty of color," the literature that focused on faculty of color was also considered.

As I reviewed the literature, key themes emerged among the various manifestations of anti-Blackness used to devalue Black scholarship. The primary themes that emerged were racially charged higher education environments, racialized hurdles to persistence, epistemic injustice and exclusion, and discriminatory barriers to professional advancement. These themes, referred to as "expressions of anti-Blackness," are used to structure the chapter.

Overview of Anti-Blackness

Scholars define anti-Blackness as the product of a social system grounded in the historical ideology that portrayed Blacks as property during the chattel slavery period and countered any visibility of Black social life (Sexton, 2016; Sharpe, 2016). Anti-Blackness theory can be operationalized by individuals and organizations as actions, beliefs, or mind-sets that attempt to dehumanize Black people and eradicate Black social life from society in order to reinforce White hegemonic practices and thus maintain political, epistemological, and economic stability (Bledsoe & Wright, 2019). Due to the impact of race on society and social interactions, anti-Blackness influences areas of higher education from student and academic affairs to business services. For the purposes of this chapter, anti-Blackness theory will be applied to understand the systemic forms of oppression that limit Black scholarship within higher education.

The United States has a long and brutal racist past. The categorization of Africans as "nonhumans" was introduced during the colonial period when Africans were enslaved and thought of as property by the colonizers (Ferreira da Silva, 2015; Wilderson, 2010). Within the United States, the concept of race as a social construct was also introduced during this period (Cornell & Hartmann, 1998). Once adopted as a social norm within US culture, race was used to preserve a financial structure and retain power and privilege for European colonizers (Sonn & Green, 2006). Since the founding of the United States, racism has permeated everyday life through legislation, economic structures, and social conventions. Governmental policies and legal precedents shaped societal structures centered on Whiteness and non-Whiteness, particularly regarding nationality and accompanying rights (Greenwald et al., 2009; Rothstein, 2017).

In practically any postcolonial community within the United States, the extent of a person's Blackness could dictate their assigned social status based on White European cultural norms. "Blackness" is predominantly a societal label used to describe individuals of African heritage or convey assumptions about their shared life experiences. Dei

(2018) defined Blackness beyond phenotype to include an understanding of ways that Black bodies are objectified and an awareness of the past and present Black experience.

Despite the diversity of experiences of Black individuals, the concept of Blackness has purposefully been collapsed over time to reflect a one-dimensional racial identity. The Black racial identity has been repressed, appropriated, and devoured, per the prevailing group's preferences and desires. *Anti-Blackness* is the term used to describe this phenomenon. Anti-Blackness is a mind-set that originates from perceptions of Black inferiority (Feagin, 2006/2013; James & Turner, 2017; Nighaoui, 2017).

Anti-Blackness has exposed a perplexing position wherein "Blackness is . . . fashionable and can be appropriated, packaged, commodified, and consumed [by non-Black people]" while being regarded as disgusting and abhorrent (Dei, 2018, p. 120). The negative perceptions of and assumptions about Blackness fuel outcomes for Black communities related to daily lived experience that may involve poverty, limited access to education, and barriers to upward mobility. Anti-Black attitudes are expressed through beliefs, behaviors, acts of discrimination, stereotyping, and bias against people who are Black. These attitudes negatively influence the perception of Black scholarship (Grier-Reed et al., 2018).

Fundamental anti-Black frameworks have been installed in the state's financial, societal, political, intellectual, legal, health care, and religious structures throughout US history. People of color are rigorously oppressed by voting restrictions (Jones & Williams, 2018), poor educational facilities (Kozol, 1991/2012), housing schemes (Gonda, 2015; Rothstein, 2017), biased courts and judicial frameworks (Allen, 2014), medical centers (Tawa et al., 2012), and job markets (Perna et al., 2007). These and other incidences of racism are based on profound social preconceptions (Kendi, 2019) about people of color, such as limited credibility and lack of intellectual capacity. The various forms of racism affect all non-White people, but Indigenous and Black people have experienced the worst persecution and oppression in US history (Hoberman, 2012).

Theoretical Framework

Anti-Blackness theory has garnered heightened attention due to the advent of the Black Lives Matter (BLM) movement following the murder of Trayvon Martin (Toporek, 2013). In light of current social and racially charged events related to excessive police brutality, BLM has gained significant attention throughout academia and society at large. BLM initiatives and public protests have entered every corner of society and subsequently centered anti-Blackness theories to frame their beliefs and arguments. Scholars across multiple disciplines are using anti-Blackness theory to frame their research and participate in the movement through scholarship, acknowledging the heightened demonstrations of violence and the associated "lack of value" placed on Black bodies (Sharpe, 2016).

Scholars use anti-Blackness theory to reveal the underpinnings of social norms intended to diminish, obscure, or devalue Black experience; reinforce the notion of Black people as property and less than human; and avoid inclusion of Black social life while upholding White dominant institutionalized systems (Hartman, 1997; Sharpe, 2016). Anti-Blackness theory acknowledges the racist encounters experienced by Black scholars within higher education. It serves as a lens that uncovers the power and influence of White supremacy and White hegemony over higher education practices and policies and the academic environment. Acknowledging that the United States was founded on racist principles, anti-Blackness theory explores the racist structures underpinning social systems and social interactions.

Anti-Blackness theory also acknowledges the infusion of White hegemony throughout US social systems, including higher education. Considering that colleges and universities are microcosms of broader society, White hegemony significantly influences the higher education environment and related social institutions (Hughes, 2013). Events of racism and discrimination that occur in broader society affect campus environments and relationships, potentially leading to demonstrations of protest and resistance on college campuses. Hughes (2013) argued that social events in broader society and within higher education institutions require ongoing critical dialogues about racism and the need for racial justice within college and university environments.

Lull (1995) argued that for hegemonic practices to be effective, those who are considered subordinate must accept the dominant ideology as the norm. White hegemony permeates society's ways of knowing and ways of being that affect both micro- and macro-social systems (Brown, 2014). Antonio Gramsci defines hegemony as the practice of domination (Bates, 1975). Therefore, White hegemony can be understood as cultural practices of White domination over "subordinate" groups who have accepted their lower-class position, which sustains White dominance as the norm (Hall, 2018; Lull, 1995). I intend to push the conversation forward by identifying specific expressions and environmental structures of anti-Blackness and Black scholarship within the context of higher education in the United States.

Anti-Blackness in Higher Education

Anti-Blackness has a profound impact on higher education in the United States, where various forms of oppression of and domination over Black lives and the Black experience persist (Ladson-Billings, 2006). The White racial paradigm, based on anti-Blackness, is "a collection of cultural narratives and symbols" (Grier-Reed et al., 2018, p. 65) that are taught, learned, and adopted in order to accept White dominant culture as the norm. An anti-Blackness mind-set conceives of Whiteness as "more virtuous, clever, moral, and honest" (Wingfield & Feagin, 2012, p. 145) than non-Whiteness, which influences the perception and minimizes the value of Black scholarship.

Geiger (2005) offers a timeline of the origin and adoption of anti-Blackness thought beginning with colonization and the establishment of colonial colleges from 1745 to 1775 in the United States. Colonialism created and reinforced a racist educational system in the early colonies. European colonialism was founded on the premise that "superior races," usually those of European descent, had the right and responsibility to civilize non-European "inferior races" (Dumas & Ross, 2016; Serequeberhan, 2010). As a result, anti-Blackness persisted during this time, influencing the educational system and the adoption of European cultural norms that affect higher education today. Throughout the colonial college era, White lawmakers and people in positions of power developed anti-Black laws and ideologies, such as dehumanizing Black people by legally defining them as less than fully human (Smith et al., 2016). The devaluation of Black people during the colonial period is directly correlated with the devaluation of Black scholarship today.

During the colonial era, Black people and those of African descent were not allowed to pursue any form of education and were relegated to a life of chattel slavery, enduring ongoing brutal, inhumane treatment (Baker, 1998; Dodge & Jarratt, 2013). Colonization influenced decades of subsequent race-based laws such as Jim Crow segregation and barriers to education.

Black Scholarship in Higher Education

Black scholarship evolved from an integrative conceptual or social devotion to the liberation of Black people and thoughts through early nineteenth-century Black researchers (Institute of the Black World, 1974). Early Black scholarship was imbued with a sentiment of practical worth as a mechanism for destroying White racist misperceptions of Black people and restoring feelings of value and visibility (Du Bois, 1903/2015; Fanon, 1967/2008; Nkrumah, 1961). Using a management and organizational perspective when examining academic institutions, Muzanenhamo and Chowdhury (2021, p. 2) define Black scholarship as "epistemic practices grounded in the social realities and locations of both individuals and communities of African descent (i.e., Black people)." Duschl and Grandy (2008, p. 99) describe epistemic practices as "the specific ways members of a community propose, justify, evaluate, and legitimize knowledge claims within a disciplinary framework."

Historically, university-based scholarship is rooted in exclusionary practices and White hegemony. White leaders in higher education often marginalize Black scholars based on their race (Cox, 2001; Nkomo & Cox, 1999). Due to this practice of marginalization, Black scholarship is frequently devalued within the academy, demonstrating an actively White-centered ideology. Particular social characteristics, such as Whiteness, being upper-class, and being male, are valued more highly in academic environments than characteristics of non-White people, restricting accessibility and entry for those who do not meet the cultural norm. As a result, the positive contributions of Black people to higher education are significantly discounted (Matias, 2016). The lack of support in academic participation has significant implications for Black scholars who are excluded from active participation in scholarship and production of knowledge (Pérez Huber & Solorzano, 2015). This fundamental lack of equity and fairness has nonetheless expanded Black scholarship into numerous interconnected conceptual frameworks, characterized by a common sense of opposition and responsibility for liberation (Blake-Beard et al., 2008; Johnson, 2008; Mukandi & Bond, 2019).

Asserting the rightful position of all humans as equal, Black scholars have traditionally mobilized and amplified the voices of non-White people opposing prejudice (Warmington, 2014). Black research, pioneered by founders such as Taylor H. Cox and Roosevelt Thomas, constitutes the cornerstone of diversification or inclusiveness studies (Dei, 2018). Black researchers such as Stella Nkomo have been invaluable in developing critical race theory (CRT), which focuses on the role of White supremacy in oppressing non-White individuals and communities (Collins, 2013; Johnson, 2008). Also of note is the contribution of Black scholarship to the essential progression of literature that expands the narrative of marginalized populations and prioritizes a focus on social justice, equity, and anti-oppression across disciplines.

Expressions of Anti-Blackness Directed at Black Scholarship in Higher Education

Racially Charged Higher Education Environments

Mustaffa (2017) describes higher education history as "violent," affirming Black scholars' experiences navigating soul wounds, empirical injustice, and racial battle fatigue. These three types of trauma provide insight into the lived experiences of Black faculty. Mustaffa explains, "The use of the term 'violence' is not a rhetorical strategy but an emphasis on how structural racism is multifaceted and has violent, material consequences for Black lives" (p. 711).

Due to the prevalence of anti-Blackness and White hegemonic practices within higher education, Black scholars are constantly navigating, countering, and healing from various forms of racist attack. In addition, Black faculty often experience expressions of anti-Blackness in the form of marginalization and exclusion from scholarly activities in the field (Diggs et al., 2009).

Racialized Hurdles to Persistence

The ongoing attacks of racism and forms of oppression experienced by Black scholars produce barriers that may lead Black scholars to depart from higher education. The hurdles created by racism and negative perceptions of Black scholarship can become insurmountable, leading one to consider other professional pathways. Soul wounds can result from such hurdles. Ladson-Billings (2006) argues that wounds on the soul are a consequence of historical distress for Indigenous people and racial minorities in the United States. According to Ivey et al. (2013), African Americans have experienced soul wounds due to individual and institutional racism since the time of slavery. Black scholars are thus entering higher education with trauma that is exacerbated by navigating the racist environment of higher education. Soul wounds can also be a result of racial struggles associated with worry, anger, depression, or sadness (Grier-Reed et al., 2020) that Black scholars experience as a result of navigating this environment. This process can become exhausting, creating wounds that destroy passion, enthusiasm, and drive to produce scholarship (Smith et al., 2007).

Personal attacks on the soul may correlate to a lack of persistence among Black faculty in higher education. It is important to understand how a wounded soul can affect a Black faculty member's ability to function in their academic environment. The constant attacks and encounters with racism can be paralyzing, causing Black faculty to leave higher education.

In the 1980s, researchers began to focus more attention on the lack of representation among minority faculty (Menges & Exum, 1983; Silver et al., 1989). Almost four decades later, the need for increased representation persists, as researchers have uncovered generations of minorities whose absence from higher education can be attributed to racism and White hegemonic practices (Gasman et al., 2011; Myers, 2002). Greater representation and retention would increase the number of Black faculty in senior positions and influence younger minority faculty's upward mobility and promotion status. Scholars have argued that the lack of representation is due to greater focus on recruitment and less on retention (Thompson, 2008; Trower & Chait, 2002).

Epistemic Injustice and Exclusion

Epistemic injustice is defined as the unfair treatment of and discrimination against individuals or groups based on their perceived capacity to know things (Byskov, 2021; Fricker, 2007). Epistemic injustice can take the form of excluding or silencing individuals who are perceived as "less than," based on their gender, sexuality, race, ethnicity, or other aspects of their sociocultural background (Byskov, 2021; Fricker, 2007). In response to these injustices, Black scholars are forced to creatively construct strategies to prove their legitimacy and experience belonging (Muzanenhamo & Chowdhury, 2021).

Epistemic exclusion, a concept that emerged from Black feminist thought (Collins, 1990/2000), is the practice of devaluing scholarship rooted in disciplinary and social identity biases, based on the argument that the scholarship does not align with the discipline (Dotson, 2012; Settles et al., 2021). Epistemic exclusion occurs even when the scholarship is characterized by intellectual complexity and rigor. Another example of epistemic exclusion can be seen in the academic hiring process. In a study by Luna et al. (2010), people of color reported feeling the need to prove their hiring was based on their credentials, not on affirmative action. This demonstrates that systems of injustice can be grounded in one's personal perceptions and beliefs regarding legal practices such as affirmative action.

Epistemic exclusionary practices can have a significant influence on Black scholars' personal well-being and professional success, causing emotional and psychological distress (Fricker, 2007). Studies examining epistemic exclusion have more often looked at faculty of color in general, not solely Black scholars. Further exploration of exclusionary practices within higher education is needed uncover the impact of these practices on Black scholars.

Discriminatory Barriers to Professional Advancement

The tenure and promotion process presents challenges for Black scholars. This is the process in which junior faculty are promoted from assistant to associate, and then to full tenured professor through a multistage peer evaluation process of their research, teaching, and service. Singh and Shifflette (1996) argue that minorities encounter unique challenges, including difficulties with the tenure and promotion process, when attempting to pursue careers within higher education. The argument is magnified in light of current political, social, and racial unrest.

Black scholars experience devaluation of their scholarship during the annual evaluation period and the tenure and promotion process. This can lead them to feel discouraged, especially when the evaluations are dehumanizing (Settles et al., 2021). Racism, White hegemony, and anti-Blackness are embedded in covert and overt standards that dictate the tenure and promotion process. The tenure system has had a greater negative impact on Black scholars at predominantly White institutions, due to the innate forms of oppression and anti-Blackness that lead to excessive stress and barriers to advancement (Kelly & Winkle-Wagner, 2017).

In his 2011 study of African American faculty, Frazier cited "lack of personal time, institutional climate, review/promotion process, marginalization of research, lack of mentoring, and covert discrimination"

(p. 2) as barriers to promotion and tenure. Working in isolation instead of as part of a community is yet another White dominant norm that does not align with Black cultural practices (Sule, 2011). The tenure process reinforces White norms, encouraging acts of self-promotion and competition that do not align with Black scholars' values of community and collaboration (Sule, 2011). Consequently, Black faculty are less likely to attain tenure and more likely to remain in entry-level, nontenured academic positions.

The following recommendations are based on the literature reviewed, as well as my expert knowledge of higher education. The recommendations are directed toward higher education leaders and policy makers who have the power, position, and privilege to effect change. Anti-Blackness is systemic and beyond the control of the Black scholar, and it thus demands the attention and responsibility of higher education leaders.

- Acknowledge the racist history of higher education and the impact on Black scholars, and take specific and public actions to counter systemic forms of oppression.
- Require cultural competency training for college and university employees to mitigate and counter all forms of anti-Blackness that may be observed, in order to diminish the racially charged environment.
- Examine existing policies and practices that directly or indirectly reinforce White hegemonic practices in order to work toward eradicating anti-Blackness within higher education environments.
- Encourage all faculty to conduct scholarship that centers social justice, equity, anti-oppression, and anti-Blackness to establish an institutional norm of creating research agendas with an equitable focus.
- Create space for Black and White scholars to work together, such as by offering research grants that require two or more scholars of different racial and ethnic backgrounds. Incorporate the grant offering as additional "points" in the tenure and promotion review.

- Provide additional self-care and spiritual healing resources for Black scholars to manage personal attacks. These resources could include personal time off, mental health services that center Blackness, and safe spaces for non-White people.
- Examine academic departments to identify exclusionary practices experienced by Black faculty.
- Incorporate annual assessment protocols for Black faculty that will identify practices of racism, exclusion, and marginalization.
- Review and modify the tenure and promotion process to remove any forms of implicit bias about Black scholarship and research that is perceived as not aligning with the broader discipline.
- Provide implicit bias training for all faculty, especially those involved in the tenure and promotion process. This will mitigate the biases that may prevent Black scholars from receiving tenure.
- Incorporate support systems such as faculty mentoring programs to promote the retention of Black faculty.

Implications for Black Scholarship and Higher Education

In this review I sought to magnify the impact of anti-Blackness and White hegemonic practices on Black scholarship and higher education. The literature uncovered the ways in which anti-Blackness is used to devalue Black scholarship. In addition, it revealed expressions of anti-Blackness that create challenges for Black scholars when navigating higher education spaces. These challenges are rooted in systemic racism and oppression that inform practices, policies, and relationships within higher education. As described by Mustaffa (2017), higher education is a violent and oppressive system that fuels the ongoing emotional and psychological attacks endured by Black scholars. Higher education was founded on anti-Black thought and perceptions that are yet to be dismantled.

Moreover, these challenges stem from a socially constructed notion of race and the historical categorization of Black people as property. As a result of racism and negative perceptions of Black scholarship,

Black scholars are forced to operate within a system that dehumanizes and devalues their contributions to research and their creation of new knowledge. The ongoing need to navigate a racist and oppressive environment can lead Black scholars to depart from higher education and pursue other careers in order to escape the volatile space and ongoing attacks on their identity.

When we view the current environment of higher education through an anti-Blackness lens, exclusionary practices that further marginalize Black scholars are revealed. These exclusionary practices have significant implications for Black scholars wishing to secure tenure and promotion as well as other forms of professional advancement (Fricker, 2007). Exclusionary practices often show up during recruitment and after hiring, which creates an ongoing environment of racism and oppression for Black scholars.

When Black scholars are free to engage in methods of research and knowledge creation that are aligned to their culture and their contributions are accepted and valued, their academic discipline is enriched by their research. The absence of Black scholars decreases the amount of scholarship published that centers the Black experience, equity, inclusion, social justice, and anti-oppression, and it limits the scholarship that is inclusive of marginalized identities. Also, lower persistence rates due to oppression and domination encountered by Black scholars affect representation within higher education. Diverse representation among faculty can have a positive impact on minoritized students, leading to enhanced engagement and a greater sense of belonging. When non-White voices are not included in all aspects of higher education, there are implications for culturally responsive policy development, student engagement, and general creativity within the curriculum. In short, the absence of Black scholarship is problematic and has significant effects on higher education, the academy, the creation of knowledge, students and faculty, and society at large.

When Black scholarship is excluded, a major body of research that focuses on social justice, equity, oppression, and the identification of hegemonic influences is never seen. This creates a gap in our epistemology, continually reinforcing racism and injustice. Additionally, a

Black perspective and Black ways of learning, knowing, and creating knowledge and information are lost across all disciplines and subject matters. This absence hinders equitable local, state, and federal legislation; the promotion of inclusion across social systems; and the centering of marginalized populations.

REFERENCES

Allen, T. W. (2014). *The invention of the White race: Vol. 2. Racial oppression and social control*. Verso Books.

Baker, L. D. (1998). *From savage to Negro*. University of California Press.

Bates, T. R. (1975). Gramsci and the theory of hegemony. *Journal of the History of Ideas, 36*(2), 351–366.

Blake-Beard, S. D., Finley-Hervey, J. A., & Harquail, C. V. (2008). Journey to a different place: Reflections on Taylor Cox, Jr.'s career and research as a catalyst for diversity education and training. *Academy of Management Learning & Education, 7*(3), 394–405.

Bledsoe, A., & Wright, W. J. (2019). The anti-Blackness of global capital. *Environment and Planning D: Society and Space, 37*(1), 8–26.

Brown, K. D. (2014). Teaching in color: A critical race theory in education analysis of the literature on preservice teachers of color and teacher education in the US. *Race Ethnicity and Education, 17*(3), 326–345.

Byskov, M. F. (2021). What makes epistemic injustice an "injustice"? *Journal of Social Philosophy, 52*(1), 116–133.

Collins, P. H. (2000). *Black feminist thought: Knowledge, consciousness, and the politics of empowerment*. Routledge. Original work published 1990.

Collins, P. H. (2013). *On intellectual activism*. Temple University Press.

Cornell, S., & Hartmann, D. (1998). *Ethnicity and race: Making identities in a changing world*. Pine Forge.

Cox Jr, T. (2001). *Creating the multicultural organization: A strategy for capturing the power of diversity* (Vol. 6). John Wiley & Sons.

Dei, G. J. S. (2018). "Black like me": Reframing Blackness for decolonial politics. *Educational Studies, 54*(2), 117–142.

Diggs, G. A., Garrison-Wade, D. F., Estrada, D., & Galindo, R. (2009). Smiling faces and colored spaces: The experiences of faculty of color pursing tenure in the academy. *The Urban Review, 41*, 312–333.

Dodge, G., & Jarratt, L. (2013). Building and sustaining a campus wide multicultural initiative. *New Directions for Student Services, 144*, 27–35.

Dotson, K. (2012). A cautionary tale: On limiting epistemic oppression. *Frontiers: A Journal of Women Studies, 33*(1), 24–47.

Duschl, R. A., & Grandy, R. E. (2008). *Teaching scientific inquiry: Recommendations for research and implementation*. BRILL.

Du Bois, W. E. B. (2015). *The souls of Black folk.* Yale University Press. Original work published 1903.

Dumas, M. J., & ross, k. m. (2016). "Be real Black for me": Imagining BlackCrit in education. *Urban Education, 51*(4), 415–442.

Fanon, F. (2008). *Black skin, White masks.* Grove. Original English translation published 1967.

Feagin, J. (2013). *Systemic racism: A theory of oppression.* Routledge. Original work published 2006.

Ferreira Da Silva, D. (2007). *Toward a global idea of race* (Vol. 27). U of Minnesota Press.

Frazier, K. (2011). Academic bullying: A barrier to tenure and promotion for African American faculty. *Florida Journal of Educational Administration and Policy, 5*(1), 1–13.

Fricker, M. (2007). *Epistemic injustice: Power and the ethics of knowing.* Oxford University Press.

Gasman, M., Kim, J., & Nguyen, T. (2011). Effectively recruiting faculty of color at highly selective institutions: A school of education case study. *Journal of Diversity in Higher Education, 4*(4), 212–222.

Geiger, R. (2005). The ten generations of American higher education. In R. O. Berdahl, P. G. Altbach, & P. J. Gumport (Eds.), *Higher education in the twenty-first century* (2nd ed., pp. 38–70). Johns Hopkins University Press.

Gonda, J. D. (2015). *Unjust deeds: The restrictive covenant cases and the making of the civil rights movement.* University of North Carolina Press.

Greenwald, A. G., Smith, C. T., Sriram, N., Bar-Anan, Y., & Nosek, B. A. (2009). Implicit race attitudes predicted vote in the 2008 US presidential election. *Analyses of Social Issues and Public Policy, 9*(1), 241–253.

Grier-Reed, T., Gagner, N., & Ajayi, A. (2018). (En)countering a White racial frame at a predominantly White institution: The case of the African American Student Network. *Journal Committed to Social Change on Race and Ethnicity, 4*(2), 65–89.

Grier-Reed, T., Maples, A., Williams-Wengerd, A., & McGee, D. (2020). The emergence of racialized labor and battle fatigue in the African American Student Network (AFAM). *Journal Committed to Social Change on Race and Ethnicity, 6*(2), 94–135.

Hall, S. (2018). The Whites of their eyes: Racist ideologies and the media. In G. Dines, J. Humez, B. Yousman, & L. Bindig (Eds.), *Gender, race, and class in media: A critical reader* (5th ed., pp. 89–93). SAGE.

Hartman, S. (1997). *Scenes of subjection: Terror, slavery, and self-making in nineteenth-century America.* Oxford University Press.

Hoberman, J. (2012). *Black and blue: The origins and consequences of medical racism.* University of California Press.

Hughes, G. (2013). Racial justice, hegemony, and bias incidents in US higher education. *Sociology and Anthropology Faculty Publications, 22*, 1–13.

Institute of the Black World. (1974). *Education and Black struggle: Notes from the colonized world*. Harvard Educational Review.

Ivey, A. E., Ivey, M. B., & Zalaquett, C. P. (2013). *Intentional interviewing and counseling: Facilitating client development in a multicultural society*. Cengage Learning.

James, C. E., & Turner, T. (2017). *Towards race equity in education: The schooling of Black students in the Greater Toronto Area*. York University.

Johnson, C. D. (2008). It's more than the five to do's: Insights on diversity education and training from Roosevelt Thomas, a pioneer and thought leader in the field. *Academy of Management Learning & Education, 7*(3), 406–417.

Jones, N. N., & Williams, M. F. (2018). Technologies of disenfranchisement: Literacy tests and Black voters in the U.S. from 1890 to 1965. *Technical Communication, 65*(4), 371–386.

Kelly, B. T., & Winkle-Wagner, R. (2017). Finding a voice in predominantly White institutions: A longitudinal study of Black women faculty members' journeys toward tenure. *Teachers College Record, 119*(6), 1–36.

Kendi, I. X. (2019). *How to be an antiracist*. One world.

Kozol, J. (2012). *Savage inequalities: Children in America's schools*. Crown. Original work published 1991.

Ladson-Billings, G. (2006). From the achievement gap to the education debt: Understanding achievement in U.S. schools. *Educational Researcher, 35*(7), 3–12.

Lull, J. (1995). *Media, communication, culture: A global approach*. Polity Press, in association with Blackwell.

Luna, G., Medina, C., & Gorman, M. S. (2010). Academic reality "show": Presented by women faculty of color. *Advancing Women in Leadership Journal, 30*. https://doi.org/10.21423/awlj-v30.a288

Matias, C. E. (2016). *Feeling White: Whiteness, emotionality, and education*. Brill.

Menges, R. J., & Exum, W. H. (1983). Barriers to the progress of women and minority faculty. *Journal of Higher Education, 54*(2), 123–144.

Mukandi, B., & Bond, C. (2019). "Good in the hood" or "burn it down"? Reconciling Black presence in the academy. *Journal of Intercultural Studies, 40*(2), 254–268.

Mustaffa, J. B. (2017). Mapping violence, naming life: A history of anti-Black oppression in the higher education system. *International Journal of Qualitative Studies in Education, 30*(8), 711–727.

Muzanenhamo, P., & Chowdhury, R. (2021). Epistemic injustice and hegemonic ordeal in management and organization studies: Advancing Black scholarship. *Human Relations, 76*(1): 3–26.

Myers, L. (2002). *A broken silence: Voices of African American women in the academy*. Greenwood.

Nighaoui, S. C. (2017). The Color of post-ethnicity: The civic ideology and the persistence of anti-Black racism. *Journal of Gender, Race, and Justice, 20*(2), 349–380.

Nkomo, S. M., & Cox Jr., T. (1999). Diverse identities in organizations. In Stewart R. Clegg, Cynthia Hardy, & Walter R. Nord (Eds.), *Managing organizations: Current issues* (pp. 88-106). Sage Publications.

Nkrumah, K. (1961). *I speak of freedom: A statement of African ideology.* Praeger.

Pérez Huber, L., & Solorzano, D. G. (2015). Racial microaggressions as a tool for critical race research. *Race Ethnicity and Education, 18*(3), 297-320.

Perna, L. W., Gerald, D., Baum, E., & Milem, J. (2007). The status of equity for Black faculty and administrators in public higher education in the South. *Research in Higher Education, 48*(2), 193-228.

Rothstein, R. (2017). *The color of law: A forgotten history of how our government segregated America.* Liveright.

Serequeberhan, T. (2010). Africa in a changing world: An inventory. *Monthly Review, 61*(8), 26.

Settles, I. H., Jones, M. K., Buchanan, N. T., & Dotson, K. (2021). Epistemic exclusion: Scholar(ly) devaluation that marginalizes faculty of color. *Journal of Diversity in Higher Education, 14*(4), 493-507.

Sexton, J. (2016). People-of-Color-Blindness: Notes on the afterlife of slavery. *Social Text, 28*(2), 31-56.

Sharpe, C. (2016). *In the wake: On Blackness and being.* Duke University Press.

Silver, J., Dennis, R., & Spikes, C. (1989). *Employment sequences of Blacks teaching in predominantly White institutions.* Southern Education Foundation.

Singh, K., & Shifflette, L. M. (1996). Teachers' perspectives on professional development. *Journal of Personnel Evaluation in Education, 10*(2), 145-160.

Smith, W. A., Allen, W. R., & Danley, L. L. (2007). "Assume the position . . . you fit the description": Psychosocial experiences and racial battle fatigue among African American male college students. *American Behavioral Scientist, 51*(4), 551-578.

Smith, W. A., Mustaffa, J. B., Jones, C. M., Curry, T. J., & Allen, W. R. (2016). 'You make me wanna holler and throw up both my hands!': Campus culture, Black misandric microaggressions, and racial battle fatigue. *International Journal of Qualitative Studies in Education, 29*(9), 1189-1209.

Sonn, C., & Green, M. J. (2006). Disrupting the dynamics of oppression in intercultural research and practice. *Journal of Community and Applied Social Psychology, 16*(5), 337-346.

Sule, V. T. (2011). Restructuring the master's tools: Black female and Latina faculty navigating and contributing in classrooms through oppositional positions. *Equity & Excellence in Education, 44*(2), 169-187.

Tawa, J., Suyemoto, K. L., & Roemer, L. (2012). Implications of perceived interpersonal and structural racism for Asian Americans' self-esteem. *Basic and Applied Social Psychology, 34*(4), 349-358.

Thompson, C. Q. (2008). Recruitment, retention, and mentoring faculty of color: The chronicle continues. *New Directions for Higher Education, 143,* 47-54.

Toporek, R. L. (2013). Violence against individuals and communities: Reflecting on the Trayvon Martin case—an introduction to the special issue. *Journal of Social Action in Counseling and Psychology, 5*(1), 1-10.

Trower, C., & Chait, R. (2002). Faculty diversity: Too little for too long. *Harvard Magazine, 104*(4), 33-38.

Warmington, P. (2014). *Black British intellectuals and education: Multiculturalism's hidden history.* Routledge.

Wilderson III, F. B. (2010). *Red, white & black: Cinema and the structure of US antagonisms.* Duke University Press.

Wingfield, A. H., & Feagin, J. (2012). The racial dialectic: President Barack Obama and the White racial frame. *Qualitative Sociology, 35*(2), 143-162.

2

Black Epistemologies Matter

Challenging Anti-Blackness in the Predominantly White Publishing World of the Academy

ERIK M. HINES, DONNA Y. FORD, JAMES L. MOORE III,
EDWARD C. FLETCHER JR., AND BRIAN L. WRIGHT

Before critiquing the anti-Blackness pervasive in white-authored academic publications, we present six all-too-familiar vignettes of our individual and combined experiences as (three) distinguished and (two)
associate Black professors at predominantly white institutions (PWIs)
and historically white institutions (HWIs) of higher education. Beyond the typical responsibilities as professors (e.g., advising, serving
on college committees, consulting, holding membership in and leading
professional organizations, teaching, conducting research, and performing service), we pay what is referred to as the "Black" or "cultural
tax" (Oliver, 2019), whereby we frequently take on the role of mentoring junior faculty of color and extra students at our own and other institutions. This tax, which we gladly pay, consumes time, sometimes
detracting from our own publishing productivity. This cultural obligation seldom counts in promotion and tenure deliberations. Later, we
return to this topic, which is also addressed in the following vignettes
that represent a sliver of common experiences—roadblocks, double
standards—that Blacks and other underrepresented scholars are bombarded with on their journey to promotion and tenure.

Black Experiences in the Academy

Not an independent scholar: A Black male assistant professor was told by administrators that he published "too much" with his doctoral adviser (twenty-one out of sixty published papers; 33%). However, a White male was given promotion and tenure the previous year with fewer publications, and twenty-three out of fifty publications (46%) with his dissertation adviser.

Low impact factor: A White male professor was granted promotion to full professor and was praised for publishing in journals with high impact factors. A Black female professor wanted to submit her dossier for promotion and tenure with the same number of publications; she was criticized for publishing in two urban journals with lower impact factors. Several faculty in her department, along with the department chair, advised her to wait another year or two and publish in higher-impact journals—that is, mainstream or White journals.

Pedigree under attack: A Black professor who moved from a historically Black colleges and universities institution was hired at a PWI with a higher salary but lower rank. A White associate professor in the same program area questioned whether the Black professor had the "pedigree" to succeed at the PWI, particularly with publishing and other scholarly endeavors. The White professor wondered whether the Black professor was a "diversity" hire.

Sailing without wind: A Black assistant professor asked several full professors and her department chairs for the number of publications required for promotion and tenure. She was told that there is no "magic" number. Frustrated and confused, she asked another new professor (White) whether he had been given a number. He responded "yes" and shared the expected number. Whatever the magic number, we know that this is a moving target once dossier materials are reviewed.

Moving targets: A Black assistant professor was informed verbally several times by the dean that four refereed articles per year ($n = 24$) were expected for promotion and tenure. When the professor submitted his dossier, he had twenty-nine, but the committee voiced criticism for having too few. He could not provide written evidence of the "four per year" target. For Black academicians, the number frequently increases, along with other criteria.

Discouraged to go up early for tenure or promotion: A Black female full professor recently moved to another institution of higher education but was given the rank of associate professor with tenure. A year after arriving, she spoke to the chair of her department about going up for early promotion. She was discouraged and told to wait another three years to be considered for a promotion. She read the faculty handbook for her department, college, and university and discovered that there are no time limits. She brought this information to the chair only to be admonished that she must be nominated by a faculty member of that rank to be considered for promotion. Another undocumented "rule" is being applied. Now, she must express her concerns and findings to the dean, knowing that she will be labeled a troublemaker.

Black Identity Scholarship

Despite the need to overcome racial barriers when seeking to publish in academic journals, we have been successful, relatively speaking, in publishing numerous manuscripts, contributing our part to the scholarly discussions of our fields. Our professional lives, therefore, contest the de facto lower rank Black research and scholarship receives compared to that of white scholarship. This binary racist and discriminatory practice, perpetuated in HWIs, serves to discredit the lived experiences of Black scholars and the approaches they use to measure, understand, and articulate perspectives that significantly influence the educational contexts and communities of color in general, and Black communities in particular. In our critique of the status quo and White privilege, we challenge what Donna Ford has termed "#scholarSHIT" that permeates many mainstream publications. #ScholarSHIT, in the guise of "scholarship," undermines Black epistemologies by ignoring, undervaluing, delegitimizing, and rendering invisible the necessity of Black scholarship and its impact on the ways of being and knowing of Black and Indigenous people of color (BIPOC) within and outside the academy.

HWIs delegitimize Black epistemologies to justify their marginalization within the broader academic ecosystem of racism and discriminatory practices. Such devaluation of scholarship is particularly pernicious for Black scholars who are often seen as not "measuring up" to white-centered publication criteria and are therefore unjustly held back from contributing to scholarship The academy's narrow view of scholarly value is upheld as an "objective evaluation" of our research and scholarship and, by extension, our intellectualism, which leads to questions about our "fit," competence, and ability to establish a national reputation to contribute to our respective fields of study and disciplines. The end result is a less than positive promotion and tenure review procedure with feedback and comments, in the guise of mere suggestions and recommendations, that leave Black scholars to second-guess their decisions to become professors, as well as their belonging in the academy—a manifestation of what is known in the literature as "imposter syndrome" (see Gutiérrez y Muhs et al., 2012). This manufactured "objective" review ultimately leads to the denial of promotion and tenure, contributing to the decrease in efforts to retain Black faculty at HWIs before and during the dual pandemic—COVID-19 and the Racism pandemic, which was sparked by the murder of George Floyd in May 2020. Unlike their White counterparts, Black faculty are contending simultaneously with two pandemics. Against this pernicious backdrop, we discuss how the experiences of Black scholars at various stages in their careers, in different and overlapping areas of study, are challenged by those who seek to maintain a knowledge hierarchy in their quest to retain power and privilege. The vignettes that opened this chapter capture several examples. Specifically, we discuss and challenge how White hegemony operates in ways that undervalue Black identity in scholarship, discounting our individual and collective knowledge that is used to advance equity in education and identifying it as less important than White scholarship in terms of its ability to add value to the research literature.

Black Faces in White Spaces: Demographics in HWIs

The enrollment patterns of Black and White college students were different during the pandemic (2019–2020 and 2020–2021), which comes as no surprise given previous and ongoing inequities in academic settings, and the P–12 to higher education pipeline (see *Journal of Blacks in Higher Education*, 2021).

The National Student Clearinghouse Research Center reported that college enrollments continued to fall in 2021 after a decrease the previous year due to the COVID-19 pandemic. Undergraduate enrollment dropped 3.2% between 2020 and 2021. Undergraduate student numbers fell by 6.5%. First-year enrollments declined by 3.1%, while the decline was 3.9% among traditional-age students.

The researchers found that, when disaggregated by race and ethnicity, Black enrollments decreased 5.1% during this timeframe. This is slightly deeper than the decline for Whites. Black enrollments in two-year community colleges lowered by 11.4%, which was somewhat similar to White students. Noteworthy is that between 2019 and 2021, Black enrollment in community colleges dropped a whopping 33.4%. White enrollments were down 20.3% during the same period.

A litany of factors—systemic, structural, and individual barriers—are responsible for the stark differences in Black and White higher education representation, and in the larger issue of recruitment and retention, which we term *desegregation* and *integration*, respectively. The aforementioned students' enrollment helps to predict and explain the abysmally low representation of Black faculty in the ivory tower. Next, we explore the racially unjust experiences of those "fortunate" enough to survive and become professors—despite barriers seldom encountered by White faculty concerning publishing in mainstream journals and meeting promotion and tenure requirements at HWIs.

Faculty Demographics

The racial, ethnic, and gender distribution of faculty varied by academic rank at degree-granting postsecondary institutions in the fall of 2018. According to the US Department of Education, National Center for Education Statistics (NCES, 2020), among full-time professors, slightly more than half (53%) were White males, 27% were White females, 8% were Asian/Pacific Islander males, and 3% were Asian/Pacific Islander females. Black males, Black females, and Hispanic males each accounted for an abysmally low 2% of full-time professors, for a total of 6%. Each of the following groups represented 1% or less of full-time professors: Hispanic females, American Indian/Alaska Native individuals, and individuals of two or more races.

Among full-time assistant professors, slightly more than one-third (34%) were White males and even more (39%) were White females. By comparison, 7% each were Asian/Pacific Islander males and Asian/Pacific Islander females, while 5% were Black females. Black males, Hispanic males, and Hispanic females each accounted for 3% of full-time assistant professors, while American Indians/Alaska Natives and individuals of two or more races accounted for 1% or less.

Themes of Injustice

In this section, we present a few common themes that depict the experiences of far too many Black and other minoritized faculty (and students).

You have to be twice as good to get promotion and tenure: The myth of meritocracy pervades the ivory tower (and many other disciplines). Faculty of color bear the weight of thinking that they must publish at least twice as many publications compared to their White faculty counterparts to ensure they are awarded tenure or promotion. There is a fear and realization that their White faculty peers and administrators will be unjustly critical and will deeply scrutinize their work. These sentiments lead minoritized scholars to experience higher stress and workloads than their peers, resulting in a work-life imbalance and occupational stress and fatigue (e.g., racial battle fatigue; Wilson, 2014).

Results from an analysis conducted by Smith and Witt (1993) indicated that Black faculty report higher levels of occupational stress (in general) than their White counterparts, especially in research and service activities. The source of this stress is the unequal distribution of "extra-academic" assignments among Black faculty, which limits their access to the more traditional faculty tasks and roles. This creates pressure to perform in ways not expected of White faculty. The stress from teaching (e.g., course design, selection of materials, creation of assignments, assessment, student evaluations), research and scholarship (e.g., publishing in top-tier journals), and service activities (e.g., journal review, consulting, presentations) experienced by Black faculty results in a much larger "faculty stress index" compared with White faculty—a double standard the vignettes, shared at the beginning of this chapter, gave voice to.

We have to be strategic in our timing when seeking promotion and tenure: Faculty, particularly those who aspire to pursue the full professor rank, often must factor in issues of timing, quality, and quantity when seeking promotion. There is often a fear among faculty of color that they will be compared to their White peers using highly subjective criteria that lacks clearly defined metrics; this gives rise to the concept of "fit," which remains a very subjective and White-centered concept and opens the door to racial prejudice and discrimination. Consequently, Black faculty seeking promotion during the same academic year as White counterparts become ensnared in this White-centered language and are compared to White faculty who often have published less but are considered "good citizens" and a better "fit" with the White culture of the college or department. Thus, even if promotion and tenure committee members review Black faculty with "stronger" scholarship records than their White peers, this positions Black faculty members as an intellectual threat rather than an asset. The predictable and unjust result decreases the chances of faculty members of color being awarded promotion or tenure. Several of the vignettes illustrate this.

You're not an independent scholar: The themes described herein are not mutually exclusive. In the promotion and tenure process, more than one barrier can be confronted. Arguments about having a professional identity independent of one's former doctoral adviser and committee members contribute to the "single authorship" roadblock.

As previously discussed, faculty of color are sometimes held to different standards when it comes to publishing. In particular, some are told to write single-authored manuscripts, which can take longer to produce and require more time to get published; conversely, White faculty are encouraged to write with multiple authors, a task with a shorter time to completion and publication, and one that demonstrates collaboration—a smoke screen for "good citizenship" and playing by spoken and unspoken rules. Relatedly, White faculty early in their careers as assistant professors have increased probabilities of being published due to coauthoring with a senior scholar. Name recognition carries weight in the publishing world. Another consideration often discounted, if considered at all, is that Black and other scholars of color (including doctoral students) often have a difficult time finding common research interests with fellow White faculty. This decreases opportunities to collaborate and coauthor articles, chapters, books, and grants. This physical isolation is compounded by scholarly isolation.

Moving targets when seeking to meet and exceed promotion and tenure requirements: Often, faculty of color face unclear expectations regarding the process of pursuing promotion or tenure; this is depicted in several of the vignettes presented earlier. They frequently are told by promotion and tenure committee members, as well as administrators and fellow faculty, that they do not have enough years of service within the institution to climb the ranks, even when their records exceed their White colleagues'. Other issues, such as the number of required or recommended peer teaching evaluations, become tactics that administrators and promotion and tenure committees use to dissuade faculty of color—who second-guess themselves, their credentials, and their productivity—from seeking promotion and tenure.

For Us, by Us: R.A.C.E. Mentoring

The ivory tower can often be a lonely and discouraging place for faculty of color. Social injustices run deep and are entrenched within academia. Faculty of color, more specifically Blacks, often lament microaggressions, stereotypes, and the "Black" or "cultural" tax that takes its toll, both personally and professionally, and frequently pushes them out of the academy. Similar to trends in P–12 settings, educators of color in postsecondary contexts represent less than 10% of the profession. In essence, we are an anomaly, and the implications of this are clear and dire, as evidenced by persistent achievement, access, and expectation gaps that hinder Black scholars' recruitment and retention in HWIs. This is compounded by a lack of institutional support, as illustrated in the vignettes.

Scholars of color, at all stages and ranks, but particularly during doctoral training, frequently struggle to not just survive but *thrive* in the academy. Too many fail to earn their doctoral degree, with many wearing the ABD (all but dissertation) as a badge of honor, but in some cases as evidence of defeat. Blacks often receive inadequate mentoring, substandard in comparison to the hand-holding and coddling White students receive, which leaves far too many doctoral scholars of color lost, bewildered, angry, indignant, and defeated. This indignation is justified but dismissed by those with decision-making power using the myth of meritocracy and color-blind or culture-blind notions of success, followed by a myriad of problems steeped in victim blaming, as noted in the classic *Presumed Incompetent: The Intersections of Race and Class for Women in Academia* (Gutiérrez y Muhs et al., 2012). This book was not the first treatise on how the non–status quo, along with others grappling with oppression and double standards, experience the field called higher education. *The Chilly Classroom Climate: A Guide to Improve the Education of Women* (Sandler et al., 1996), which focused on females, was also telling, but not enough was addressed and disclosed about females of color.

The Facebook group R.A.C.E. (research, advocacy, collaboration, and empowerment) Mentoring was created by Donna Y. Ford, Michelle Trotman Scott, and Malik S. Henfield in 2013 to tackle the numerous thorny and contentious issues and challenges in higher education. The founders began by intentionally attending to the needs of students of color enrolled at mostly PWIs, as well as those who attended historically Black colleges and universities, while keeping the unique nuances and challenges of each setting in mind. We wanted scholars of color to thrive in both.

Fondly called RM, the group's charge and challenge are to affirm the dignity and worth of scholars of color. Additionally, RM recognizes that there are scholars outside higher education who can and do support Black faculty and students to increase and provide opportunities for research and service. Examples are P–12 educators and administrators, community organizations, and corporations that agree to be places for research studies and grants, along with service opportunities (e.g., membership, leadership, consulting, blogging, and presentations). It truly takes a village, and this village has to include the voices of BIPOC and their allies. It also requires that college and university officials use their voices and actions to respond in a manner that is in the spirit of advocacy—proactive, justice oriented, and culturally responsive and responsible.

In the spirit of research, advocacy, collaboration, and empowerment, RM has a book series, hosts several webinars annually, has annual conferences, and provides a space to be our authentic selves (Ford et al., 2017). We cannot wait for HWIs to fully embrace us and our work; we must find ways and means to persist and thrive in spite of the challenges we face.

In summary, the purpose and goals of RM apply to minoritized journals, such as the *Journal of Negro Education*, the *Journal for Multicultural Education*, the *Journal for Women and Minorities in Science and Engineering*, *Urban Education*, the *Urban Review*, the *Journal of Black Psychology*, the *Journal of Multicultural Counseling and Development*, the *Journal of African American Males in Education*, the *Journal of Family Strengths*, and the *Journal of Minority Achievement, Creativity, and Leadership*. These journals provide publication outlets to counter rejections from mainstream journals. They also give voice to our work so that we are not silenced—not only are our voices heard in writing, but our issues are shared, giving a platform to antiracist, culturally responsive, and equity-based scholarship in the academy and beyond.

REFERENCES

Ford, D. Y., Trotman Scott, M., Goings, R., Wingfield, T., & Henfield, M. (Eds.). (2017). *R.A.C.E. mentoring through social media: Black and Hispanic scholars share their journey in the academy.* Information Age.

Gutiérrez y Muhs, G., Niemann, Y. F., González, C. G., & Harris, A. P. (Eds.). (2012). *Presumed incompetent: The intersections of race and class for women in academia.* University Press of Colorado. https://doi.org/10.2307/j.ctt4cgr3k.

Journal of Blacks in Higher Education. (2021). How Black enrollments in higher education have been impacted by the global pandemic. November 1, 2021. https://www.jbhe.com/2021/11/how-black-enrollments-in-higher-education -have-been-impacted-by-the-global-pandemic/.

NCES (US Department of Education, National Center for Education Statistics). (2020). Characteristics of postsecondary faculty. In *The condition of education 2020*, NCES 2020-144 (pp. 150-153). NCES.

Oliver, B. (2019). The hidden "Black tax" that some professionals of color struggle with. *Fast Company*, February 5, 2019. https://www.fastcompany.com/90296371/.

Sandler, B. R., Silverberg, L. A., & Hall, R. M. (1996). *The chilly classroom climate: A guide to improve the education of women.* National Association for Women in Education.

Smith, D. G., & Witt, P. A. (1993). Examining the stress–strain relationship among faculty: A qualitative analysis. *Journal of Higher Education*, 64(4), 389–412.

Wilson, W. (2014). Racial battle fatigue. In A. N. Villalpando & D. Solorzano (Eds.), *The Wiley Blackwell encyclopedia of race, ethnicity, and nationalism* (pp. 1-5). John Wiley & Sons.

3

What Black Social Scientists Want to Say to Reviewer #2

Resisting Race-Conscious Devaluation
of Black Scholars and Black Scholarship
Once and for All

TERRELL L. STRAYHORN

> In order to get beyond racism, we must first take account of race.
> There is no other way. —JUSTICE HARRY BLACKMUN

It was a typical day on campus at the predominantly White institution (PWI) where I worked as a full-time, tenured professor in the College of Education and Human Ecology. After teaching my graduate seminar and surviving several remarkably long meetings—one of departmental faculty and the other with collaborators in the College of Engineering—I retreated to my office to check email, grade papers, and prepare to leave campus for the day. As Outlook reconnected with the Exchange server, emails flooded my inbox from campus colleagues, centers, students, conferences, and national associations, to name a few. A furtive glance at the screen revealed an email from *"The Journal of . . . ,"* a phrase that always seemed to catch my eye. Once the download deluge completed, I searched to find the journal's email and quickly opened it. It was an editor's decision about a "recent submission"—and by that I mean a manuscript that I submitted for review and possible publication nearly a year ago, quite typical of academic publishing these days. Excitement stirred within as I scanned the email hoping for an "accept" or "minor revisions" outcome. My chest lowered and my breathing slowed as I crossed the phrase "major revisions." Knowing that the paper still stood a chance at publication, I read on to the reviewer's comments:

> While a respectable study with obvious worthy implications for improving policy and practice . . . [,] the author has little to nothing to say by studying Blacks only without comparing them to White students.

This is an excerpt of comments shared by "Reviewer #2" in response to the fairly extensive manuscript based on a rigorous empirical survey study that I conducted several years ago. In short, the project was based on a longitudinal survey of African American college students attending PWIs and historically Black colleges and universities (HBCUs) located in the United States. Along with several other key questions, the purpose of the longitudinal analysis was to estimate differences in postcollege outcomes among Black PWI graduates and their same-race HBCU peers—that, by design, was the *intentional* comparison to test for within-group differences.

Despite several pages of in-depth discussion of the study's design, analytic sample, key variables, and coverage of prior literature attempting to document measurable differences between Black graduates of PWIs and HBCUs, Reviewer #2 fell prey to the salacious assumption that "all Black students are the same, far more similar than different"—this we now call the fallacious belief in racial homogeneity. Echoing decades of similar racist critiques, the external peer reviewer implies that the academic study of Black life in America generally, and "Blacks in education" specifically, depends on—even requires—comparing them with Whites as the presumed objective standard by which all others must be judged. To do anything else is to have "little to nothing to say," regardless of one's theoretical grounding, methodological sophistication, and anti-deficit lens.

I wish that I could say this was the first and last time an external peer reviewer—almost always camouflaged as "Reviewer #2"—raised such offensive, suspicious, unbalanced, unwarranted, and racist criticisms cloaked as critique, but that would be a lie. In fact, this has happened on more than a dozen occasions almost exclusively at some of the most highly regarded scholarly journals in education and social sciences. That alone is troubling and worthy of the attention granted in this chapter, but it is even more disappointing that such scholarly vitriol is often passed along *uncritically* from reviewer to editor, then from editor to (Black) author, subtly implying that one reviewer's unqualified feedback is now an unquestionable fact to which the author must attend. Not only is this aggravating and inequitable, but it's exactly how structural racism perpetuates itself within academe.

Several problems flow from this uncertain predicament. Space limitations will not allow for a full discussion of every issue—including the erosion of a Black scholar's sense of self and scholarly efficacy at the hands of such intellectual microaggressions—that is, everyday insults to one's ideas and mind—but several deserve mention. For instance, circulating the belief that the value of Black scholars, Black students, and Black scholarship rests entirely on "Black versus White" comparisons only perpetuates the imbalanced, inequitable regime that *Black-centered*, antiracist, equity-minded studies were designed to resist. It is like telling a vegan that one cannot discuss or appreciate plant-based diets without also eating meat—it simply does not make sense. But they share another point in common: they can both be offensive to an entire way of life, a worldview, and an approach to engaging and understanding the world around them.

When editors *uncritically* pass along feedback that reinforces historical binaries, that upholds canonical perspectives, and that forces cross-racial comparisons that perpetuate the hierarchy of oppression, they subject scholars of color—namely Black scholars—to yet another form of oppression and marginalization. One (White) scholar (probably wearing an "I'm woke" T-shirt) conjures up a half-baked, fictitious opinion that now gets reproduced and circulated through the coveted peer-review process as fact or grand theory. That lands on the Black scholar's desk in the form of a decision letter rendering the manuscript "rejected" or in need of "major revisions," to name a few options. Though it is hard to remember in the moment, "rejected" refers to the manuscript *in its current form*, not the project, the study's sample, or the scholar—it can be difficult to separate the incident from identity. If the manuscript is not rejected, the author has the opportunity to address concerns from reviewers by making major revisions to it. And most, like myself, will feel compelled to respond to "Reviewer #2" not because we agree with their Eurocentric assessment but because we believe in the worth of the project, the impact of the study, and desire to publish our scholarship in highly ranked journals that both provide academic prestige, standing, and broad circulation, as well as fulfill professional obligations and institutional requirements.

To interrogate the reviewer's race-based comments in a way that both exposes their underlying assumptions and facilitates a *critical conversation* about Black scholarship in a White academy, I utilize critical race theory (CRT) as a necessary heuristic for analysis. After delineating CRT in the next section, I employ its core tenets to lay bare the problems, contradictions, and limitations of Reviewer #2's racist evaluation that reflects how Black scholarship is viewed through the "White gaze" of the academy. A final section points to affirmative actions that hold promise for improving the condition and consideration of Black scholarship in the future.

Critical Race Theory: A Frame for Conversation

CRT is an important framework that has proved effective for critically considering issues related to race and racism in law, business, politics, and education, to name a few fields (Crenshaw, 1995; Ladson-Billings, 2003). It is an intellectual movement (Roithmayr, 1999) that emerged in the mid-1970s from the writings of predominantly Black critical legal studies scholars (Bell, 1992; Crenshaw, 1995). Generally presented as a starting point for developing a critical "race consciousness," CRT directs close explanatory attention to how race privileges Whiteness and disadvantages others, especially those attributed with Blackness.

Scholars generally agree that CRT has several core tenets. First, it involves centering race and racism, while also acknowledging their connection to other forms of oppression and subjugation (e.g., class, gender). A critical ontology ensures that race stays at the center of the lens as a driving force adjusting the aperture through which the researcher views a subject or phenomenon. With its intentional and un apologetic emphasis on race *and racism*, CRT facilitates analyses of social phenomena from a starting point that is race conscious and admits the existence of a fundamentally unequal society where structures and processes systematically deprive some while privileging others.

Second, CRT challenges traditional dominant ideologies and critiques liberalism. For instance, it rejects prevailing systems of ideals that form the basis of economic and political policies such as meritocracy, objectivity, color blindness, race neutrality, and "leveling the playing field" perspectives. In prior research, CRT has been instrumental in interrogating existing orthodoxies of fairness, racial harmony, homogeneity, equal opportunity, and multiculturalism (Ladson-Billings, 1998).

The third tenet of CRT acknowledges the value of experiential knowledge—in other words, it identifies experiences as valid resources and knowledge sources to supplement and challenge established epistemologies. For example, CRT places a premium on "the Black voice" that is all too often devalued, inadequately represented, or ignored in traditional methodologies, epistemologies, and social science studies. Recent CRT criticisms, however, caution against essentializing "the Black experience" through recognition of "the Black voice," as if *the voice* played on a single note. Instead, CRT encourages counterstory methods that center racialized voices and present competing versions of reality. Counterstories are race-centered research tools that reflect embodiment of the African proverb "Until the lion tells its story, the tale of the hunt will always glorify the hunter."

Other core tenets of CRT hold that it is a transdisciplinary approach to the development of theory and praxis in relation to race and racism in society (Stovall, 2005), thereby resisting ahistorical, apolitical, classless, and unidisciplinary models of analysis. Consequently, it has the potential to interrupt and transform social science, jurisprudence, structures, and racial power to further an agenda of racial emancipation (Roithmayr, 1999) and social justice (Villalpando & Solórzano, 2005).

In short, CRT offers an alternative way of knowing and an accessible lexicon—that is, words and phrases—for talking about *and through* difficult concepts like race, racism, and systematic oppression. As a framework, CRT can be used effectively to generate a useful theoretical vocabulary for practicing progressive politics, theorizing, and understanding essential formations of racial power and ideologies.

Putting CRT into Practice: A Rejoinder to Reviewer #2

Before employing CRT as a tool for challenging and responding to Reviewer #2's comments, I owe it to future readers—especially early-career underrepresented researchers—to admit openly that I did *not* enter the White academy as a Black scholar knowing that I could disagree with a reviewer *through my revision* and still stand a chance at publication. This lack of knowledge was in part due to years of internalized racism, living as a Black boy-turned-man in the South, and the balance between "time and opportunity," as they say. While my doctoral adviser, Don Creamer (a White male Texan) taught me much about the field—how to carry out my dissertation, how to negotiate a book contract, and how to interview for a tenure-track faculty position at a research university—it was Sylvia Hurtado (a Latina eminent scholar at UCLA) who empowered me to know that I could "speak up, talk back, and argue for my approach to the topic as an expert voice." While I learned so much from Don in formal classrooms and advising meetings, I received the gift of this advice from Sylvia over informal coffee and conversation at a conference. This simply goes to show that mentoring matters and it occurs in every nook and cranny of life.

It is virtually impossible to describe the gravity and weight that Sylvia's words carried *to* and *for* me. That a leading scholar, who is also a person of color, would advise me to speak up (recognizing that I have a voice), to talk back (affirming that I have something important to say), and to argue for my approach as an expert (no longer just a student) was life-changing—no, *game-changing*—transporting me from the sunken place shackled by the weight of "major revisions" to the place of powerful possibilities energized by the opportunity to inform, improve, and reprove an academy that wasn't built with me in mind. Her sage advice aligned with my own epistemological view of the world—that communities of color are both creators and producers of knowledge (too) and thus should be central to talking back to and resisting Western constructions of their lived experiences. Though living miles apart, together we made good sense.

To address Reviewer #2's comments, I had to fully understand the sentiments of his feedback. So, yes, that required a close, careful reading and rereading of his fairly lengthy evaluation, including the parts that were (and are) racially offensive, insensitive, "unwoke," and blatantly inconsistent with the aims of a journal that purportedly "welcomes submissions from all methodological traditions and disciplines" . . . where scholars find their voice (paraphrased). It is impossible to mount an informed response to critique without first leaning in to hear, listen to, and understand the perspective, no matter how dissonant, inconsistent, or unusual. Denying Reviewer #2 the space to air this perspective is no better than downplaying my methodological choice as a mistake or error—it is simply replacing one form of tyranny with another. To square up my response, I found it useful to outline the reviewer's incendiary comments on the left side of my notebook paper and frame my response to each comment on the right side. CRT was instrumental in this exercise, as it provided language, definitions, and propositions for presenting the main points of my rebuttal. The accompanying figure presents a visual illustration.

For the sake of brevity, I highlight a handful of points here that structured my response to the reviewer's comments, but this list is by no means exhaustive. In fact, readers of this chapter will likely see other refutations that could (and likely should) have been raised to challenge this perspective. Rather than judging this as missing the mark, readers are encouraged "to speak up, talk back, and argue for [your own] approach," especially for Black scholarship in a White academy. One of the first issues that I tackled in my written response was the reviewer's nod to the *respectability* of the study. I was puzzled

Framing My Argument: Critical Race Theory

- Race and racism are endemic in society and, thus, should be at center
- Challenges traditional dominant ideologies
- Acknowledges experiential knowledge

While a respectable study with obvious worthy implications for improving policy and practice, the author has little to nothing to say by studying Blacks only...

ANONYMOUS REVIEWER

Side-by-Side Analysis

While a respectable study	• respectability politics • what qualifies study as respectable? by whom?
...with obvious worthy implications for improving policy and practice	• despite minor APA issues typical of many manuscripts, the reviewer admits the study has capacity to create change
the author has little to nothing to say by studying blacks only	• Voice and race linked to disempower or silence • new racism
by studying blacks only without comparing them to White students	• erroneous assumption about race • whiteness in educational research • capitalization

Side-by-side analysis of reviewer's comments.

over the word choice. What makes a study respectable, per se? And what would a *disrespectful* study look like? I could not resist mental images of White male-like bodies looking down on Black and Brown ones, threatening them to avoid direct eye contact—"Don't look at me, boy. . . . You're not on my level," as they would shout in some of the horrific movies we watched in social studies depicting Black life in America pre-1950s. Was it that the study was deemed respectable because it did not rock the intellectual boat? It failed to challenge preexisting assumptions or break from traditional disciplinary boundaries; it simply preserved the status quo and avoided *direct eye contact* with Western constructions of comparative analysis in social science research by analyzing data without first theorizing race, racism, and a race-centered way of knowing.

In response, I called out the term *respectable* and linked it to the historical and current literature on respectability politics and race from sociology, law, and economics. I invited the editor into my situation by asking a set of rhetorical questions: *What makes a study respectful? And what makes a study disrespectful?* Nodding to the terrifying pre-1950s social exchanges between White men and African Americans, I challenged any race-neutral interpretation of the comment and affirmed my right to know and how to know (i.e., epistemology). Rather than leaving it to chance, I added an entire section to the paper directly explaining my methodological decision to use longitudinal survey data, with appropriate proxies for potentially confounding variables, to study the labor market outcomes of Black college graduates, comparing Black PWI and Black HBCU graduates *without* reference to White students. I explicitly noted that I was consciously debunking and resisting dominant expectations to compare Blacks to Whites, which renders White students as the standard by which all other success is measured.

A second point that the reviewer made is found in their comment that the study has potential for improving education policy and practices despite "minor APA issues" typical of many manuscripts about race. At first glance, I was struck by the connection between race and, say, the use of running headers in keeping with the APA's most recent edition of the *Publication Manual*. But upon further reflection, I realized that the reviewer's comments revealed elements of a deeper racialized discourse (and flawed mind-set) that has a propensity to fall prey to confusing facts with fiction, typos with typologies, and incidents with identities. Without intervention, such perspectives disguise the White academy as objective, color-blind, or race-neutral and can leave one wondering whether mistakes happen when studying race or whether *studying race* is a mistake. Both conclusions are wrong, problematic, and an unfortunate by-product of race and racism being permanent fixtures in society often enacted through informed perspectives, unsubstantiated claims, and inequitable practices and processes (Bell, 1992).

In response, I pointed out the reviewer's comment about the frequency of APA infelicities in manuscripts about race and placed the burden of proof on the reviewer or editor. I wrote, "I was both struck and confused by the reviewer's comment that 'minor APA issues [are] typical of many manuscripts about race.' Does the reviewer *believe* this is correlation, causation, or genetic? Are journal data readily available to support this assertion?" Knowing that the questions would likely go without response, I then turned to thank the reviewer for acknowledging the study's obvious implications for improving policy and practice in education. I urged the editor to consider this point when making a final decision about the paper's contribution to knowledge. Recall that CRT has a clear and compelling commitment to social justice and thus that any such research must hold promise for producing social transformation that changes the material conditions of dispossessed and disempowered communities (Villalpando & Solórzano, 2005).

A third point drawn from the reviewer's comment relates to issues of invisibility, voicelessness, and disempowerment (Ellison, 1952). Notice the power and privilege that is displayed in the external reviewer's pronouncement that I, as "the author," have *little to nothing to say* "by studying Blacks only," as if to suggest that studying Black life in America generally, or higher education specifically, is a waste of time. Although I had written over thirty pages of content reporting results from a fairly complex quantitative analysis that took months to fully execute, Reviewer #2's comment silences my voice and the implied voice of my survey respondents by declaring a major contradiction—that the *respectable study* with *worthy implications* had *little to nothing to say*. And according to the reviewer, its greatest weakness perhaps was its focus on "Blacks only," a statement that eerily echoes Jim Crow segregation signs that designated public places "Whites only" and "colored only." Was it subconsciously plastered in this written evaluation to mark the "top-tier" or "highly rated" or "prestigious" journal as welcoming to some, not all?

In response, I pointed out these concerns using the interdisciplinary literature on *new racism* as a guide. New racism, or cultural racism, reifies distinctions between powerful and less powerful, visible and less visible groups using words and phrases that seem harmless (e.g., *different*) but perpetuate divisiveness through exclusion, prejudice, and hatred. Anticipating a tongue-in-cheek response that I was "being too sensitive" or "taking things out of context," I acknowledged that new racism is far less recognizable than the overt racism of the past, making it difficult to detect and easy to deny. Then, I turned to reclaim the *mean*(ing) and *frequency* of "Black voices," as well as *the weight* (i.e., regression coefficient) of their *explanatory power* (i.e., R^2) in my study, to play on several statistical terms. Through a quantitative investigation, I strove to tie statistical results to "lived experiences" in the discussion section of the revised manuscript. Wherever possible, I also avoided the phrase "Blacks only," for obvious reasons.

A fourth and final point focuses on the reviewer's insistence that Black students *must be* compared to White students, despite decades of research consistently showing differential effects of college (Mayhew et al., 2016). The reviewer's argument is based on an erroneous and limited racialized assumption that humans can be divided into biologically and phenotypically distinct races whose similarities *within group* are indistinguishable, yet differences *across groups* are pronounced. Research shows that within-group differences can be large. Comments from the reviewer also provide clear evidence of belief in a racial hierarchy that exists with White people at the top—serving as the rule by which all others are judged—and darker races (e.g., Blacks) at the bottom (Fenton, 2003). The insistence on cross-racial comparisons confirms that some dominant mind-sets can be parochial in nature and problematic in practice, perpetuating the stubbornly persistent "Black-White binary" that sustains Whiteness in education research (Deliovsky & Kitossa, 2013).

In response, I expanded my literature review to include studies that compare Black and White college students across postgraduation labor market outcomes, highlighting that few studies explore *within-group* variances. Furthermore, I enlisted the growing literature on Black men in college to bolster the argument for examining differences between Black men and women at PWIs and HBCUs. All of this was more than merely revising the manuscript or attending to the reviewer's comments, although that is undeniably important. It also served as a form of scholarly *race-conscious resistance* to canonical, dominant, Eurocentric, or Western ways of knowing that failed to honor more indigenous worldviews or align with my own epistemological beliefs about knowledge—what it is, how it is constructed, and who has the power to produce it. Indeed, Black lives matter—so, too, do their voices, in and of themselves.

Future Directions

Recall that the purpose of this chapter was to interrogate an external reviewer's race-based comments in a way that both exposes their underlying assumptions and facilitates a *critical conversation* about Black scholarship in a White academy. Specifically, I utilized CRT as an organizing heuristic for analysis and revealed through my writing how it informed my response and revision of the manuscript under question. After delineating CRT and its core tenets, I employed it to lay bare the problems, contradictions, and limitations of Reviewer #2's racist evaluation to expose how Black scholarship is all too often viewed unfairly through the "White gaze" of the academy. In this final section, I point to affirmative actions that hold promise for improving the condition and consideration of Black scholarship in the future.

First, external reviewers from all walks of life would do well to read essays like the present chapter, and others included in this volume, to familiarize themselves with the lived racialized experiences of others. Race (still) matters in society (West, 1993) and in the academy. Race, though a social construct, "is neither an essence nor an illusion" (Haney-Lopez, 2000, p. 193). Race and racism have *real* material effects on people's experiences, opportunity structures, and potential for achieving their dreams.

Rather than deny such realities, reviewers, editors, researchers, and writers alike should acknowledge race and racism as "normal, not aberrant" (Delgado, 1995, p. xiv), and to adopt antiracist perspectives and practices to overcome these effects. For instance, publishing companies and university presses should *intentionally* recruit and appoint chief editors of color and diverse editorial board members who bring Eastern, Afrocentric, and Third World views with them. Editors might also challenge racist perspectives by annotating reviewers' feedback and calling out comments that are inconsistent with the journal's commitment to person-first, assets-based, antiracist, and inclusive practices. Beyond annotation, editors reserve the right to request the removal of offensive comments, incendiary remarks, and faulty racial reasoning before passing information along to authors. This should *not* be viewed as too much work; it is *the work* of antiracist scholars.

My final word goes to fellow Black scholars living, working, striving, and thriving to *find a way or make one* through a White academy that was *not* designed for us or by us. Remember this: *You matter. You are enough. You belong here* (Strayhorn, 2019). You are important and your work adds distinctive value to the shelf of knowledge. It fills a space that could not be occupied by many others—they simply do not see what you see *and* do not know what you know. This is not a claim of intellectual superiority that maps neatly onto grade point averages, standardized test scores, and early- or midcareer awards from national professional associations. If that is your aim, I wish you many ceremonies, trophies, and honorable mentions. But even more than that, I want you to affirm your value in the field—it is too risky to leave that to others in a White academy. *You are important;* do not let anyone tell you otherwise, not even Reviewer #2. *We see you;* stay your true, authentic self. *We need you;* so practice self-care and love regularly. *Never give up;* find joy in the journey and keep shining. There's a bright side somewhere; do not give up until you find it, as the old gospel hymn reminds us. *There's a bright side somewhere.*

REFERENCES

Bell, D. A. (1992). *Faces at the bottom of the well: The permanence of racism.* Basic Books.

Crenshaw, K. W. (1995). Mapping the margins: Intersectionality, identity politics, and violence against women of color. In K. Crenshaw, N. Gotanda, G. Peller, & A. D. Thomas (Eds.), *Critical race theory: The key writings that formed the movement* (pp. 357–383). New Press.

Delgado, R. (1995). Introduction. In R. Delgado (Ed.), *Critical race theory: The cutting edge* (pp. xiii–xvi). Temple University Press.

Deliovsky, K., & Kitossa, T. (2013). Beyond Black and White: When going beyond may take us out of bounds. *Journal of Black Studies, 44*(2), 158–181.

Ellison, R. (1952). *Invisible man.* Random House.

Fenton, S. (2003). *Ethnicity*. Polity.

Haney-Lopez, I. (2000). The social construction of race. In R. Delgado & J. Stefancic (Eds.), *Critical race theory: The cutting edge* (2nd ed., pp. 163-175). Temple University Press.

Ladson-Billings, G. (1998). Just what is critical race theory and what's it doing in a *nice* field like education? *Qualitative Studies in Education, 11*(1), 7-24.

Ladson-Billings, G. (2003). *Critical race theory: Perspectives on social studies*. Information Age.

Mayhew, M. J., Rockenbach, A. N., Bowman, N., Seifert, T. A., Wolniak, G. C., Pascarella, E. T., & Terenzini, P. T. (2016). *How college affects students: 21st century evidence that higher education works* (Vol. 3). Jossey-Bass.

Roithmayr, D. (1999). Introduction to critical race theory in educational research and praxis. In L. Parker, D. Deyhle, & S. Villenas (Eds.), *Race is . . . race Isn't: Critical race theory and qualitative studies in education*. Westview.

Stovall, D. (2005). A challenge to traditional theory: Critical race theory, African American organizers, and education. *Discourse Studies in the Cultural Politics of Education, 26*(1), 95-108.

Strayhorn, T. L. (2019). *College students' sense of belonging: A key to educational success for all students* (2nd ed.). Routledge.

Villalpando, O., & Solórzano, D. G. (2005). The role of culture in college preparation programs: A review of the research literature. In W. G. Tierney, Z. B. Corwin, & J. E. Colyar (Eds.), *Preparing for college: Nine elements of effective outreach* (pp. 13-28). State University of New York Press.

West, C. (1993). *Race matters*. Vintage Books.

4

We Goin' Ultra Black?

Real Rap about Hip-Hop Pedagogy in Higher Education

H. BERNARD HALL

Way back in 2006, I was transitioning from the eighth-grade English language arts classroom to the assistant principal's office in Ypsilanti, Michigan. In between the migraines and depression that came with enforcing what I now know to be an anti-Black student code of conduct, I was doing my research on different doctoral programs. This was when I stumbled across the research profile of Marc Lamont Hill, who was a junior faculty member at Temple University in Philadelphia. After a couple more clicks and a few more scrolls, I saw it for the first time: *hip-hop pedagogy.*

Oh, shit! That's me. That's what I do! That's what I want to do . . . I think?

It was on, I was going to build my research agenda around hip-hop pedagogy. Starting with Tricia Rose's *Black Noise* (1994) and Murray Forman and Mark Anthony Neal's edited volume, *That's the Joint! The Hip-Hop Studies Reader* (2004), I spent the next six years reading every published work on hip-hop cultural studies. While I entered, and ultimately exited, the classroom without ever hearing the term *hip-hop pedagogy* (more about this later), I learned that the first peer-reviewed scholarship on hip-hop culture's role, purpose, and function in K–12 classrooms and schools was published in the early 1990s (Anderson, 1993; Baker, 1991; Jeremiah, 1992). As a research assistant, I had the privilege of contributing to Hill's book on "hip-hop-based education" (HHBE), *Beats, Rhymes, and Classroom Life: Hip-Hop Pedagogy and the Politics of Identity* (2009). In it, Hill theorizes the distinct yet interconnected instructional, dialogical, and political dimensions of HHBE using the tripartite "pedagogies *with*, *about*, and *of* hip-hop." "Pedagogies *with* hip-hop," the most common form of hip-hop pedagogy, describe the ways hip-hop cultural products (primarily printed rap lyrics as literary texts) are used to validate students' hip-hop literacies as a means of scaffolding the interests of students to the interests (i.e., curricular goals) of the teacher or school (Hill, 2009; Morrell & Duncan-Andrade, 2002; Stovall, 2006). "Pedagogies *about* hip-hop" call for teachers and students to act as "cultural critics who deploy critical literacies in order to identify and respond to structures of power and meaning within hip-hop texts" (Hill, 2009, p. 122). Through celebrations and critiques of the cultural self, teachers and students tender poignant commentaries on the violent, misogynistic, and materialistic messages propagated by rap music and American culture at large (Dimitriadis, 2001; Fisher, 2007; Hill, 2009; Stino, 1995). The third leg of the hip-hop pedagogical tripod is "pedagogies *of* hip-hop." These "reflect the various ways that hip-hop culture authorizes particular values, truth claims, and subject positions while implicitly and explicitly contesting others" (Hill, 2009, p. 120).

More recently, HHBE scholars, most notably Christopher Emdin and Bettina L. Love, have argued for a more expansive notion of *critical hip-hop pedagogy* (CHHP). CHHP pushes researchers, scholars, and teachers to consider the pedagogical potential of hip-hop cultural knowledge and products drawn from the other three core elements (deejaying, graffiti, and breakdancing), not just emceeing and rap music. Love (2018) argues for the inclusion of hip-hop's fifth element, "knowledge of self," and the importance of reconnecting Black students to their African identity and history. Furthermore, like its antecedent "critical pedagogy" (Freire, 1970), CHHP is explicit in its goals of addressing social inequities (Love, 2018). A testament to the brilliance and hustle driving their work, Emdin and Love have risen to the forefront of national discourses about urban education reform (Emdin, 2016; Love, 2019).

As KRS-One (2003), known in the Hip-Hop Nation as the Teacha, famously said, "Rap is something you do. Hip-hop is how you live." It has been fifteen years since I had that life-changing *Oh, shit!* moment, and I can now say—without question marks or ellipses—that HHBE is what I do, and hip-hop pedagogy is how I live. My teaching practices and behaviors, whether with middle school students, pre-service teachers, or doctoral students, are foregrounded in hip-hop cultural literacies, from the creative processes I use to design a lesson plan, to how I "move the crowd" (linguistically) in the classroom or lecture hall, and most importantly, *why* I move the crowd (politically). How I live, my identity as a scholar-activist, is, in the words of Nas (2020), "ultra Black." In this conversation about hip-hop pedagogy, *ultra Black* signifies unapologetic language and acts of critique and love. If you were not alive and aware in 1989 when Public Enemy's "Fight the Power" dropped, it is hard to comprehend how big of a deal it was for Flavor Flav to scream, "Motherfuck him [Elvis Presley] and John Wayne!" The substance of what he and Chuck D said—America's cultural heroes were "straight up racist"—combined with the style of how he said it, MF and all, took White America's (and my nine-year-old) breath away. The substance and style of this critique represent the essence of hip-hop pedagogy. Much to the chagrin of some of my colleagues (White and Black), I do not play the respectability politics game very well anymore. I am not hesitating, qualifying, or apologizing for calling out what is "simple and plain": White supremacy and anti-Blackness are embedded in K–12 schools and teacher education. Due to the White academy's unwillingness or inability to respond to inequalities that Black scholarship has made simple and plain, hip-hop pedagogy is invaluable because it screams the truth in ways that the White academy cannot ignore.

Ultra-Black hip-hop pedagogy is also about unapologetic love; what I would describe as deliberate acts of collective cultural self-care. Whether it is through my money and time or, in this case, my teaching and research, I support Black "shit." I am unwavering in my professional and personal commitments to improving the educational and lived experiences of Black youths. There is an urgency to hip-hop pedagogy because White supremacy and anti-Blackness are not only embedded in White institutions; they have been internalized by Black people too. It takes deliberate acts of love and knowledge of self to unlearn lessons like these. Questions persist about whether the White academy shares this urgency or is capable of unlearning what has been internalized for so long.

This brings me to the subtitle and focus of this chapter: "Real Rap about Hip-Hop Pedagogy in Higher Education." In my ethnographic research on hip-hop-based educators in urban English language arts classrooms, the words *real talk*, or my preferred variant, *real rap*, were invoked in a number of different ways. In one instance, "Real Talk" was the name of the large-group classroom discussion led by a young, Black male hip-hop educator. Here, real talk signified the importance of speaking candidly and being true to one's thoughts and beliefs, without fear of what others might think. It also signified that the content of the conversations, whether drawn from the curricular text or individual and collective lived experiences, may be difficult to discuss. From my observations of and interviews with the teacher and students, it was evident that this kind of honesty, safety, and "realness" was missing from the majority of the educational spaces they frequented, and it fostered a different level of engagement, one that reflected the academic and cultural needs of the participants.

In this chapter, I will engage in critical conversations, or *real rap*, about the challenges and tensions scholars who specialize in hip-hop cultural studies and HHBE face in this "White man'z world" (Shakur, 1996) known as higher education. As you may have already noticed through my occasional use of uncensored expletives and the numerous hip-hop cultural references I weave into my prose, this conversation will be in my most authentic voice. The "first verse" of this rap will center on higher education's (and White America's) genuine and voyeuristic interests in hip-hop culture. In the second verse, without fear of reprisal, I will talk about HHBE and the anti-(ultra) Blackness that functions in teacher education. The conversation will conclude with reflections and insights for scholars and researchers committed to fighting the (hegemonic) powers from within the power.

Why am I doing this? I think it is worth repeating: this kind of honesty, safety, and "realness" is missing from most of the educational spaces we frequent. One of my goals is to make the private public; to take those isolated conversations we have with our comrades within the walls of our Hip-Hop Theories, Praxis, and Pedagogies Special Interest Group meetings at the American Educational Research Association Annual Meeting (shout-outs to Lauren Leigh Kelly and Daren Graves), and in office hours and group texts with our mentors or mentees, and put them on blast. I want the aspiring doctoral student or junior faculty member who picks up this book to know the professional, cultural, and emotional risks and rewards that come with goin' ultra Black in the ivory tower. To a lesser extent, I am also doing this for our White colleagues—the "real" ones. By giving them access to this chapter, I am, as Ta-Nehisi Coates does in *Between the World and Me* (2015), giving them an opportunity to interrogate some of the power and privileges they enjoy.

First Verse: Higher Education's Genuine and Voyeuristic Interests in Hip-Hop

As a point of departure, I begin with the realest of rap, taken from Cornel West's (2021) recent letter of resignation from Harvard University: "With a few glorious and glaring exceptions, the shadow of Jim Crow was cast in its new glittering form expressed in the language of superficial diversity." Personally, I do not know a single Black, Brown, or queer scholar who did not holler #*Facts!* (or some similar affirmation) upon reading West's words. I could copy and paste the entire letter, but I find this passage particularly salient to the challenges faced by hip-hop scholars.

The questions surrounding the authenticity of higher education's interests in hip-hop studies and HHBE stem from White America's complicated history of consumption and production of Black culture.

From jazz and rock and roll to the Black Arts movement and rap music, it is evident that White America loves our shit. Over the past forty years, we have witnessed the domestic and international appeal of hip-hop to non-Black people as an authentic medium to learn about the marginalization of others and express personal experiences of oppression (Kahf, 2012; Pardue, 2013; Tiongson, 2013). This is where my hope and optimism as a HHBE scholar and teacher educator come from. In the spirit of cross-cultural exchange, I teach and research to make the strange familiar. Teaching and learning with and about hip-hop is strange to cultural outsiders who possess no physical or psychological connections to the hood (Emdin, 2016). So, too, is the idea of living in an America that is "like a jungle sometimes" (Flash et al., 1982/1994); where teachers, police officers, and politicians do not always have the best interests of the people they serve in mind. Teachers cannot teach what they do not know and cannot "fight the power(s)" they do not see. Hip-hop provides a means of cross-cultural exchange that helps outsiders know and see.

However, we also know that some of the White kids who listened to Wu-Tang and Tupac with us when we were teenagers are now listening to Sean Hannity and Tucker Carlson in their forties. White America loves hip-hop culture when it is objectified and reduced to rap music, especially the popular violent, misogynistic, and materialistic variety when it is time to turn up before the football game or at the party. But what about when it is time to turn up for justice? Hip-hop is *our* shit; and it is way more than just rap music. It is our history, our politics, our identity. "Passing through" hip-hop culture as a phase of teenage rebelliousness is cultural voyeurism (Hawthorne, 1989). Consuming or producing hip-hop cultural knowledge and products in ways that disconnect it from the racialized systems of oppression they were born out of is cultural voyeurism.

This is why hip-hop scholars such as myself are skeptical about higher education's interests in hip-hop studies and HHBE. Unfortunately, to borrow from West, the language and acts of superficial diversity are more conspicuous than the exceptions. Higher education definitely wants the "hip"—the new faces of color and trendy buzzwords on their websites, "cool" courses in the catalog, and packed special lectures. But they do not necessarily want the "hop"—the actions, especially when the commitments to social justice and critiques of White supremacy are directed toward senior faculty members and internal policies and practices. Many of us have dealt with the pre— and post–job offer bait-and-switch. During the interview process, search committee chairs genuinely encourage us to present our ambitious, action-oriented teaching, and research agendas. Once the offer is extended, the meeting with the dean often comes with a warning to "play it safe" until after tenure.

Speaking of tenure, the vast majority of hip-hop scholars are hired into "old-school" departments or schools like sociology, English, and education that are deeply entrenched in the traditions of the academy. When considering where to place my work, I find myself wrestling with the tensions between selecting a prestigious academic journal because of its reputable impact factor and aiming for a lesser-known journal because I believe in supporting Black shit and making an impact in my community. Some of the tensions are the result of microaggressions I have had to endure in the feedback from reviewers and editors of those "prestigious" academic journals. Sampling from the title of Rudolfo Anaya's poem "Take the Tortillas Out of Your Poetry" (1995), I have been reminded to "take the flow out of my academic writing" on a number of occasions. I am well aware of the conventions of the academic genre and importance of writing with your audience in mind, but the irony of reviewers telling me that the prose I use in articles about the intersections of hip-hop pedagogy and English education is "too poetic" is not lost on me.

The pressure to secure external research grant money is also palpable. Admittedly, this has been one of the most significant tensions I have had to negotiate in my transition from my previous position as a tenured faculty member at a public teaching institution to my current tenure-track position at a private research institution. You're telling me that my work is only important to the extent that it brings in extramural support? The purpose of doing research is to secure funding (Gallup & Svare, 2016)? I am fortunate to have a small but solid group of Black faculty mentors who have put me on to the grant game. Yet I feel like the aspiring musical artist torn between signing with a major record label and staying independent. I want to earn tenure *and* I want to maximize my impact in my field, as well as my community. The more money I bring in, the more time and support I will have to devote to accomplishing my professional and personal goals—I get it. At the same time, I am very uncomfortable with the idea of bureaucrats with purse strings determining the merits of my HHBE research.

We felt West's frustrations in part because even in higher education, arguably the most "progressive" of White spaces, the shadows of Jim Crow continue to loom over Black scholars. Yes, we are getting the interviews. Yes, in some cases we are getting the jobs. And yes, getting the job also means getting the isolation and hypervisibility that comes with being the only one (or one of a few). Yes, getting the job means getting the microaggressions in emails and meetings. It means getting *extra* jobs like serving on diversity, equity, and inclusion and search committees. For hip-hop scholars in particular, the jobs come with concerns about being objectified as a commodity used to expand higher education's consumer base and increase profits. The jobs also come with the risks of being perceived as *over Black*, and not worth the trouble. If Harvard can push Cornel West out, we are all in trouble— real rap.

Second Verse: Hip-Hop Pedagogy and Anti-(Ultra-) Blackness in Teacher Education

I must admit that the concept of *hegemony* was completely foreign to me when I graduated from my master's and teacher certification program in 2004. I was part of the first cohort of "highly qualified" teachers produced by the University of Michigan under the policy of No Child Left Behind. It was not until I left the classroom and entered the urban education PhD program at Temple University that I understood why this concept was missing from my teacher preparation. The power, and danger, of hegemony lies in how the rhetoric of "common sense" is used, quite masterfully, to present the interests of the privileged as the interests of the universal. *Who would argue against having highly qualified teachers? Who would argue for leaving children behind?* It certainly was not part of my preparation as a teacher, but I felt the same "common-sense-ness" about teaching and learning "with, about, and of" hip-hop in a racially diverse middle school English language arts classroom. As Ladson-Billings (1995a) puts it, it was "just good teaching."

At its core, hip-hop pedagogy is a counterhegemonic project that questions some of the most "sacred" social relations and discourses circulating in and around K–12 schools and teacher education. Drawing from the past and present history of Negro miseducation (Woodson, 1933), hip-hop pedagogy begins from an ideological standpoint that "they schools" (Dead Prez, 2000) have never had the political, economic, and social interests of Black children in mind. HHBE scholars question hegemonic conceptions of what it means to be a teacher and student. We push back against the idea of teachers as technocratic content specialists, reframing teaching and learning as hip-hop "cultural work" (Giroux, 1992). Hip-hop pedagogies are rooted in the knowledge and practices of youths, in many cases youths deemed illiterate by schools' Eurocentric standards of achievement and conduct. In my field of English education, the "texts" created and literacies employed by MCs question hegemonic notions of curriculum and the ideologies undergirding what teachers and schools put forth as "official knowledge." Hip-hop pedagogy is also more than just textual analysis (Hall, 2017). My teacher research on hip-hop English language arts pedagogies has demonstrated how the hip-hop cultural practices of freestyling, ciphering, and sampling can work to reimagine the writing process (Hall, 2016). When it comes to the purpose of schooling, what it means to be a teacher, and the notions of knowledge critiqued and loved in the classroom, hip-hop pedagogy questions the unquestionable.

In the next section, I will employ some of the tenets of critical race theory (CRT) to articulate why and how hip-hop pedagogy remains relegated to the margins of teacher education.

Interlude: Critical Race Theory and the Powers We Fight in Teacher Education

The tenets of CRT—racism as embedded in US institutions, Whiteness as property, interest convergence, critiques of liberalism, counterstories, and majoritarian narratives—help us to understand the ways anti-(ultra-)Blackness functions in teacher education. CRT argues that racism is a permanent component of American life, embedded in our political, economic, social, and educational structures (Bell, 1980; Ladson-Billings & Tate, 1995). By extension, teacher education and teacher educators (regardless of their race) are complicit in racism. CRT asks us to look beyond the overt, discriminatory language or acts of individuals to analyze how racism functions, both consciously and unconsciously, at cultural, organizational, and policy levels. Teacher education, unlike other spaces in higher education, is in a particularly compromised position because it is beholden to hegemonic state and federal educational policies that serve the interests of the privileged. Evidence of disparate racial inequities is undeniable, yet teacher education continues to focus on subject-specific content, instructional planning, and rudimentary competencies (Cochran-Smith & Fries, 2001). Of course, many teacher educators are transforming syllabi and courses in an effort to impart prospective teachers with the knowledge, skills, and dispositions to accomplish the goals of academic achievement *and* racial justice. However, these additive approaches do little to disrupt the hegemonic goals of teacher education (Banks, 2020). The perpetual resistance to racial and cultural dimensions of teaching and learning, at programmatic levels, suggests that the teacher education system is not broken; it is working as it was designed.

The second tenet of CRT, Whiteness as property, provides insight into how teacher education was designed. For much of this nation's history, Whiteness was a prerequisite for owning property and, therefore, the right to vote. Whiteness also comes with the power to exclude "non-Whites" from the privileges of democracy. CRT scholars have applied this idea of property to various aspects of education (Ladson-Billings & Tate, 1995). With that said, I pose the question,

What "property" do Whites protect for themselves in teacher education? I argue that they are protecting hegemonic notions of the teaching profession. The discourses about teaching as a profession are not
arbitrary, objective, or neutral. They are "always framed within articulations and experiences occupied by someone[,] and to the degree
that they are implicated in organizing the future for others they are
always located in moral and political interests" (Giroux, 1992, p. 232).
Historically, Black people have been systematically excluded from
positions to organize the future of teacher education. Contemporar-
ily, the articulations and experiences of HHBE scholars regarding
teaching as justice-oriented cultural work have been excluded because
they disrupt the neutrality of Whiteness (Marx, 2004) that prevents
issues of race and racism from entering teacher education discourse
(Milner, 2008). Excluding HHBE and racial discourses from teacher
education curriculum works to preserve White property rights of
"use and enjoyment" (Ladson-Billings & Tate, 1995).

Interest convergence, the third tenet of CRT, further explains why
teacher education is resistant to change. Despite the rhetoric of diversity, equity, and inclusion; mission statements; and "statements of
solidarity," progress for people of color does not happen unless it con-
verges with the interests of White people (Bell, 1980). When examining the negative impacts on the Black teacher workforce (Walker,
2001), the consequences of White teachers' low expectations of Black
students, and disproportionate disciplinary actions White school administrators imposed on Black students (Irvine & Irvine, 1983), some
would argue that Brown v. Board of Education's (1954) desegregation of
public schools made racial inequalities worse. In the wake of the tragic
murder of George Floyd at the hands of Derek Chauvin, a White police officer in the Minneapolis Police Department, the volume of calls
for antiracist teacher education has increased in terms of both the
quantity and the degree of loudness. Why? Because the moral outrage
of this injustice politically and economically incentivized K–12 schools
and teacher education to do so (Delgado & Stefancic, 2021). As a HHBE
scholar who was doing antiracist teaching and learning long before it
was called antiracist teaching and learning, I cannot help but be

cynical. On one hand, I have certainly seen an increase in demand for my work as a professional developer; and, in the words of Jay Z (2001), "I'm overcharging niggas for what they did to the Cold Crush." On the other hand, there is no amount of money a school or district can pay me to perpetuate the "one-and-done" approach to professional development. This butterfly will not be pimped (Lamar, 2015) by his university to create hip-hop-based "microcredentials" that serve the interests of the neoliberal learning economy (Ralston, 2021). Time will reveal whether teacher education's commitments to antiracist teaching and learning are genuine or merely an attempt for progressive Whites to "look 'woke'" (Love, 2021).

The final tenet of CRT that I will touch on in this conversation on anti-(ultra-)Blackness in teacher education is counter-storytelling and acknowledgment of majoritarian narratives. Beginning with Grandmaster Flash and the Furious Five's "The Message" (Flash et al., 1982/1994), and later with Public Enemy's "Fight the Power" (1989), rap music has provided narratives of people of color that counter dominant narratives about freedom and equality. Through my explanations of how anti-(ultra-)Blackness functions in teacher education, I have illuminated some of the institutional and cultural microaggressions that West referred to as "shadows." Delgado (1993, p. 666) writes, "Majoritarians tell stories too. But the ones they tell—about merit, causation, blame, responsibility, and social justice—do not seem to them like 'stories' at all, but the truth." In the spring of 2020, it was in the moral, political, and economic interests of K–12 schools and teacher education to position themselves on "the right side of justice." As the political pendulum swings back to the right in response to the election of President Joe Biden, majoritarian narratives about the "CRT threat" have become a weapon in a larger culture war (Strauss, 2021). The stories told about CRT, antiracist teaching, and culturally relevant pedagogy (Ladson-Billings, 1995b) on Fox News, in school board meetings, and in state and federal legislatures are designed to protect the political and educational property rights of Whites. Conservative pundits, parents, and lawmakers use the hegemonic language of "color blindness" to profess that they are not racist but at the same time make it clear that they are not the least bit interested in combatting, let alone acknowledging, how structural racism persists in school policies and practices. This country and its schools are theirs; and they are working just fine for them. They have earned the right to control their country and schools because they are "real patriots" and work harder than Black people. Far from being a catalyst for addressing nationwide racialized disparity, racial inequity is appropriated by white supremacist ideologies as proof of the intellectual and cultural inferiority of Black people. No, they do not say that, but it is in between the lines of every story conservatives tell about why America, and its educational, criminal justice, health care, and economic systems, are not structurally racist.

Historically speaking, higher education has always been a progressive stronghold across the different battles of the American culture wars. As HHBE scholars, we find ourselves having to fight against both the conservative and progressive camps. While conservatives have made it clear where they stand and what they are willing to do to protect their property, the resistance from White progressives is subtler and more passive (and more frustrating). Most of our colleagues in teacher education would acknowledge that structural racism persists in school policies and practices. They would reject explicit and implicit arguments for White supremacy. But teacher education programs are still theirs and they are working just fine for them. Think about how adding the words and worlds of Nas or Lil Baby to curriculum challenges English educators' property rights in the academy. What about hip-hop-based culturally sustaining approaches to STEM education (Champion et al., 2020)? How would the remediation system-complex (special education, bilingual education, etc.) respond to arguments that these well-intended programs designed to address racial inequalities perpetuate racial inequalities (Capper, 2019)? This is why West's metaphor of the shadows of Jim Crow is so appropriate for this conversation about HHBE scholars in teacher education. The shadows are less ominous than the clouds, but the darkness persists.

Outro

In this chapter, I have highlighted some of the challenges and tensions HHBE scholars face when fighting the hegemonic powers from within teacher education. In conclusion, I offer a few recommendations for the aspiring HHBE scholar goin', *and stayin'*, ultra Black in higher education.

Fifteen years ago, I entered the teacher education game with a naïve notion of HHBE going mainstream. After seeing firsthand how cultural voyeurism operates in the ivory tower, and how anti-Blackness functions specifically in teacher education, I have come to understand how problematic the idea of mainstreaming HHBE is. Emdin (2018) encourages HHBE scholars to stop looking for acceptance from the people and institutions that failed us in the first place. HHBE scholars play a vital role as counter-storytellers in traditional academic spaces. Our stories in the classroom and academic journals tell teacher education about itself, revealing harsh, uncomfortable truths about who and what has been silenced, ignored, and forgotten. We must embrace the radical possibilities of our praxis in the margins. We can do dope, influential work with teacher and community partners in "transformative third spaces" (Gutierrez, 2008) and "informal learning contexts" (Vadeboncoeur, 2006) at the margins of K–12 schools. Though often marginalized in traditional academic spaces, we can do dope, "scientifically rigorous" teacher research on our practices and behaviors in these third spaces and informal learning contexts.

This brings me to my second recommendation, for which I draw from the teachings of J. Cole (2010):

> 'Cause you either play the game or watch the game play you
> And be that broke muthafucka talkin' 'bout "I stayed true"

I turn to J. Cole because he is recognized for his ability to succeed according to the traditional standards of the music industry while maintaining his principles. Every musician and poet wants to be heard, and most scholars, especially those in tenure-track positions, want tenure. Admitting this does not mean that you are not keepin' it real.

Wanting to pay off some of your student loans while combatting social injustice does not make you a "sellout." One of my goals in writing this chapter has been to paint a picture of the playing field (White academia) and some of the unwritten rules that govern it. With this insight, my hope is that HHBE scholars are better equipped to play the game so they can ultimately change the game.

Exactly how do we change the game? Real rap: it means grindin'. It means writing extra narratives that explicitly connect the dots between our research, teaching, and service; our statements of expectations; and the mission of our departments and schools for evaluation committees. It means volunteering for some of the extra "gatekeeping" jobs with the purpose of infiltrating those influential evaluation and search committees. It means being reviewers for the prestigious journals and professional associations, as well as collaborating with other HHBE scholars to create our own. Most importantly, it means never letting this game play you.

REFERENCES

Anaya, R. (1995). Take the tortillas out of your poetry. In J. D. Womack & R. Torres (Eds.), *Voces: An anthology of Nuevo Mexicano writers* (pp. 71–73). University of New Mexico Press.

Anderson, E. (1993). Positive use of rap music in the classroom. *Teaching English in the Two-Year College, 20*(3), 214–221.

Baker, H. (1991). Hybridity, the rap race, and pedagogy for the 1990s. *Black Music Research Journal, 11*(2), 217–228.

Banks, J. A. (2020). Approaches to multicultural curriculum reform. In J. A. Banks & C. A. McGee Banks (Eds.), *Multicultural education: Issues and perspectives* (pp. 233–258). John Wiley & Sons.

Bell, D. A. (1980). Brown v. Board of Education and the interest-convergence dilemma. *Harvard Law Review, 93*(3), 518–533.

Capper, C. A. (2019). *Organizational theory for equity and diversity: Leading integrated, socially just education.* Routledge.

Champion, D. N., Tucker-Raymond, E., Millner, A., Gravel, B., Wright, C. G., Likely, R., Allen-Handy, A., & Dandridge, T. M. (2020). (Designing for) learning computational STEM and arts integration in culturally sustaining learning ecologies. *Information and Learning Sciences, 121*(9/10), 785–804.

Coates, T.-N. (2015). *Between the world and me.* Spiegel & Grau.

Cochran-Smith, M., & Fries, M. K. (2001). Sticks, stones, and ideology: The discourse of reform in teacher education. *Educational Researcher, 30*(8), 3–15.

Cole, J. (2010). See world [Song]. On *Friday night lights*. Dreamville/RocNarion.

Dead Prez. (2000). They schools [Song]. On *Let's get free*. Loud Records.

Delgado, R. (1993). Rodrigo's sixth chronicle: Intersections, essences, and the dilemma of social reform. *New York University Law Review, 68*, 639–674.

Delgado, R., & Stefancic, J. (2021) Introduction. In R. Delgado & J. Stefancic (Eds.), *Critical race theory: An introduction* (3rd ed., pp. 1–17). New York University Press.

Dimitriadis, G. (2001). *Performing identity/performing culture: Hip-hop as text, pedagogy, and lived practice*. Lang.

Emdin, C. (2016). *For White folks who teach in the hood . . . and the rest of y'all too: Reality pedagogy and urban education*. Random House.

Emdin, C. (2018). Introduction. In C. Emdin & E. Adjapong (Eds.), *#HipHopEd: The compilation on hip-hop education: Vol. 1. Hip-hop as education, philosophy, and practice* (pp. 1–11). Brill Sense.

Fisher, M. T. (2007). *Writing in rhythm: Spoken word poetry in urban classrooms*. Teachers College Press.

Flash, G., Melle, M., Williams, S., Robinson, J., McLees, D., & Clayton, R. (1982/1994). The message [Song]. On *The best of Grandmaster Flash, Melle Mel & the Furious Five: Message from beat street*. Rhino.

Forman, M., & Neal, M. A. (Eds.). (2004). *That's the joint! The hip-hop studies reader*. Routledge.

Freire, P. (1970). *Pedagogy of the oppressed* (30th anniversary ed.). Continuum.

Gallup, G. G., & Svare, B. B. (2016). Hijacked by an external funding mentality. *Inside Higher Ed*, July 25, 2016.

Giroux, H. (1992). *Border crossings: Cultural workers and the politics of education*. Routledge.

Gutierrez, K. (2008). Developing a sociocultural literacy in the third space. *Reading Research Quarterly, 43*(2), 148–164.

Hall, H. B. (2016). Welcome to the 'shop: Insights and reflections from teaching hip-hop-based spoken word poetry for social justice. *English Teaching, Practice and Critique, 15*(3), 394–410.

Hall, H. B. (2017). Deeper than rap: Expanding conceptions of hip-hop culture and pedagogy in the English language arts classroom. *Research in the Teaching of English, 51*(3), 341–350.

Hawthorne, S. (1989). The politics of the exotic: The paradox of cultural voyeurism. *NWSA Journal, 1*(4), 617–629. http://www.jstor.org/stable/4315958.

Hill, M. L. (2009). *Beats, rhymes, and classroom life: Hip-hop pedagogy and the politics of identity*. Teachers College Press.

Irvine, R. W., & Irvine, J. J. (1983). The impact of desegregation process on the education of Black student: Key variables. *The Journal of Negro Education, 52*(4), 410–422.

Jay Z. (2001). Izzo (H.O.V.A.) [Song]. On *The blueprint*. Rocafella Records.

Jeremiah, M. (1992). Rap lyrics: Instruments for language arts instruction. *Western Journal of Black Studies, 16*(2), 98–102.

Kahf, U. (2012). Arabic hip-hop: Claims of authenticity and identity of a new genre. In M. Forman & M. A. Neal (Eds.), *That's the joint! The hip-hop studies reader* (2nd ed., pp. 116–133). Routledge.

KRS-One. (2003). 9 elements [Song]. On *Kristyles*. Koch Records.

Ladson-Billings, G. (1995a). But that's just good teaching! The case for culturally relevant pedagogy. *Theory into Practice, 34*(3), 159–165.

Ladson-Billings, G. (1995b). Toward a theory of culturally relevant pedagogy. *American Educational Research Journal, 32*(3), 465–491.

Ladson-Billings, G., & Tate, W. F. (1995). Toward a critical race theory of education. *Teachers College Record, 97*(1), 47–68.

Lamar, K. (2015). *To pimp a butterfly.* Aftermath Entertainment.

Love, B. L. (2018). Knowledge reigns supreme: The fifth element, hip-hop critical pedagogy & community. In C. Emdin & E. Adjapong (Eds.), *#HipHopEd: The compilation on hip-hop education: Vol. 1. Hip-hop as education, philosophy, and practice* (pp. 38–43). Brill Sense.

Love, B. L. (2019). *We want to do more than survive: Abolitionist teaching and the pursuit of educational freedom.* Beacon.

Love, B. L. (2021). How to make anti-racism more than a performance [Opinion]. *Education Week,* January 12, 2021. https://www.edweek.org/leadership/opinion -empty-promises-of-equity/2021/01.

Marx, S. (2004). Regarding whiteness: Exploring and intervening in the effects of white racism in teacher education. *Equity & Excellence in Education, 37*(1), 31–43.

Milner IV, H. R. (2008). Critical race theory and interest convergence as analytic tools in teacher education policies and practices. *Journal of Teacher Education, 59*(4), 332–346.

Morrell, E., & Duncan-Andrade, J. M. R. (2002). Promoting academic literacy with urban youth through engaging hip-hop culture. *English Journal, 91*(6), 88–92.

Nas. (2020). Ultra Black [Song]. On *King's disease*. Mass Appeal Records.

Pardue, D. (2013). Who are we? Hip hoppers' influence in the Brazilian understanding of citizenship and education. In M. L. Hill & E. Petchauer (Eds.), *Schooling hip-hop: Expanding hip-hop based education across the curriculum* (pp. 137–154). Teachers College Press.

Public Enemy. (1989). Fight the power [Song]. On *Fear of a Black planet*. Def Jam Recordings.

Ralston, S. J. (2021). Higher education's microcredentialing craze: A postdigital-Deweyan critique. *Postdigital Science and Education, 3*, 83–101. https://doi.org/10 .1007/s42438-020-00121-8.

Rose, T. (1994). *Black noise: Rap music and Black culture in contemporary America.* Wesleyan University Press.

Shakur, T. (1996). White man'z world [Song]. On *The don killuminati: The 7 day theory*. Death Row Records/Interscope Records.

Stino, Z. (1995). Writing as therapy in a county jail. *Journal of Poetry Therapy, 9*(1), 13–23.

Stovall, D. (2006). We can relate: Hip-hop culture, critical pedagogy, and the secondary classroom. *Urban Education, 41*(6), 585-602.

Strauss, V. (2021). The culture war over critical race theory looks like the one waged 50 years ago over sex education. *Washington Post*, July 25, 2021. https://www.washingtonpost.com/education/2021/07/25/critical-race-theory-sex-education-culture-wars/.

Tiongson, A. T., Jr. (2013). *Filipinos represent: DJs, racial authenticity, and the hip-hop nation.* University of Minnesota Press.

Vadeboncoeur, J. A. (2006). Engaging young people: Learning in informal contexts. *Review of Research in Education, 30,* 239-278.

Walker, V.S. (2001). African-American teaching in the South: 1940-1960. *American Educational Research Journal, 38*(4), 751-779.

West, C. [@CornelWest]. (2021). This is my candid letter of resignation to my Harvard Dean. I try to tell the unvarnished truth about the decadence in our market-driven universities! Let us bear witness against this spiritual rot! [Letter attached] [Tweet]. Twitter, July 12, 2021. https://twitter.com/CornelWest/status/1414765668222869508.

Woodson, C. G. (1933). *The mis-education of the negro.* First Africa World.

PART II

Using Aspects of Anti-Blackness to
Interrogate Racism on the Campuses
of Higher Education Institutions

5

Epistemic Exclusion

A Form of Scholarly Devaluation That Is a Barrier to the Inclusion of Black Faculty

MARTINQUE K. JONES, ISIS H. SETTLES, NICOLE T. BUCHANAN,
AND KRISTIE DOTSON

Despite institutional efforts to increase faculty diversity, Black faculty remain underrepresented within academia. Black Americans represent approximately 13% of the US population (US Census Bureau, 2020) but only 6% of full-time faculty (US Department of Education, 2019). Beyond the racial biases that impede the successful hiring of Black faculty (e.g., Sensoy & DiAngelo, 2017), we assert that the underrepresentation of Black faculty may be due, in part, to a revolving door of Black faculty, who are successfully hired but not retained and promoted in their academic positions. In the current chapter, we put forth *epistemic exclusion*, scholarly devaluation that is rooted in invisible biases built into formal systems of evaluation and informal economies that influence faculty interactions, as an understudied factor that may help to explain these negative outcomes. This chapter is divided into three components. First, we will detail the theory of epistemic exclusion, framing it within Black feminist theory (Collins, 1989, 2000) and critical race theory (Ladson-Billings, 1998; West, 1995); these theories locate the cause of racism in systems of inequality at multiple levels (e.g., society and the university) rather than individual animus, and emphasize the role of meritocracy and individualism as beliefs that support such systems. Second, we will review our research on epistemic exclusion and highlight findings that show how it is experienced among Black faculty, as well as its impacts. Finally, we will offer recommendations to disciplinary gatekeepers, institutions, and faculty for addressing epistemic exclusion.

Theoretical Foundations

The theory of epistemic exclusion builds on two critical theories, Black feminist theory (Collins, 1989, 2000) and critical race theory (Bell, 1980; Crenshaw, 1988; Delgado, 1995; Ladson-Billings, 1998; West, 1995). Black feminist theory offers a framework useful for understanding *how* epistemic exclusion emerges, whereas critical race theory provides insight into *why* epistemic exclusion persists and does not upend easily. In the sections that follow, we provide a brief summary of the theories foundational to understanding epistemic exclusion and detail how the theories converge.

As applied to epistemology, Black feminist theory (Collins, 1989, 2000) considers how the intellectual contributions and voices of marginalized individuals are systematically oppressed, which elevates some knowers (often White men) and reifies particular beliefs about knowledge acquisition (e.g., valuing researcher neutrality). Black feminist theory also challenges the status quo in knowledge production by naming and elevating Black women (and other marginalized individuals) as agentic creators of knowledge and highlighting that knowledge can be extracted from various sources, including life experiences. The theory of epistemic exclusion grapples with similar concepts (knowers and knowledge production) and posits that faculty of color are a group whose knowledge and ways of knowing are constantly under question; in fact, this is how epistemic exclusion works—specific faculty are deemed illegitimate scholars because of who they are (Black, woman, etc.), and the topics they study and the research methods they use are devalued.

Like Black feminist theorists (Collins, 1989, 2000; Crenshaw, 1989; Dotson, 2012, 2014), critical race theorists (e.g., Delgado, 1995; Ladson-Billings, 1998; West, 1995) have long acknowledged how pervasive societal forces, such as racism, infiltrate and shape the academic landscape. There are five tenets of critical race theory: racism is a systemic and pervasive force in society; societal perspectives (e.g., liberalism and meritocracy) render racism and other forms of oppression invisible and thus obscure its systemic roots and effects; equity advancements are only permitted when they benefit White Americans (i.e., interest convergence); Whiteness is constructed as property that results in material benefits and therefore leads those who benefit from White privilege to defend it; and people of color have perspectives on racism that are distinct from White individuals', making it imperative that their stories and perspectives are elevated to counter popular narratives based on White individuals' experiences. Together, these tenets reinforce that race and racism are not aberrant forces in society but rather reflect the status quo of societal systems (Delgado, 1995). The theory of epistemic exclusion also recognizes that the marginalization of certain faculty in higher education is endemic and rooted in systemic forces (e.g., disciplinary-based biases) that privilege specific scholars and types of scholarship over others. Similar to critical race theory, epistemic exclusion theory points to how commonly held perspectives, such as meritocracy and neoliberalism, maintain exclusion by making this form of marginalization invisible. Epistemic exclusion theory is also testimony driven, meaning it seeks to contest the master narrative that academia and the processes used to evaluate scholars are free of bias, and elevates the accounts of faculty who have experienced this form of exclusion. Thus, critical race theory helps us understand that epistemic exclusion persists because it is embedded within systemic processes, maintained through widely held beliefs about meritocracy, and rendered invisible because the experiences of those subject to epistemic exclusion are often minimized, denied, or subjected to cultural gaslighting.

Theory of Epistemic Exclusion

The theory of epistemic exclusion (Dotson, 2012, 2014; Settles et al., 2021) challenges preexisting notions about who may be considered a legitimate scholar and what is considered quality scholarship. The theory puts forth that attitudes about scholars and their scholarship are informed by two forms of bias. First, disciplinary biases contribute to certain types of scholarship being privileged and others being devalued. For many fields and disciplines, research that is objective (and presumed to be free of bias), generalizable, and quantitative is privileged and labeled mainstream. Second, identity-based biases lead to individuals in certain social identity groups being privileged and others being marginalized. For Black scholars, negative stereotypes about their intellect and work ethic (e.g., Ghavami & Peplau, 2013; Sue, 2010) may contribute to their exclusion; these racial stereotypes are also gendered (e.g., women do not excel in math and science; Heilman, 2001) and may be informed by other marginalized statuses a Black faculty member holds (e.g., sexual minority or working-class background).

The theory of epistemic exclusion posits that these two forms of bias, and the narrative created as a result, contribute to the systematic exclusion of faculty of color, in particular Black faculty. Black faculty, alongside other marginalized scholars, commonly engage with research in ways considered to be outside the disciplinary norm or that are seen as failing to meet research "gold standards" (e.g., studying marginalized groups, focusing on race and racism, using qualitative methods; Bernal & Villalpando, 2002; Gonzales, 2018). As a result, their scholarship is perceived as lacking quality or rigor and, in some instances, considered "me-search" (de la Luz Reyes & Halcon, 1988, p. 302). Further compounding the devaluation of their scholarship is their membership within a marginalized social group (e.g., Black Americans). Said differently, the negative stereotypes about Black faculty shape and contribute to the devaluation of their scholarship; for instance, if there is a stereotype that Black people are poor scholars and use community-based methods, then community-based methods are also perceived as poor-quality scholarship. The impact of identity-based bias persists even when scholars conduct research within the disciplinary mainstream and leads to their work being perceived as having lower quality because of their social group (e.g., race and gender; Dotson, 2012, 2014).

Phenomenology of Epistemic Exclusion for Black Faculty

To illustrate the phenomenology of epistemic exclusion among Black faculty, and specifically how it may manifest through formal processes and informal economies, we draw on qualitative data from 30 self-identified Black faculty extracted from a larger study of 118 faculty of color about "workplace and work-life experiences" (for additional details, see Settles et al., 2019; Settles, Jones, et al., 2021). In this study, participants were asked open-ended questions that covered several topics related to faculty experiences, such as the departmental environment, departmental policies and procedures, and factors contributing to career success and job satisfaction. None of the interview questions specifically asked about epistemic exclusion or other themes presented in this chapter. Therefore, the data presented here are likely an underestimate of faculty experiences with epistemic exclusion. All the Black faculty sampled worked at the same research-intensive, predominantly White university. Of the faculty sampled, just over half were women and working in fields related to STEM (science, technology, engineering, and math), and there was representation of faculty across ranks. For a full listing of faculty demographics, see table 5.1.

Experiences of Epistemic Exclusion

Among our sample of Black faculty, epistemic exclusion was common, with over half ($n = 17$, 56.7%) reporting some form of it. These rates were similar across Black women ($n = 10$, 58.8%) and Black men ($n = 7$, 53.8%). A relatively smaller percentage of assistant professors ($n = 6$, 50.0%) reported epistemic exclusion compared with associate ($n = 6$, 60.0%) and full ($n = 5$, 62.5%) professors, and it was more commonly

Table 5.1.
Demographic Characteristics of Black Faculty in the Sample

Characteristic	n	%
Gender		
Woman	17	56.7
Man	13	43.3
Sexual orientation*		
Lesbian, gay, or bisexual	1	3.4
Heterosexual	28	96.6
Nationality		
Born in the United States	25	83.3
Born outside the United States	5	16.7
Rank		
Assistant professor	12	40.0
Associate professor	10	33.3
Full professor	8	26.7
Academic discipline		
Science, technology, engineering, and math	17	56.7
Arts and humanities	13	43.3

Source: Adapted from Settles, Jones, et al., 2020.
  * One participant did not respond to this question.

reported by faculty in arts and humanities fields ($n = 8$, 61.5%) compared with those in STEM-related fields ($n = 9$, 52.9%). Further, our data suggest that epistemic exclusion is experienced by Black faculty through formal processes and informal economies within departments, institutions, and disciplinary fields.

Formal Processes of Epistemic Exclusion

Formal processes of epistemic exclusion refers to bias against scholarly work that occurs in formal evaluation processes, such as annual reviews or promotion and tenure reviews, and contributes to a scholar's marginalization. Formal epistemic exclusion highlights seemingly neutral judgments about what scholarly work is meritorious that, in fact, reflect disciplinary and identity-based biases. Among the seventeen Black faculty who reported experiencing any epistemic exclusion, most indicated encountering some form of exclusion in formal processes ($n = 14$, 82.4%), and these experiences were equally represented among Black women ($n = 8$, 47.1%) and Black men ($n = 6$, 46.2%). Across ranks, 50% of Black faculty reported formal epistemic exclusion: assistant ($n=6$), associate professors ($n=5$), and full professors ($n=4$). Faculty in STEM-related fields ($n=6$, 35.3%) reported less formal epistemic exclusion than those in arts and humanities ($n=8$, 61.5%). Based on our data, Black faculty experienced formal processes of epistemic exclusion in their department and in the profession broadly (e.g., journal and grant review).

Multiple faculty members noted that their work was considered lower quality by colleagues in their department because of their scholarly focus (e.g., race, ethnicity, and gender) or the methods they used in their research. In fact, one faculty member noted how research that centered on issues of race and gender was considered less valuable in their department:

> A lot of it comes down to the idea [of] what work is valuable and what work is fluff. . . . The way it pans out in our department is that the stuff that is deemed as valuable is the traditional science stuff and the stuff that isn't really valued tends to be stuff that deals with women and race. . . . Yeah, so there's just a hierarchy that's reified around here.—Black woman, associate professor (unpublished source)

Similarly, faculty noted that their research was seen as having less quality because of the methods they used, such as qualitative work being seen as less rigorous than quantitative research. One Black man who was an assistant professor mentioned that because he does not conduct quantitative research, his work is undervalued and not understood by those in his department: "I don't feel valued in the department. I don't think people understand the kind of research I do. I don't think it's viewed as research because of the type of methodology I use. It's a very highly quantitatively inclined department" (Settles et al., 2021, p. 498).

Above and beyond the devaluation faculty experienced as a result of subjective criteria of quality, faculty were also subject to negative evaluations because the performance standards in their department were often based on metrics (e.g., journal impact factor or grant dollars accrued) that created or reinforced narrow disciplinary values. One external criterion used to evaluate faculty research quality was grant-getting; faculty who secured grant funding were valued more than others, often in proportion to the amount of funding they received. For instance, one faculty member stated,

> It seems that the more grant money you have, the better the treatment. When I've had very large grants in the department, it just seemed like I could do no wrong and when you have modest grants or no grants, then you're not disrespected but you certainly don't have the same level of clout.—Black woman, full professor (Settles et al., 2021, p. 498)

Further contributing to experiences of exclusion among Black faculty was the extent to which evaluation standards within their department were misapplied or shifted to become less attainable, or had always been ambiguous or unclear. One Black woman who was an assistant professor explained how the number of publications necessary for a positive review shifted over time:

> The first year I was here, everybody I asked gave me a different number [of publications] and they were all bigger and bigger and bigger. And then I asked the same person again, they gave me a bigger number. . . . It was like . . . the carrot keeps moving [laughs]. I decided that I had no other choice, besides to run and sprint, right? Get as much out as I could and do everything I could within reason and see where the chips fall.—Black woman, assistant professor (Settles et al., 2021, p. 499)

Unfortunately, faculty noted that even when they met the shifting and elusive standards for a positive review in their department, they were still negatively evaluated. One faculty member recounted the experiences of another Black faculty member in their department who, after a series of unfair tenure and promotion review processes, was denied tenure:

> The same happened with an African American man, he and a White man went up for tenure at the same time. He [the African American man] had two books, double-digit articles, very prolific writer, and was actually denied tenure the first time going up. And they told him to wait a year cause at that time this White person that was going up had

roughly a third or half of the publications that he had at that time. And so when you have such disparities in how the law or the "expectations" are applied, then how can one feel that is a fair process?—Black man, assistant professor (unpublished source)

Informal Economies of Epistemic Exclusion

Informal economies of epistemic exclusion are composed of perceptions and interactions that contribute to the epistemic exclusion of scholars of color outside formal processes. This form of exclusion commonly occurred in informal spaces, such as in the hallway or faculty meetings, and emerged in three primary forms—lack of scholarly legitimacy, lack of scholarly recognition, and lack of scholarly comprehensibility—that are described here. Relative to the number of faculty who reported experiencing exclusion via formal processes, fewer reported experiencing exclusion through informal economies ($n = 8$, 47.1%). Somewhat fewer Black women ($n = 4$, 23.5%) reported experiencing this form of exclusion compared with Black men ($n = 4$, 30.8%). In terms of rank, associate professors ($n = 4$, 40.0%) reported more informal exclusion than assistant ($n = 2$, 16.7%) or full professors ($n = 2$, 25.0%). In addition, as with formal epistemic exclusion, faculty working in STEM-related fields ($n = 4$, 23.5%) reported less informal epistemic exclusion than those in arts and humanities ($n = 4$, 30.8%).

For Black faculty in our sample, exclusion via informal economies in some cases emerged as critiques of the scholar's legitimacy, and specifically in instances in which the scholar's competence, expertise, knowledge, or credibility was questioned or denied. For instance, one faculty member observed that despite his scholarly accomplishments, faculty in his department questioned his legitimacy, and subsequently the salary he earned:

I think they believe that I'm making the money because I'm Black and that it's some type of racial privilege that plays into it because, you know, god forbid that I be smart enough and good enough to deserve my compensation, my salary. Of course it's a hand me down, hand me out because I'm Black right? . . . I publish more, I'm on more committees, you know, I sit with more students or as many students, I do as much, I speak around the country. . . . And these faculty question my compensation and their argument is a racial argument that, you know, my compensation is because I'm Black.—Black man, associate professor (unpublished source)

Although the faculty member in this example felt that he received appropriate compensation for his scholarly efforts, Black faculty more commonly reported a lack of recognition. They experienced invisibility such that their scholarly accomplishments were overlooked or minimized. For example, one faculty member noted that despite receiving a large external grant, his work was not acknowledged by his department:

The college has this research newsletter. They tell you to send your [news] whatever it is. So I sent it to my department when I got my R01 [National Institutes of Health Research Project Grant]. What I noticed is that when the newsletter came out, the White women who received grants that were not as significant as mine and another person who received a grant that was equal to the prestige of mine, they were all on the newsletter and I was not. When I mentioned it, it was as if it was my fault when I knew what I had done [sent in the news]. But nobody wanted to own up.—Black man, associate professor (unpublished source)

Black faculty also indicated facing a lack of comprehension regarding their work, in which there was a denial of its understandability, familiarity, and disciplinary inclusion. Said differently, these faculty were excluded on the basis of their work being perceived as incomprehensible. As it pertains to their scholarly work being perceived as beyond the disciplinary center, one faculty member stated, "I *have* had the experience of being treated like the work I do is ancillary, of people kind of not really getting it, not being able to understand why it's important, and so just kind of being dismissive about it" (Black woman, associate professor; Settles et al., 2019, p. 69).

Although exclusionary experiences did not vary for women and men, our data demonstrated meaningful differences in experiences of exclusion by rank and discipline. In terms of rank, associate professors reported the most informal epistemic exclusion, perhaps because of the novel demands of this new career stage, including greater expectations of national scholarly recognition, which may create challenges for successfully navigating the academic system. Faculty in arts and humanities were more likely than STEM faculty to experience epistemic exclusion, perhaps because of the range of scholarly output in the arts and humanities (e.g., artwork, books, and journal articles) or because of the greater societal devaluation of these fields (Belfiore, 2015). These patterns highlight the connection of epistemic exclusion to disciplinary norms and to the role of power and privilege in the process.

The Impact of Epistemic Exclusion

Findings from our qualitative data (Settles et al., 2019; Settles et al., 2021) indicate that faculty of color, and specifically Black faculty, experience both work-related and psychological consequences as a result of epistemic exclusion. For some, experiences of exclusion prompted them to limit or reorient their scholarly focus to one that may be considered more "mainstream." In one instance, a faculty member mentioned shifting their community-based and social justice–oriented program of research to an area or topic better aligned with their university's values. Unfortunately, a shift of this magnitude tended to undermine productivity, as faculty were forced to develop a new line of research and forge new collaborative relationships with others who may not view them as legitimate collaborators. Epistemic exclusion also contributed to limited opportunities for merit-based salary increases and backlash for those who were successful despite racialized and gendered barriers. Psychologically, faculty reported that experiences of exclusion were associated with feelings of frustration, a sense of isolation, and uncertainty, specifically about their competence.

Faculty reported coping with epistemic exclusion and its effects in two primary ways (Settles et al., 2021). Some faculty felt a need to directly respond to experiences of exclusion, and thus coped by being assertive (e.g., responding when treated as illegitimate or incompetent and advocating for respect or recognition when it was not freely given). Seeking validation and social support from others outside their department or university (e.g., faculty in different professional organizations) was another strategy that faculty used to cope with exclusionary experiences.

The effects of epistemic exclusion on faculty of color were further evidenced in our subsequent quantitative study of this phenomenon (Settles et al., 2022). Results of this study showed that women and faculty of color experienced more scholarly devaluation than White faculty. Additionally, experiences of epistemic exclusion were associated with lower job satisfaction and less positive perceptions of the climate of their department, which in turn were related to greater intentions to leave the university. These study results point to how the impacts of epistemic exclusion are multifaceted, thereby shaping how faculty perceive their work environments and the extent to which they feel inclined to remain at a specific institution. In addition to these job-related outcomes, epistemic exclusion may result in fewer opportunities for the development of professional collaborations or positive personal relationships.

Our work also identified consequences of epistemic exclusion that extend beyond the individuals targeted to include the institutions and disciplinary fields within which they work (Settles et al., 2021). Importantly, faculty in our studies noted that institutions experience reputational harm as more people learn that an institution is not supportive of Black faculty and the scholarship they produce. Moreover, our participants observed that epistemic exclusion resulted in faculty leaving the institution. Economic data highlight the costs associated with faculty coping with mistreatment and eventually leaving the institution. Workplace mistreatment costs US institutions over $64 billion every year (Namie & Namie, 2009) due to several factors, such as lost time and diminished productivity, disengagement and withdrawal from teaching and research endeavors, and premature retirement. An average of 3.9 hours per week is spent coping with, reacting to, and strategizing on how to deal with workplace mistreatment, over 50 work weeks, this equals 195 hours, or 5 weeks, per year (Hollis, 2015). If we presume a faculty salary of $50,000 a year, this would mean that nearly $10,000 of their salary is spent on workplace mistreatment instead of teaching and research. When faculty leave the institution, these costs are exacerbated. Faculty turnover costs an institution approximately 150% of the faculty member's salary due to lost productivity for the employee before leaving and for those involved in the hiring search once they leave—advertising the position, interviewing, recruiting, and retraining—and overtime to people (e.g., administrative staff) covering portions of the faculty's work (Hensen, 1997; Zhang, 2016). As a result, a faculty member earning $50,000 a year will cost $75,000 to replace (Hollis, 2015).

Further, we suggest that epistemic exclusion produces disciplinary inertia by maintaining narrow conceptions of appropriate scholarly work in the field (i.e., disciplinary norms). One example of how this occurs is in graduate training. Graduate students are educated within disciplinary norms that influence what knowledge they are exposed to, which scholarly endeavors they are encouraged or discouraged to pursue, and whether they are equipped to conduct research that moves beyond disciplinary centers. If disciplinary norms are narrow as a result of epistemic exclusion, this limits the possibilities for a field's growth in the long term. An exhaustive list of the numerous examples of the ways epistemic exclusion fosters disciplinary inertia is beyond the scope of this chapter. Nonetheless, it is likely that disciplines rife with epistemic exclusion will also produce less innovative scholarship over time.

Overall, the theory of epistemic exclusion and studies illuminating this phenomenon bring to bear the negative impacts of this exclusion on Black faculty as well as other faculty of color. Because of epistemic exclusion, Black faculty may not be hired, retained, or promoted; in evaluative processes, they are at particular risk of their scholarship being devalued and, because of their identity, their legitimacy as experts in their field being questioned. Considering the greater frequency at which formal, relative to informal, epistemic exclusion was reported by faculty and its impacts (e.g., decreased productivity and limited opportunities for merit-based salary increases), the pervasive nature of disciplinary and identity-based bias at a structural level is even more apparent. As articulated in the critical theories framing epistemic exclusion (e.g., Collins, 1989, 2000; Dotson, 2012, 2014; Ladson-Billings, 1998; West, 1995), experiences of exclusion are not accidental, nor do they occur in isolation, but rather are predictable and repetitive, and they stem from systems that privilege certain groups and not others. Further, our data show that epistemic exclusion is both systemic and interpersonal, such that faculty of color may be mistreated by their colleagues and experience frustration and a limited sense of belonging as a result. These experiences of exclusion add another layer to the marginalization and workplace mistreatment Black faculty already experience (e.g., invisibility and racial discrimination; Buchanan & Settles, 2019; Constantine et al., 2008; Pittman, 2012), in particular those in predominantly White institutions (Kelly et al., 2017).

Recommendations for Addressing Epistemic Exclusion

Our current understanding of epistemic exclusion and its impact on Black faculty has implications for academic institutions seeking to reduce this form of exclusion and, in turn, better support Black faculty. A major conclusion derived from this body of work, and its framing within Black feminist theory (Collins, 1989, 2000; Crenshaw, 1989; Dotson, 2012, 2014) and critical race theory (e.g., Bell, 1980; Crenshaw, 1988; Ladson-Billings, 1998; West, 1995), is that it highlights the need for systemic and institutional change and suggests that seemingly objective forms of evaluation (e.g., annual review) are not objective but in fact reflect forms of bias that act to disproportionately affect Black faculty negatively. Therefore, we offer recommendations to mitigate epistemic exclusion and its impact at three levels—the discipline or field, institutions, and faculty.

Across all three levels, discussions about the characteristics of "good" scholarship (i.e., objectivity and generalizability) that privilege those adhering to the disciplinary mainstream are necessary for raising awareness of disciplinary assumptions and norms that undergird epistemic exclusion. Disciplinary gatekeepers, institutions, and faculty may consider questions such as, "What is considered 'good' scholarship?" and "In what ways do discipline-specific and institutional policies and practices privilege certain types of scholarship?" It is equally important that all parties consider what they deem to be of lesser quality and the shared characteristics of scholarship and scholars within this category. Such discussions will illuminate how seemingly objective practices introduce bias into evaluation processes. Because both disciplinary and identity-based biases contribute to epistemic exclusion, efforts should also be placed on exploring and addressing faculty biases shaped by racial and gender stereotypes (e.g., implicit bias training). Additional awareness of epistemic exclusion may also be gained by reading scholarly works written by faculty of color who narrate their personal experiences in the academy (Buchanan, 2020; Settles, 2020) and qualitative works illuminating the experiences of Black faculty more broadly (Griffin et al., 2013); readings of this sort may be particularly helpful for Black faculty who are contending with experiences of exclusion.

At the disciplinary level, we recommend shifts in disciplinary norms and values, and subsequently practices and policies that may lessen epistemic exclusion. To start, mainstream journals can communicate the importance and contribution of scholarship on marginalized groups (e.g., Black Americans) and scholarship that addresses social issues (e.g., racism and poverty); this may be accomplished through changes, such as rewording the journal description to incorporate these foci and showcasing research that aligns with the new values of the journal. Additionally, new journal policies and practices may be warranted, such as being more open and receptive to works not traditionally considered by the journal (e.g., scholarship using mixed methods or critical ethnography), updating the standards for research and publication to include explicit mention of diversity considerations (e.g., noting the implications of study findings for marginalized groups; Buchanan & Wiklund, 2020), and soliciting marginalized scholars to serve as editors and editorial board members (Buchanan et al., 2021; Settles et al., 2020).

To lessen epistemic exclusion at an institutional level, actions similar to those just noted can be taken. Institutions and departments should update their mission statements to more clearly indicate their support of scholarship focused on marginalized groups and social issues, as well as their significance. That support should be mirrored in institution-specific practices and policies, such as grants and funding opportunities for faculty engaged in scholarship centered on marginalized communities and incentivizing the pursuit of research that may be considered outside the disciplinary mainstream. Moreover, systems of accountability and rewards can facilitate these efforts. For example, institutions can regularly survey faculty perceptions of the institutional climate and scholarly marginalization given the consequences of epistemic exclusion for Black scholars and institutional retention efforts. Institutions must also act on the results of these surveys and take action to stop workplace mistreatment and marginalization, particularly given their increased frequency among junior faculty, as well as research that shows these behaviors are commonly cited reasons for junior faculty departure (Hollis, 2017). Institutions can also reward those departments that are actively improving the working conditions for Black faculty, such as through incentives to support departments that seek to gain greater awareness of epistemic exclusion and shift their values and policies accordingly.

For Black scholars, our suggestions are threefold. First, we encourage Black scholars who may be contending with epistemic exclusion to realize that they are not alone and that their experiences of exclusion are a manifestation of a larger institutional system that is biased against specific scholars and scholarship. Second, because epistemic exclusion is a shared experience among many Black faculty, we suggest that Black scholars seek mentorship from peers and senior faculty within and beyond the institution who may have successfully navigated key evaluative milestones (e.g., promotion and tenure) and the academic landscape in general. Third, considering the psychological impacts of epistemic exclusion, we recommend that Black scholars be proactive in attending to their mental and physical health, and thus assert their boundaries and needs, engage in self-care, and solicit support as needed (Buchanan & Jones, 2023).

REFERENCES

Belfiore, E. (2015). "Impact," "value" and "bad economics": Making sense of the problem of value in the arts and humanities. *Arts and Humanities in Higher Education, 14*(1), 95–110. http://dx.doi.org/10.1177/1474022214531503.

Bell, D. A., Jr. (1980). Brown v. Board of Education and the interest-convergence dilemma. *Harvard Law Review, 93*(3), 518–533.

Bernal, D. D., & Villalpando, O. (2002). An apartheid of knowledge in academia: The struggle over the "legitimate" knowledge of faculty of color. *Equity & Excellence in Education, 35*(2), 169–180. http://dx.doi.org/10.1080/713845282.

Buchanan, N. T. (2020). Researching while Black (and female). *Women & Therapy, 43*(1/2), 91–111. https://doi.org/10.1080/02703149.2019.1684681.

Buchanan, N. T., & Jones, M. K. (2023). Value-driven service and the right to say no. In K. Richmond, I. H. Settles, S. A. Shields, & A. I. Zelin (Eds.), *Feminist scholars on the road to tenure: The personal is professional* (pp. 169–184). Cognella Academic Publishing.

Buchanan, N. T., Perez, M., Prinstein, M., & Thurston, I. (2021). Upending racism in psychological science: Strategies to change how our science is conducted, reported, reviewed, and disseminated. *American Psychologist, 26* (7), 1097–1112. https://doi.org/10.1037/amp0000905.

Buchanan, N. T., & Settles, I. H. (2019). Managing (in)visibility and hypervisibility at work. *Journal of Vocational Behavior, 113*, 1–5. https://doi.org/10.1016/j.jvb.2018.11.001.

Buchanan, N. T., & Wiklund, L. (2020). Why clinical science must change or die: Integrating intersectionality and social justice. *Women & Therapy, 34*(3–4), 309–329. https://doi.org/10.1080/02703149.2020.1729470.

Collins, P. H. (1989). The social construction of Black feminist thought. *Signs, 14*(4), 745–773. http://dx.doi.org/10.1086/494543.

Collins, P. H. (2000). Gender, Black feminism, and Black political economy. *Annals of the American Academy of Political and Social Science, 568*(1), 41–53. http://dx.doi.org/10.1177/000271620056800105.

Constantine, M. G., Smith, L., Redington, R. M., & Owens, D. (2008). Racial microaggressions against Black counseling and counseling psychology faculty: A central challenge in the multicultural counseling movement. *Journal of Counseling & Development, 86*(3), 348–355. https://doi.org/10.1002/j.1556-6678.2008.tb00519.x.

Crenshaw, K. W. (1988). Race, reform, and retrenchment: Transformation and legitimation in antidiscrimination law. *Harvard Law Review, 101*(7), 1331–1387. https://doi.org/10.2307/1341398.

Crenshaw, K. (1989). Demarginalizing the intersection of race and sex: A Black feminist critique of antidiscrimination doctrine, feminist theory and antiracist politics. *University of Chicago Legal Forum, 1989,* 139–167. http://chicagounbound .uchicago.edu/uclf/vol1989/iss1/8.

de la Luz Reyes, M., & Halcon, J. (1988). Racism in academia: The old wolf revisited. *Harvard Educational Review, 58*(3), 299–315. http://dx.doi.org/10.17763/haer.58.3 .9257765135854643.

Delgado, R. (1995). *Critical race theory: The cutting edge.* Temple University.

Dotson, K. (2012). A cautionary tale: On limiting epistemic oppression. *Frontiers, 33*(1), 24–47. http://dx.doi.org/10.5250/fronjwomenstud.33.1.0024.

Dotson, K. (2014). Conceptualizing epistemic oppression. *Social Epistemology, 28*(2), 115–138. http://dx.doi.org/10.1080/02691728.2013.782585.

Ghavami, N., & Peplau, L. A. (2013). An intersectional analysis of gender and ethnic stereotypes: Testing three hypotheses. *Psychology of Women Quarterly, 37*(1), 113–127. http://dx.doi.org/10.1177/0361684312464203.

Gonzales, L. D. (2018). Subverting and minding boundaries: The intellectual work of women. *Journal of Higher Education, 89*(5), 677–701. http://dx.doi.org/10.1080 /00221546.2018.1434278.

Griffin, K. A., Bennett, J. C., & Harris, J. (2013). Marginalizing merit? Gender differences in Black faculty D/discourses on tenure, advancement, and professional success. *Review of Higher Education, 36*(4), 489–512.

Heilman, M. E. (2001). Description and prescription: How gender stereotypes prevent women's ascent up the organizational ladder. *Journal of Social Issues, 57*(4), 657–674. https://doi.org/10.1111/0022-4537.00234.

Hensen, F. (1997). What is the cost of employee turnover? *Compensation and Benefits Review, 29*(5), 17–18.

Hollis, L. P. (2015). Bully university? The cost of workplace bullying and employee disengagement in American higher education. *Sage Open, 5*(2), 1–11. https://doi .org/10.1177/2158244015589997.

Hollis, L. (2017). This is why they leave you: Workplace bullying and insight to junior faculty departure. *British Journal of Education, 5*(10), 1–7. https://ssrn.com /abstract=3030905.

Kelly, B. T., Gayles, J. G., & Williams, C. D. (2017). Recruitment without retention: A critical case of Black faculty unrest. *Journal of Negro Education, 86*(3), 305–317. https://doi.org/10.7709/jnegroeducation.86.3.0305.

Ladson-Billings, G. (1998). Just what is critical race theory and what's it doing in a nice field like education? *International Journal of Qualitative Studies in Education, 11*(1), 7–24. https://doi.org/10.1080/095183998236863.

Namie, G., & Namie, R. (2009). *Bully at work: What you can do to stop the hurt and reclaim your dignity on the job.* Sourcebooks.

Pittman, C. T. (2012). Racial microaggressions: The narratives of African American faculty at a predominantly White university. *Journal of Negro Education, 81*(1), 82 92. https://doi.org/10.7709/jnegroeducation.81.1.0082.

Sensoy, Ö., & DiAngelo, R. (2017). "We are all for diversity, but . . .": How faculty hiring committees reproduce Whiteness and practical suggestions for how they can change. *Harvard Educational Review, 87*(4), 557–580. https://doi.org/10.17763 /1943-5045-87.4.557.

Settles, I. H. (2020). Meaningful moments: How mentors and collaborators helped transform career challenges into opportunities. *Women & Therapy, 43*(1–2), 58–73. https://doi.org/10.1080/02703149.2019.1684674.

Settles, I. H., Buchanan, N. T., & Dotson, K. (2019). Scrutinized but not recognized: (In)visibility and hypervisibility experiences of faculty of color. *Journal of Vocational Behavior, 113*, 62–74. https://doi.org/10.1016/j.jvb.2018.06.003.

Settles, I. H., Jones, M. K., Buchanan, N. T., & Brassel, S. T. (2022). Epistemic exclusion of women faculty and faculty of color: Understanding scholar(ly) devaluation as a predictor of turnover intentions. *Journal of Higher Education, 93*(1), 31–55. https://doi.org/10.1080/00221546.2021.1914494.

Settles, I. H., Jones, M. K., Buchanan, N. T., & Dotson, K. (2021). Epistemic exclusion: Scholar(ly) devaluation that marginalizes faculty of color. *Journal of Diversity in Higher Education, 14*(4), 493–507. https://doi.org/10.1037/dhe0000174.

Settles, I. H., Warner, L., Buchanan, N. T., & Jones, M. K. (2020). Understanding psychology's resistance to intersectionality theory using a framework of invisibility and epistemic exclusion. *Journal of Social Issues, 76*(4), 769–813. http://dx.doi.org/10.1111/josi.12403.

Sue, D. W. (2010). Microaggressions in everyday life: Race, gender and sexual orientation. In D. W. Sue (Ed.), *Racial/ethnic microaggressions and racism* (pp. 137–159). Wiley.

US Census Bureau. (2020). QuickFacts: United States. https://www.census.gov /quickfacts/fact/table/US/POP010220#POP010220.

US Department of Education. (2019). Table 315.20. Full-time faculty in degree-granting postsecondary institutions, by race/ethnicity, sex, and academic rank: Fall 2015, fall 2017, and fall 2018. https://nces.ed.gov/programs/digest/d19/tables /dt19_315.20.asp.

West, C. (1995). *Critical race theory: The key writings that formed the movement.* New Press.

Zhang, Y. (2016). A review of employee turnover influence factor and countermeasure. *Journal of Human Resource and Sustainability Studies, 4*, 85–91. http://dx.doi .org/10.4236/jhrss.2016.42010.

6

Building Black Spaces for Black Epistemological Inclusion

BLANCA ELIZABETH VEGA

In 2009, I walked into a class called "Introduction to African American Education" at Teachers College, Columbia University. This course was the only one taught at this institution of higher education to help us understand how African American students have been educated historically in the United States. In the class, I met four Black women who were also going through their doctoral journeys. We began a friendship that has since lasted over a decade. For me, this class also provided an opportunity to meet other students who shared scholarly and intellectual interests in a very White space. As an Ecuadorian American woman who identifies as Afro-descendant and was born and raised in New York City, my relationship with race is rooted in the knowledge that anti-Black racism is a specific form of racism that often becomes lost in notions of diversity. Thus, to be entrenched in Black scholarship within a White space was important for my spirit. For the purposes of this chapter, Black scholarship is defined as Black "epistemic practices grounded in the social realities and locations of both individuals and communities of African descent (i.e., Black people)" (Muzanenhamo & Chowdhury, 2021, p. 2). In predominantly White

institutions (PWIs), Black spaces where Black scholarship is cultivated are that much more important but, unfortunately, very scarce.

Classrooms can be Black spaces where Black scholarship is intentionally constructed. I acknowledged this class, the Introduction to African American Education course, as a Black space, and also a space
that cultivated Black scholarship. It was taught by a scholar and his-
torian who also identified as a Black woman, indicating that the Black
space intentionally sought to cultivate Black scholarship. Additionally,
the majority of students in the class identified as Black. Being in a
space that elevated Blackness to an accurate perspective and not one
filled with deficits and lies countered some of the effects we were all
feeling at a PWI. The class became a generative space, one where the
women I met understood the importance of creating and cultivating
more Black spaces. Thus, in 2011, they invited me to be a part of their
writing group, an extension of the Black space created for us in the
classroom. As an extension of Black scholarship, the writing group supported and graduated a number of Black and Afro-descendant scholars.
We not only shared our writing; we shared knowledge about the
PWI, about supportive and nonsupportive professors, and about how to
write and finish a dissertation in spite of the many ways our scholarship
about race and Black people was dismissed, discounted, ignored, and
mistrusted. Our space countered that. We worked collaboratively—a
value deeply rooted in communal traditions that resisted the capitalist
notions of individualism. We celebrated our wins together, attended
each other's milestones, and pulled together when one of our sisters
was in trouble. In many ways, our space, our Black space, was not
the norm at our doctoral institution. Yet here we were engaged in a
centuries-old tradition of creating and nurturing Black spaces, a form
of refuge, in itself an act of hope in a White supremacist society.

Purpose and Overview of This Chapter

For reasons such as building community, seeking information from
other Black students, and learning to be politically active on campus,
Black spaces (both physical and online) provide a sense of intellectual

safety and an environment for the development of Black scholarship for many Black students (Osei, 2019). Given that higher education and other social spaces are mostly White (Anderson, 2015), Black spaces in higher education serve as important resources for Black students yet lack attention in higher education. The purpose of this chapter is to explore how to cultivate more Black spaces, with particular attention to the development of Black scholarship. I theorize that the unavailability of Black spaces indicates that Black students, administrators, and faculty experience resource deprivation in higher education, which contributes to epistemic exclusion (Settles et al., 2020). Epistemic exclusion is "a form of scholarly delegitimization rooted in disciplinary biases about what types of research are valued as well as social identity-based biases against individuals from marginalized groups" (p. 2).

To counter epistemic exclusion, Black spaces that foster the development of Black scholarship, such as writing groups, Black student organizations, and Black studies programs or departments, must be cultivated, supported, and funded by the institution to demonstrate racial care (Harper, 2017). Doing so will support Black scholars in their intellectual development and counter negative stereotypes about their academic abilities. To demonstrate how Black scholarship spaces counter epistemic exclusion in higher education, I first review the literature on Black spaces. I then discuss how Black spaces function to support Black intellectualism in higher education, using research from a study on racial conflict at a Hispanic-serving institution (HSI) (Vega, 2021). Next I describe BlackCrit theory, which centers Black people in critical race theory (CRT) to build on the work of supporting and nurturing Black spaces in higher education. Finally, I provide recommendations for higher education and student affairs (HESA)* professionals and leaders to help them recognize the importance of

---

* HESA professionals include university-trained managers, administrators, and leaders who are in charge of the functions of the university such as admissions, human resources, financial aid, and residence life. They are not in charge of the teaching and research functions of the institution but may have some administrative responsibilities in these areas.

Black spaces and how to best support such spaces, despite the potential conflict they pose in higher education. While it is important for faculty to participate in the cultivation of Black spaces, HESA professionals and leaders have institutional and organizational knowledge and resources that can help these spaces thrive in PWIs.

Black Spaces and White Higher Education

For this chapter, institutions of higher education, specifically HWIs and HSIs, are racialized organizations that are conceptualized as "White spaces" where "Black people are typically absent, not expected, or marginalized when present" (Anderson, 2015, p. 10). White spaces and the dangers they pose to students of color continue to be reported on in the media (see Cobb, 2018; Wootson, 2018). Sociologists (see Anderson, 2015), journalists (see Cobb, 2018), and education researchers (see Vega, 2019) have explored problems associated with spaces that are historically White. Cobb (2018) warned that in White spaces, "implicit biases often have a way of becoming explicit ones" (para. 10), reminding us that White spaces are often protected by the law. Of educational spaces, Nxumalo & ross (2019) said the following: "Black schooling [is] situated within . . . the afterlife of school segregation, where Black students remain systematically dehumanized and positioned as uneducable" (p. 505).

I extend this work to higher education as a White space, where Black students in many ways continue to be dehumanized and deemed inadmissible. This is supported by research that has demonstrated that Black students report hostile racial climates, racial discrimination, and racial microaggressions (Allen & Solórzano, 2001; Dancy et al., 2018; George Mwangi et al., 2018; Hurtado & Ruiz Alvarado, 2015; Mensah & Jackson, 2012). These conflicts often lead to confrontations with campus police (Wootson, 2018), a lowered sense of trust between Black students and administrators (Vega, 2021), and various other disruptions to academic life. Ideologies such as anti-Black racism pervade White spaces and "[serve] to reinforce the ideological and material 'infrastructure' of educational inequity—the misrecognition of students and communities of color, and the (racialized) maldistribution of educational resources" (Dumas & ross, 2016, p. 432).

By contrast, Black spaces have been organized since as early as 1862 (Jerkins, 2019). Also known as "counterspaces" in higher education, these spaces "serve as sites where deficit notions of people of color can be challenged and where a positive collegiate racial climate can be established and maintained" (Solorzano et al., 2000, p. 70). For many students of color, counterspaces in higher education provide a place where they feel free from microaggressions and other forms of prejudice and discrimination in spaces that have historically privileged White people. Counterspaces are places where students of color can exchange what Harper (2013) calls "peer pedagogies," providing each other with valuable information about how to navigate often hostile racial campus climates. Despite how valuable Black spaces are in institutions of higher education, they continue to be defunded, removed, and unsupported (Vega, 2019). Nxumalo and ross (2019) describe Black spaces in the following way:

> In conceptualizing Black space in education, kihana ross (forthcoming) offers a consideration of Black space in education as what Christina Sharpe (2016) calls "wake work" (2016, p. 20), or "ways of seeing and imagining responses to terror in the varied and various ways that our Black lives are lived under occupation; ways that attest to the modalities of Black life lived in, as, under, and despite Black death" (2016, 20). Black space in education interrogates the ways Black students and educators enact educational fugitivity through the social production of Black space in the margin; ross suggests Black space in education manifests as search, as destination, as departure, as fugitivity, as the margin, as underground, as outer space, as submarine. (p. 508)

In her work, ross (2019) theorizes Black educational fugitive spaces, where Black students and educators create spaces to free themselves from the oppressive practices of educational institutions and, at the same time, find refuge in these spaces. Refuge is necessary in White spaces such as PWIs where students and scholars feel epistemologically excluded. Derrick Bell's "The Space Traders" (1992), an important tale of interest convergence and the lack of commitment to Black people in the United States, extends the idea of White spaces by providing an image of how Black people are understood in these spaces, as just bodies to be traded away. Thus, Bell conveys an important message: if we do not do the "wake work," if we do not see Black people as more than just Black bodies, dehumanization of Black people will continue to be normalized.

Thus, my focus on Black spaces is purposeful. Nxumalo and ross (2019) wonder what these Black spaces might look like if we acknowledge the central tenet of CRT offered by Bell and others—that racism is permanent—yet simultaneously recognize that we continue to use White spaces for education. Black spaces counter the negative effects of White spaces and invite racial contestation, a pushback against dehumanization and a reclamation of humanity for Black people. Unlike in White spaces, Black students in Black spaces are recognized and seen for their full humanity as resources are distributed equitably. In a sense, Black spaces are necessary for the physical, cultural, and intellectual survival of Black people in a very White world.

Black Scholarship in White Spaces

Despite the various contributions of Black scholars to our understanding of social life globally and in the United States, Black scholarship and Black scholars remain vulnerable to epistemological attacks, particularly in White spaces. "Black scholars . . . are marginalized based both on their race, and on their research on Black social realities . . . [and are] socially located as less powerful, less knowledgeable . . . less acceptable and—more broadly—rather untrustworthy in relation to White scholars" (Muzanenhamo & Chowdhury, 2021, p. 2). Thus, attacks on Black scholars and Black scholarship in White spaces are consistent with White supremacist and anti-Black logic, and they are unfortunately typical in higher education.

These attacks have historical precedents and have been documented among historians, educational researchers, and journalists. From the legal segregation of Black people into underresourced schools, to separate-but-equal laws, to post–civil rights era racism, the attack on Black intellectualism is part of American history. The most recent attack of CRT came about at the end of the Trump presidency and during the wake of the George Floyd protests. Scholars such as Kimberlé Crenshaw explained that a backlash would occur in the form of attacking educational curriculum (Wallace-Wells, 2021). Curriculum is often used as a mechanism of backlash from a rise in racial protests because children are on the receiving end of curriculum (Kingkade, 2020). When public figures argue that White children may have negative feelings in response to learning about White supremacist histories, they prioritize White children's safety and trade away racial justice for Black people. Thus, centering Black scholars and Black scholarship in conversations about building more equitable environments allows for a better understanding of how these environments or White spaces contribute to Black epistemological exclusion and ultimately jeopardize racial justice.

For these reasons, Black scholars have called for a focus on Black scholarship (see Fenwick, 2016). Additionally, scholars who have written on the Black intellectual tradition have provided a few ways to consider Black scholarship. According to Marable (2000), the Black intellectual tradition describes the living reality of Black life from the perspective of Black people, corrects inaccurate histories of Black people in the United States, and suggests plans to improve the conditions faced by Black people due to racism. It is transformative in that it lays out hopes and plans for the improvement of social, political, and educational lives of Black people in the United States. Fenwick (2016) adds that deficit perspectives of Black people must be interrupted, and one way to do so is by sharing research that accurately portrays the lived experiences of Black people and not entering conversations or work about Black people by using deficit perspectives such as negative statistics of Black students (Boutte et al., 2021, p. 2). Teresa (2019) notes that spaces that specifically encourage development of Black scholarship, such as newspapers and other media outlets focused on the lived experiences of Black people (read: noncooperative spaces), are especially important for the intellectual development of Black students. The question then remains: How do Black spaces encourage Black scholarship? In what ways can higher education administrators deter or support the development of Black spaces that are committed to cultivating Black scholarship? To explore this further, I will examine data from my research on Black spaces and organizational conflict.

The Case of an Administrative Closure
of a Black Space at an HSI

In an article I published titled "Lessons from an Administrative Closure: The Curious Case of Black Space at an MSI [minority-serving institution]" (Vega 2019), I wrote about a specific example that emerged from my study on racial conflict. A thirty-year-old student center used by Black student activists and community organizers was closed without warning to the students and other stakeholders of the center. The center had always been riddled with controversy because it was named after a freedom fighter who fought against racial injustice. White students had attempted to shut down the center throughout its history but were not successful. When it was finally closed, it was because the administration had overtaken it to use for university purposes.

The center was an office space that belonged to a public HSI, and some students, faculty, and administrators considered it a Black space. One midlevel administrator who managed a center for the academic affairs department described the space as "an antagonistic space from an administration perspective where in the last decades they either have tried to change the name or just take over the space." Other administrators expressed a desire for the space to expand student services. While members of multiple Black student organizations, community activists, and faculty used the space, administrators who were part of the decision to close the center believed it could be used for broader student needs. Given the power that the administration had over the members of the community who used the space, it was determined that the center needed to be closed and renovated for the needs described by student services administrators.

Black Spaces as a Source of Organizational Conflict

Black spaces have meaning in White spaces, specifically higher education. Black spaces, while providing joy to Black students, can signal a threat to White stakeholders. Dover et al. (2016) found that the White participants they studied felt threatened by feelings of anti-White discrimination. White participants felt they would be treated unfairly in a job search and even exhibited physiological conditions that suggested stress when applying to jobs with pro-diversity messages. This corroborates Hurtado et al.'s (1998) earlier finding that increased diversity often leads White students to perceive that fewer resources are available for them. Additionally, organizational conflict theorists have suggested that a scarcity of resources is another cause for conflict (Burke, 2006; Pondy, 1967; Tolbert & Hall, 2009). These perceptions, while seemingly innocuous, have serious consequences for making policies and conceptualizing practices that distribute resources along the lines of race. While more resources should be redistributed to Black people—especially in higher education, given all the evidence—the threat that Whites and other groups feel may contribute to the resource deprivation experienced by Black people.

My research on racial conflict suggests that administrators do not see racism as students do. This is a reflection of US society, in which not only do members (such as those in my study) disagree about how severely or frequently racism manifests, but they even disagree about whether it exists (Vega, 2021). To understand how conflict operates in an organization, I used De Dreu and Gelfand's (2008, p. 6) definition of organizational conflict: "a process that begins with how an individual or group perceives differences and opposition between itself and another individual or group about interests and resources, beliefs, values, or practices that matter to them." Using this definition, I studied racial conflict at two racially distinct universities, one an MSI, which is also identified as an HSI, and the other a PWI. In this study, I found that the HESA professionals with whom I spoke were very aware that racism and racist incidents exist, but their responses differed from the those of students I interviewed. While administrators felt that the incidents were not severe—often describing them from a historical perspective—students felt that they occurred every day and were triggered by structural racism, such as a lack of faculty and administrators of color and no curriculum speaking to the experiences of people of color. This finding has been corroborated by studies demonstrating that higher education leaders believe racism is an important consideration for higher education, but when asked about racism on their own campuses, they often replied with thoughts about its severity on other campuses instead.

The administrators I asked about the takeover of the student center told me that the center was important for the university for many reasons: it could serve more students if it was a student services center, not merely a space used by the Black student organization; student services are typically underfunded in the larger organizational scheme; those who used the center were not just Black students but also members of the surrounding community, whom the university did not think it had to prioritize over its own students and campus stakeholders. In addition to all these reasons, the university had been experiencing a decline in Black student enrollment for ten years at the time of my study, which the administration may have felt in various ways. Black students, on the other hand, felt the center was one more resource that had been taken away from them, since they had no access to Black faculty or a Black studies program. While Black students strongly felt this was an example of racial conflict, administrators did not see it as such. Rather, it was a necessary intervention for the greater good of the university and the majority of university students. In many ways, as already noted, this story and others like it are reminiscent of Bell's "The Space Traders." While Black people were not being traded away, Black student learning, comfort, and joy indeed were, primarily to create a space that served "all" students, even though Black students already faced a dearth of intellectual and student services that are often guaranteed to all university students.

As this example illustrates, one source of organizational conflict is the scarcity of resources. Diversity rhetoric in higher education often signals to White and other students that Black students are given more attention than they themselves receive. Yet diversity research in higher education has suggested that while practices to address inequities are plentiful, actual change does not easily come about, and race and racism are being phased out of diversity initiatives (Milem et al., 2005). Additionally, researchers who study Hispanic Serving Institutions (HSIs) found that a disproportionate number of resources are being directed toward Latinx students who identify as Mestizo or White while Afro-descendant and Indigenous Latinx students are further marginalized (Brooms, 2022; Kovats Sanchez, 2021; Pirtle et al., 2021; Vega et al., 2022). Thus, while organizations may be experiencing a scarcity of resources, Black students may be most deprived because of the false perception that diversity policies and practices are hyperfocused on Black students.

In a sense, Black spaces become a source of organizational conflict, one that administrators must acknowledge in order to recognize, protect, and cultivate these spaces. Ignoring this conflict could end Black spaces while upholding the values of a neoliberal diversity that does not serve the interests of Black people (ross, 2019). How might university leaders and administrators learn to recognize this kind of conflict? One way is by understanding race-based organizational conflict and identifying seemingly innocuous administrative decisions. Using a lens of anti-Black racism through BlackCrit theory provides an even clearer view of the ways racism operates against Black students, faculty, and administrators. One such operation, which the example of the student center discussed earlier clearly depicted, is through resource and epistemological deprivation. Black spaces are not only a physical resource for Black scholars, they are also intellectual ones, where Black scholars learn about protests that have targeted demands such as increasing Black faculty, encounter the histories and experiences of Black people within their collegiate institutions, and continue to develop Black intellectualism. My research suggests that while administrators accept the existence of racial conflict, they have yet to fully address these issues and demands after decades of protest. Why? How can university leaders recognize racism, yet still feel powerless (Harper & Hurtado, 2007) in addressing it?

BlackCrit and Supporting, Cultivating, and Protecting Black Spaces

BlackCrit theory centers Blackness and Black people in CRT and explains the particular ways racism affects Black people in the United States (Dumas & ross, 2016). Whereas CRT interrogates practices and policies associated with White supremacy, it does not address the specific ways that anti-Blackness manifests, especially in educational spaces. Ross (2019) explained that the tenets of BlackCrit are influenced by CRT but vary in specific ways: anti-Blackness is the ideology that is central to how social life is organized and "signals the broader antagonistic relationship between blackness and possibility of humanity" (p. 3); "Blackness exists in tension with neoliberal and multicultural imagination" (p. 3), as neoliberal logics often invisibilize and dehumanize Black people in the name of diversity; and Black liberatory space is a place where resistance to revisionist history is cultivated, accurate history and events are told, and liberation is conceptualized.

Using BlackCrit theory to analyze the case I detailed earlier in this chapter can help retell the story of an administrative closure of a Black space and its contribution to epistemological deprivation. While the institution I studied was a designated MSI, at the time of the study, the Black student population in higher education was steadily decreasing. This has been corroborated by US studies overall: Black student enrollment in higher education declined by almost 10% between 2010 and 2017 (Zahneis, 2019) and continues to stagnate or decline at most public flagship institutions (Lumpkin et al., 2021). As these numbers decline and as fiscal pressures increase, particularly during a time of crisis such as the COVID-19 pandemic, other resources, such as Black studies departments and Black student centers, may be in danger. Protecting these resources also means protecting the intellectual development of Black students and scholars. Rather than committing epistemic exclusion, administrators can consider Black epistemic inclusion in their work on racial diversity and improving racial climates on their campuses. By valuing epistemic inclusion for Black scholars specifically, administrators may understand racial conflict to be more than just interpersonal in nature or overtly physical in other instances.

Valuing Black epistemological inclusion would allow administrators to recognize Black spaces as valuable to the intellectual development of Black scholars in their institutions. The administrators in my study felt the student center space could have been used by more students; however, if administrators had applied a BlackCrit lens to this situation, they would have recognized the decline of Black students at their institution. Not only was there a decline in Black student enrollment, but there was also a decline in support for Black students. Administrators could have reviewed the state of Black students at MSIs and HSIs rather than simply understanding it to be an issue related to diversity.

Applying a BlackCrit analysis to the administrative closure of the center as a Black space, administrators would have recognized how incredibly important the center was to Black students, administrators, faculty, and community organizers who were confronting the erasure of Blackness at their institution. Instead, administrators believed the center was not useful to the larger student population. They must explore how they contributed to Black epistemological deprivation by suggesting that more students could benefit from the space and using that as a rationale for taking over a Black space. This space was one where Black people could understand the nuances of anti-Black racism, resist revisionist histories, review accurate perspectives, and envision better possibilities and futures for themselves and their communities by engaging in activism. If the administrators had had a full understanding of Black student life at their institution, they may have approached the matter differently and protected this Black space.

Recommendations

Higher education leaders play a critical role in either supporting or defunding Black spaces, since Black spaces are often a source of organizational conflict for HESA administrators who experience scarcity of resources and space (Vega, 2019, 2021). Using BlackCrit theory, HESA administrators can learn how Black spaces on their campuses contribute to Black epistemological inclusion and explore their significance to Black scholarship. These recommendations for Black spaces are offered in the spirit of hope, which is critical to change—or, if no change occurs, to at least ensure we are not replicating any systems of domination (hooks, 2004). In higher education, "*critical hope* reflects the ability to realistically assess one's environment through a lens of equity and justice while also envisioning the possibility of a better future" (Bishundat et al., 2018, p. 91). The following are suggestions for HESA professionals and leaders to build Black spaces committed to Black epistemological inclusion and the development of Black scholarship at PWIs and other institutions such as HSIs to counter the devaluation of Black students in higher education.

- HESA professionals and leaders should adopt a BlackCrit perspective to analyze Black spaces and their role in contributing to Black epistemological inclusion. This is especially salient in PWIs. Additionally, HESA professionals at other types of institutions (e.g., MSIs) could consider BlackCrit perspectives in their work to ensure that Black students, administrators, and faculty are being served. Applying racially and culturally relevant lenses and perspectives of minoritized populations within MSIs would prevent a flattening of various identities and the development of a "minority" monolith.
- HESA professionals and leaders should center Black epistemological inclusion in conversations about diversity. Practices related to diversity are more harmful to Black scholarship and Black scholars than they are helpful because they typically erase the experiences of Black people. Centering Black scholarship

and valuing Black epistemological inclusion involves two things: (1) recognizing that Black epistemological exclusion exists in White spaces such as PWIs and (2) moving past the understanding that racial conflict is largely interpersonal and individual and instead focusing on institutional and structural racism.

- HESA professionals and leaders should explore existing Black spaces on campuses. Where are they? Who uses them? Black spaces provide a place for fugitivity (ross, 2019) from larger White spaces. HESA professionals should protect these spaces by ensuring their existence and providing them with resources. Additionally, faculty or administrators who work within Black spaces supporting Black epistemological inclusion should be given some release from their day-to-day employment activities.

- HESA professionals and leaders should document Black epistemological deprivation. This includes a lack of Black studies departments, Black faculty, and Black HESA administrators. In PWIs that already have dedicated Black spaces, HESA professionals could document how these spaces are funded in relation to other spaces or services on campus. Are they being equitably funded and supported? Where are the disparities, and what are the plans to ameliorate them? Additionally, HESA professionals at PWIs could document admissions and enrollment rates of Black students within a designated time period. What are the trends? What can the PWI learn from those trends?

- HESA professionals and leaders should support the liberatory and visionary needs of Black students, Black faculty, and Black HESA professionals. Black spaces prevent Black epistemological deprivation. They demonstrate to Black scholars that their knowledge is valued. Within Black spaces, Black scholarship is cultivated, but so is hope because plans and activities geared toward liberation from White supremacy are acknowledged and developed.

Conclusion

White spaces continue to threaten Black epistemological inclusion and the development of scholarship by Black people. The purpose of this chapter was to explore how Black spaces in White academia counter the epistemological exclusion that is the very foundation of White spaces. By using a BlackCrit perspective on race-based organizational conflict, I explored how a Black space, while providing a source of Black epistemological inclusion for Black and Afro-descendant people, caused organizational conflict on a postsecondary campus. The closure of a Black space indicates resource deprivation for Black people. I argue that Black spaces, while not serving all members of a postsecondary campus, should not be intended to do so given the resource deprivation experienced by Black people in predominantly White spaces. This resource deprivation is in actuality epistemological deprivation experienced by Black scholars, to the detriment of the whole campus community. I call on HESA administrators to add Black epistemological inclusion as a value toward building more equitable and more just environments.

REFERENCES

Allen, W., & Solórzano, D. (2001). Affirmative action, educational equity and campus racial climate: A case study of the University of Michigan Law School. *La Raza Law Journal, 12*, 237–363.

Anderson, E. (2015). The White space. *Sociology of Race and Ethnicity, 1*, 10–21. https://doi.org/10.1177/2332649214561306.

Bell, D. (1992). The space traders. In *Faces at the bottom of the well: The permanence of racism*. Basic Books.

Bishundat, D., Phillip, D. V., & Gore, W. (2018). Cultivating critical hope: The too often forgotten dimension of critical leadership development. *New Directions for Student Leadership, 2018*(159), 91–102.

Boutte, G., & Bryan, N. (2021). When will Black children be well? Interrupting anti-Black violence in early childhood classrooms and schools. *Contemporary Issues in Early Childhood, 22*(3), 232–243.

Brooms, D. R. (2022). What's going on here? Black men and gendered-antiblackness at a Hispanic-Serving Institution. *Race Ethnicity and Education*, 1–20. https://doi .org/10.1080/13613324.2022.2154371.

Burke, W. W. (2006). Conflict in organizations. In M. Deutsch, P. Coleman, & E. C. Marcus (Eds.), *The handbook of conflict resolution: Theory and practice* (pp. 781–804). Jossey-Bass.

Cobb, J. (2018). Starbucks and the issue of White space. *New Yorker*, June 4 and 11, 2018. https://www.newyorker.com/magazine/2018/06/04/starbucks-and-the-issue-of-white-space.

Dancy, T. E., Edwards, K. T., & Davis, J. E. (2018). Historically White universities and plantation politics: Anti-Blackness and higher education in the Black Lives Matter era. *Urban Education, 53*(2), 176–195.

De Dreu, C. K., & Gelfand, M. J. (Eds.). (2008). *The psychology of conflict and conflict management in organizations* (pp. 3–54). Lawrence Erlbaum.

Dover, T. L., Major, B., & Kaiser, C. R. (2016). Members of high-status groups are threatened by pro-diversity organizational messages. *Journal of Experimental Social Psychology, 62*, 58–67. https://doi.org/10.1016/J.JESP.2015.10.006.

Dumas, M. J., & ross, k. m. (2016). "Be real Black for me": Imagining BlackCrit in education. *Urban Education, 51*(4), 415–442. https://doi.org/10.1177/0042085916628611.

Fenwick, L. T. (2016). Blacks in research: How shall we be portrayed? *Urban Education, 51*(6), 587–599.

George Mwangi, C. A., Thelamour, B., Ezeofor, I., & Carpenter, A. (2018). "Black elephant in the room": Black students contextualizing campus racial climate within U.S. racial climate. *Journal of College Student Development, 59*(4), 456–474.

Harper, S. R. (2013). Am I my brother's teacher? Black undergraduates, peer pedagogies, and racial socialization in predominantly White postsecondary contexts. *Review of Research in Education, 37*(1), 183–211. https://doi.org/10.3102/0091732X12471300.

Harper, S. R. (2017). Racially responsive leadership: Addressing the longstanding problem of racism in higher education. In J. S. Antony, A. M. Cauce, & D. E. Shalala (Eds.), *Challenges in higher education leadership: Practical and scholarly solutions* (pp. 145–156). Routledge.

Harper, S. R., & Hurtado, S. (2007). Nine themes in campus racial climates and implications for institutional transformation. *New Directions for Student Services, 2007*(120), 7–24.

hooks, b. (2004). *Teaching community: A pedagogy of hope.* Routledge.

Hurtado, S., Milem, J., Clayton-Pedersen, A., & Allen, W. (1998). Enhancing campus climate for racial/ethnic diversity: Educational policy and practice. *Review of Higher Education, 21*(3), 279–302. https://doi.org/10.1353.rhe.1998.0003.

Hurtado, S., & Ruiz Alvarado, A. (2015). Discrimination and bias, underrepresentation, and sense of belonging on campus. HERI Research Brief. Higher Education Research Institute. https://vtechworks.lib.vt.edu/bitstream/handle/10919/83064/DiscriminationBiasCampus.pdf?sequence=1&isAllowed=y.

Jerkins, M. (2019). "For us, by us": Inside the new social spaces for people of color. *New York Times*, March 9, 2019. https://www.nytimes.com/2019/03/09/nyregion/social-clubs-nyc-people-of-color.html.

Kingkade, T. (2020). How one teacher's Black Lives Matter lesson divided a small Wisconsin town. NBC News, October 24, 2020. https://www.nbcnews.com /news/us-news/how-one-teacher-s-black-lives-matter-lesson-divided-small -n1244566.

Kovats Sánchez, G. (2021). "If we don't do it, nobody is going to talk about it": Indigenous students disrupting Latinidad at Hispanic-Serving Institutions. *AERA Open, 7.* https://doi.org/10.1177/23328584211059194.

Lumpkin, L., Kolodner, M., & Anderson, N. (2021). Flagship universities say diversity is a priority. But Black enrollment in many states continues to lag. *Washington Post,* April 18, 2021. https://www.washingtonpost.com/education /2021/04/18/flagship-universities-black-enrollment/.

Marable, M. (2000). Black studies and the racial mountain. *Souls: Critical Journal of Black Politics & Culture, 2*(3), 17–36.

Mensah, F., & Jackson, I. (2012). Whiteness as property in science teacher education. Presentation at Sixth Annual Critical Race Studies in Education Conference, May 30, 2012. Teachers College, Columbia University, New York.

Milem, J., Chang, M., & Antonio, A. (2005). *Making diversity work on campus: A research-based perspective.* Association of American Colleges and Universities.

Muzanenhamo, P., & Chowdhury, R. (2021). Epistemic injustice and hegemonic ordeal in management and organization studies: Advancing Black scholarship. *Human Relations.* Advance online publication. https://doi.org/10.1177 /00187267211014802.

Nxumalo, F., & ross, k. m. (2019). Envisioning Black space in environmental education for young children. *Race Ethnicity and Education, 22*(4), 502–524. https://doi.org/10.1080/13613324.2019.1592837.

Osei, Z. (2019). Seeking a community, Black students turn to online chats. *Chronicle of Higher Education,* January 29, 2019. https://www.chronicle.com/article /Seeking-a-Community-Black/245569.

Pirtle, W. N., Brock, B., Aldonza, N., Leke, K., & Edge, D. (2021). "I didn't know what anti-Blackness was until I got here": The unmet needs of Black students at Hispanic-Serving Institutions. *Urban Education,* 1–28. https://doi.org/10.1177 /00420859211044948.

Pondy, L. R. (1967). Organizational conflict: Concepts and models. *Administrative Science Quarterly, 12,* 296–320.

ross, k. (2019). Revisiting BlackCrit in education: Anti-Black reality and liberatory fantasy. Center for Critical Race Studies in Education at UCLA: Research Briefs, 17.

Settles, I. H., Warner, L., Buchanan, N. T., & Jones, M. K. (2020). Understanding psychology's resistance to intersectionality theory using a framework of invisibility and epistemic exclusion. *Journal of Social Issues, 76*(4), 769–813. http://dx.doi.org/10.1111/josi.12403.

Solorzano, D., Ceja, M., & Yosso, T. (2000). Critical race theory, racial microaggressions, and campus racial climate: The experiences of African American college students. *Journal of Negro Education, 69*(1/2), 60–73. http://www.jstor.org/stable /2696265.

Teresa, C. (2019). Twentieth-century Black press scholarship: New analytical approaches, growing momentum. *American Periodicals: A Journal of History & Criticism, 29*(1), 96–102.

Tolbert, P. S., & Hall, R. H. (2009). *Organizations: Structures, processes and outcomes.* Routledge.

Vega, B. E. (2019). Lessons from an administrative closure: The curious case of Black space at an MSI. *Frontiers in Education, 3,* article 88.

Vega, B. E. (2021). "What is the real belief on campus?" Perceptions of racial conflict at a minority-serving institution and a historically White institution. *Teachers College Record, 123*(9), 144–170.

Vega, B. E., Liera, R., & Boveda, M. (2022). Hispanic-Serving Institutions as racialized organizations: Elevating intersectional consciousness to reframe the "H" in HSIs. *AERA Open, 8.* https://doi.org/10.1177/23328584221095074.

Venegas, E. M., Koonce, J. B., Lancaster, L., Bazan, J., & Garza, A. (2021). Diversifying the "HSI bubble": Black and Asian women faculty at Hispanic-serving institutions. *Race Ethnicity and Education.* Advance online publication. https://doi.org/10.1080/13613324.2021.1924139.

Wallace-Wells, B. (2021). How a conservative activist invented the conflict over critical race theory. *New Yorker,* June 18, 2021.

Wootson, C., Jr. (2018). A Black Yale student fell asleep in her dorm's common room. A White student called police. *Washington Post,* May 11, 2018. https://www.washingtonpost.com/news/grade-point/wp/2018/05/10/a-black-yale-student-fell-asleep-in-her-dorms-common-room-a-white-student-called-police/?utm_term=.a2c192acf3d4.

Zahneis, M. (2019). Why has Black-student enrollment fallen? *Chronicle of Higher Education,* August 18, 2019. https://www.chronicle.com/article/why-has-black-student-enrollment-fallen/?cid2=gen_login_refresh&cid=gen_sign_in.

7

Facing Racial Microaggressions in the Academy

Sustaining Oneself through a Womanist Consciousness

SHERON FRASER-BURGESS

Seminal literature in higher education recounts the persisting oppressive conditions that African Americans and Black and Indigenous people of color confront in higher education. Dancy et al. (2018) detail the "plantation politics" pervading policy and practice in predominantly White institutions of higher education, predicated on Black people as property. Mustaffa (2017) offers a historiography of anti-Black violence in the higher education system—from the colonial era, through the Civil War and its aftermath, and into the mid- to late twentieth century—and the structural, cultural, and direct or interpersonal moves that have reinscribed the racial hierarchy of the broader society in these institutions (Pittman, 2012).

Racial microaggressions are one type of racial violence that can have a debilitating effect on the Black psyche inclusive of racial battle fatigue (Jones, 2021; McCabe, 2009; Midgette & Mulvey, 2022; Smith et al., 2016) Their persisting effects support Afro-pessimism's hypothesis of insuperable racism in US society (ross, 2020; Wilderson, 2020). Taking a narrator-as-third-person perspective, this chapter details a narrative reflection on confronting racial microaggressions in higher education. Modeling self and situational inquiry to overcome the internal conflict that Black women experience in facing racial microaggressions (Jones, 2021), it sheds light on the Black female academic's generative internal dialogue that can foster imperviousness to the catastrophic White normative gaze and ways of resisting regimes of delegitimization. The chapter argues that there are philosophical resources that womanist thinking offers in its onto-epistemology and onto-ethics to sustain oneself. A generative internal voice can therefore persist.

Afro-pessimism in Higher Education

Grant, Woodson, & Dumas (2020) put forward a "radical analytic" that invites an examination of the Black condition through the lens of Black suffering, Black fugitivity, and Black futurity. According to this Afro-pessimism, anti-Blackness is an immutable fact about the world because the perpetual subjugation of the Black race, in one form or another, is necessary for all other theories to survive. In contesting the theoretical and structural facets of society and its institutions, Grant, Woodson, & Dumas's (2020) edited work identifies the material conditions that are the persisting markers of the permanence of anti-Blackness in educational institutions, practice, and policy. Dumas (2016, p. 12) states that "in all the theorizing on antiblackness, there is a concern with what it means to have one's very existence as Black constructed as problem—for White people, for the public (good), for the nation-state, and even as a problem for (the celebration of) racial difference."

Racial microaggressions (Pittman, 2012; Sue et al., 2007) are one manifestation of anti-Blackness that exemplifies Afro-pessimism in higher education. Harris et al. (2021, p. 531) define racial microaggressions as "subtle acts of racism that are so normalized and slight they are hard to identify, address, and redress." Pittman's (2012) research focuses on the forms that are evidenced in typical interpersonal interactions in the Black faculty experience. They can exact a heavy toll on Black faculty members. Jones (2021) found that Black women experienced internal conflict about the veracity of their subject experience when they encountered microaggressions and tried to verify that the behaviors in question qualify as or are motivated by racism. Constantine (2008, p. 349) noted that members of the White dominant culture who exhibited the most insidious forms fail to be conscious of or recognize the "racist origins or implications of their actions."

Narrative Self-Reflection as Womanist Inquiry

The focus of this chapter is a Black female faculty member's narrative self-reflection on her experience of an extended series of interpersonal interactions with White colleagues at a predominantly White institution of higher education. The narrative begins when a social justice book club for faculty members is convening to read Monique Morris's (2016) *Pushout: The Criminalization of Black Girls in School*. At the outset, the narrator/protagonist expresses optimism that the book club will be a space where she feels welcome, only to note that the antagonist of these microaggressions is one of the attendees. Salient to this emerging social constitution of the book club is that, in attempting to resolve a long-standing inter-faculty conflict, the narrator's home department in her college installed a new chairperson of the department, who happens to be the antagonist. Documented and recorded as the narrator was determining whether this antagonist and others were engaging in racial microaggressions, the narrative is a form of situational inquiry. However, as the narrator must resolve the internal conflicts that arise, it is also a self-inquiry.

Goodall (2009), writing on narrative as a qualitative inquiry method, proposes that personal narratives offer an episteme that has the power to affect perceptions of reality, to alter opinions, and to mediate choices of action in each situation. Goodall writes,

> The basic idea is that when we engage in writing or telling a story, we create alternative pathways to meaning that are imaginative and analytical; that are guided by a narrative (rather than propositional) rationality; and that are relational—in the production of meaning, they

connect the teller of the tale to the listener or reader of the story. The very act of writing a story, or telling a tale in public or just to a friend, changes not so much how or what we know (although telling a good story well can certainly do that), it *alters* the way we think about what we know and how we know it. (2009, p. xiv)

Narratives represent an account of reality and by their exposition can fulfill an epistemological aim of discovery.

Womanist thinking offers philosophical resources to the Black academic, and narrative inquiry can direct the narrator to these areas of psychic strength. Rossini (2021, p. 3) writes that a narrative is also a "reflexive turn onto myself; a turn formed of my stories and within kindred moments of dialogical engagement. . . . The narrative turn becoming the construct of my being in the world; yet, one which is also paradoxical as the inward turn is also outward in ethos." One can locate the "summonses" of narrative by identifying and turning to the imperative of the narrative. This chapter aims to demonstrate that through narrative inquiry, one can identify womanist thinking at work. It evidences the way that affective and dispositional responses to embodied suffering and striving can act as immaterial and regulative forces that generate an ethic of self-sustenance.

Womanist thinking as a stance in the world originated in Alice Walker's literary representation of the Black woman's way of being considering centuries of oppression and subjugation. Walker (1983) described womanist ways of the world in *In Search of Our Mothers' Gardens* and proposed four definitions. The first meaning was that of being in opposition to "girlish" frivolity, or not being serious; being a Black feminist or woman of color. Its second manifestation is loving other women, platonically or not, or being passionate about "women's culture." Third, being womanist is to have particular objects of love — for example, music, the moon or dancing, and the "struggle." Lastly, Walker (1983) distinguishes womanist thinking as metaphorically "purple" compared with (White) feminism's "lavender" (xi–xii). Although Walker, in defining womanist thinking, does not purport to describe the necessary and sufficient conditions of its assertion, the theory conforms to the generally accepted view of philosophy, broadly, as a systematic and internally consistent account of the human condition.

One model of theorizing human moral worth and thought, in terms of embodiment that instantiates somatic value, is the onto-ethics of womanist Katie Cannon. Cannon seminally developed an ethic that has "ontological commitments" to inform its subaltern ethics (Howe, 2003, p. 283). One precept asserts the dignity of Black women as an inference from the moral facts from colonization to the antebellum period. Cannon (1988/2006) maintains that, while Black women's existence consistently has been one of struggle against forces determined to dictate their existential condition as objects and their ontological condition of subjugation to the White normative gaze, there is a dignity imputed by the universe that ultimately bears witness to all forms of justice and God, in whose divine gaze all are objects of radical love. This axiom harks back to Anna Julia Cooper (1896/2022) and her assertion of the inherent moral worth of Black women as a counterpart axiom to a similar proclamation about the male gender.

Cannon's onto-ethics, typical of the womanist worldview, shows first that the immanence of suffering, as a culturally formative immaterial influence on the body, can supervene to elicit affective states that express the best of the human condition. Howe (2003, p. 278) argues, in his discussion of the subaltern ethics and the attendant ontology, that "one cannot avoid the question of ontology" and must ask the teleological question of the human condition: "What are the sources of hope and joy—of feistiness—that allow one to assert a positive existence beyond the dismal situation one is given"?

Womanist scholars interpret the collective and historical significance of the lived experiences of the Black woman in the North American African diaspora as a way of being that reveals "the ethical values that the Black community has construed for itself" (Cannon, 1988/2006, p. 3). For instance, a womanist theological ethic presupposes that these values reflect that "Black women live moral wisdom in their real-lived context that does not appeal to the fixed rules or absolute principles" of Eurocentrism. Instead, "Black women's analysis and appraisal of what is right or wrong and good" is "moral counsel that can liberate and empower them to live out a spirituality that prevails through the oppressive social, economic, and political conditions" (Cannon, 1988/2006, p. 4). The end goal is to embody the forms of love and hope that Walker identifies in *In Search of Our Mothers' Gardens*. Similarly, Collins (1996) framed womanist conceptualization in terms of offering an alternate standpoint for knowing comparable to Black feminism. On this view, centering Black women's experiences highlights "the potential for oppressed people to possess a moral vision and standpoint on society that grows from their situation of oppression" (p. 11).*

This is a frame of reference that the womanist theological ethic has adopted in its theorization of womanism and its underlying ontological claims about the subject. Cannon (1988/2006) conceptualized the womanist ethic in a way that reflects dialectical engagement with anti-Blackness; the womanist ethic or womanist theological ethic problematizes the prevailing Eurocentric philosophical conception of the subject that embeds Western intellectual thought as a legacy of the Enlightenment (hooks, 1992; Peters & Tesar, 2016).

The Narrative Inquiry

A Diversity Book Club

The email announcement stated that the College of Education book club had selected a text about young Black female lives. And Black female faculty nursed hopes that maybe, just maybe, they could finally have *the* long sought-after conversation about race in the intimate space of conversations about these important matters of racism and inequity. As they would discover, nothing could have been further from the truth. Over a twelve-month period that included President Barack Obama's last months in office, the resignation of a dean over racially insensitive comments in the college, and the election of Donald

---

* Collins (1996, p. 12) discounts the claim that such a standpoint can be "privileged" or complete on its own.

Trump as president, the space would prove remarkably impervious to critical self-reflection on ways that racial inequality is perpetuated in the academy in general. Instead, it seemed to exemplify the typical legitimization exercise in which White women engage. By attending, they show their social justice credentials, but in discourse they neither acknowledge nor surrender any of their power or positionality in being White, female academics in positions of influence and able to wield that power to the detriment of the Black female body.

Prologue

Andrea skimmed the names in the listserv and swallowed hard. Unbelievably, not only was Rebecca's name listed, but she had replied that she would attend, as if she cared about the racialized ways in which Black girls in middle school and high school were being criminalized through excessive disciplinary practices. Andrea knew intimately that Rebecca resisted acknowledging the structural workings of racism in the lives of Black women. More importantly, Andrea resented the loss of the potential for a confessional space that this book club had represented. How could she share her experience when one of the causes of this racially hostile environment was there?

Act I (Two Years Previously): The New Department Chair and Old Tropes of White Duplicity

Andrea spotted Rebecca with a group of faculty members from her department. She dreaded convocations even after thirteen years of working for this university. In the large auditorium filling up with faculty members, where would she sit? The answer was, of course, anywhere; but the expectation was that one would sit somewhere in the vicinity of the other members of one's department. Andrea dreaded this thought. How could she withstand the cold stares and dismissive looks of her colleagues? However, as she walked down the aisle in the general direction of a few familiar faces, the sight of Rebecca signaled a space that was not hostile. Indeed, Rebecca looked up as Andrea approached. Simultaneously, three or four others walked up to the rows at the same time, and suddenly there was the awkwardness of there being more people than empty spaces. In a tacit acknowledgment of her new role as interim department chair, Rebecca stood up and directed the movement of the small group into a new row, and as luck would have it, Andrea's seat in the shuffle placed her next to Rebecca.

Scarred by years of marginalization, Andrea wanted to believe that with Rebecca there would be a fresh start. Perhaps her label as the department's resident angry Black woman would be a thing of the past. Was there a chance that this White woman understood the way that institutional racism unfolded in the academy? Would she be willing to be an ally? News of Rebecca's coming to the department was welcomed by Andrea, with good reason. Although they were from different departments, she and Andrea shared a social history. Their children both attended a local elementary and middle school together. Andrea remembered pleasant encounters at school events, socializing at lazy summer barbecues and chilly autumn parties that were warmed by the fellowship of shared parental joys, bottles of wine, insider stories about the college, and gossipy conversations about the middle school happenings.

Rebecca came to Andrea's department at a time when the faculty were incredibly polarized. The last department chair, Jezzie, had been asked to step down. One half of the group welcomed Rebecca as the lesser of two evils. The other half resented her being imposed on them. The dean had asked Jezzie to step down rather than assume her fourth three-year term. Although there was no official word on the exact nature of the incidents that precipitated the decision, the talk in the department was that a combination of decisions that clearly reflected abuse of her power in the use of department funds were contributing factors. Also, there was her long-standing feud with a Black female faculty member, Andrea, who had filed a lawsuit against the university on these grounds.

Before the university convocation began, Rebecca and Andrea engaged in small talk. There were the requisite pleasantries about their respective children before the provost spoke. When there was applause, they chitchatted about university issues. When a faculty member from her former department walked up to receive the faculty of the year award, Rebecca shared confidences about the questionable quality of his scholarship and his excessive reliance on doctoral students. Although this talk was not the kind of conversation that Andrea sought, preferred, or encouraged, she listened in a quiet hope that it was a sign that Rebecca viewed her as a part of the team. Maybe, she thought to herself, she could begin to flourish rather than merely survive.

Maintaining this belief took some resolve and was counter to the misgivings that were surfacing in light of a tumultuous start to the academic year, which was a remnant of her acrimonious relationship with Jezzie. Andrea had watched her fall-semester schedule all summer nervously. In one of her last retaliatory acts as department chairperson, Jezzie had engineered a five-day teaching load, which, for Andrea, who commuted over one hour each way to work, would have been a considerable commitment of time. A simple alteration to one of her class offerings would have allowed her to teach on just two days. It was the kind of modification that faculty requested and received often. Just three weeks before the semester, Rebecca had emailed to inform her that one of her classes, which was required for Ph.D. students had an insufficient number of students who had registered. If this class was canceled, then a five-day schedule was unavoidable, based on the courses that were already being offered. The email exchange with Rebecca suggested that the only way to circumvent this outcome was for Andrea to locate someone to teach one of two alternative courses offered. Andrea pondered this dilemma and the daunting task of recruiting a faculty member to teach the course.

Andrea soon discovered through emailing students who were previously registered for the Ph.D. course that they had been advised not to take the course by their dissertation committee chairs, who were all faculty who were part of Jezzie's faction. Faced with this act of aggression and the prospect of such a burdensome schedule, Andrea contemplated going on medical leave. To manage this contentious environment, she had been in therapy for the last two years continuously.

Ironically, after being informed that Jezzie would no longer be chair-person, she ended the sessions. The five-day teaching load still pend-ing, she scheduled a meeting with Rebecca to begin the process of acquiring and completing the paperwork to submit the request for medical leave. At the time, the absurdity of the situation was lost on Andrea. For although Rebecca entertained all of the options and of-fered Andrea the chance to find someone to teach one of the courses so that she would not have the more onerous slate, it should not have been Andrea's responsibility to do so. Moreover, as she faced the like-lihood of going on medical leave, having to seek out someone to re-place her was not the best use of her overtaxed mental and emotional resources. Nevertheless, with the prospect of working with Rebecca to achieve a mutually beneficial compromise, Andrea did so and suc-ceeded in achieving a more reasonable schedule. In the end, she was assigned an online course in a section in a disciplinary area outside her expertise instead of an in-person course that met three times a week. Two weeks before the semester started, she was expected to pre-pare the syllabus for this course. Andrea accepted the compromise and decided not to take the medical leave.

The experience generated some unease for Andrea about Rebecca's objectivity, primarily because in discussing the issue of the doctoral class, Rebecca insisted on repeating a narrative that did not acknowl-edge that there could be bad actors who engineered the situation. She addressed the situation as solely a problem of scheduling and not of the broader issue of Jezzie's use of her power to misinform students and to undermine Andrea's teaching this course in the Ph.D. program. Now it seemed that, under the guise of there being a crisis, Andrea had been maneuvered nicely into teaching a course in a subsection of the department that sorely needed someone; but she was entirely with-out the background knowledge and previous experience in this edu-cation field and the semester would begin on Monday.

Convocation over, Andrea walked to the meeting of the college fac-ulty where the dean would celebrate accomplishments and discuss the strategic course for the year. That tedious time having ended, soon she made her way to the department meeting, where, in a flurry of activity, committees were established and the chair people were selected. However, it would have been a mistake to understand the matter-of-fact way that the details unfolded as indicating that they were insignificant. Before the actual voting, it was likely that coalitions had been sought and secured. At stake were the promotions of friends and their denial to enemies of the promotion and tenure committee, for example. Of critical importance was the constitution of the salary committee, because salary increases were 100% merit based. Typically, factions sought to have a majority presence on this committee in order to ensure that they would receive their raises. Andrea took all of this department politics for granted and was resigned to her own powerlessness in this process. She was aligned with no one and therefore was only a single voice. Walking into the room, which contained six tables, she once again faced the choice of where to sit. It was a question of who could at least be polite to her. When the meeting began, Andrea could see that Jezzie sat at a table diagonal to her closest to the refreshments. When Andrea walked over to get lunch, Jezzie's simmering anger was evident as she wheeled her chair out of the way to avoid even being close to Andrea.

When the meeting began, Rebecca, in her first presentation as the new chair, sought to acknowledge the contentiousness of the department's past, without being explicit, and reassure the faculty that it was possible to set a new course. Facing Jezzie and with her back to Andrea, she issued words of reassurance to Jezzie and everyone else. "I will keep you safe!" she said. "I know how this is done; I have worked in difficult spaces before, and I am confident that I have the skills to defuse this conflict. Your safety is my utmost concern!" There was no mistaking who the direct target of her reassurance was. Andrea sank in her seat and her eyes stung with burning tears. She thought to herself, What did she mean? Was she referencing Jezzie's claim that she feared that Andrea would shoot her? This had been a widely circulated accusation that was not substantiated by any facts but that Jezzie repeated invoked. The accusation savaged Andrea's standing in the department just by its mere intonation. Andrea wondered also whether Rebecca intended to give credence to Jezzie's fear. Did she not know that Jezzie was drawing on the standard tropes of White female fragility in order to center herself and her experiences? She was the one being victimized, Jezzie was insisting.

Andrea suddenly felt that an official signal had been sent that she would be the subject of surveillance in order to reassure Jezzie. In that moment, Andrea believed that Rebecca had claimed the department's space as the purview of the dominant group and she had been put in her place as a troublemaker. She endured the rest of the meeting in shocked silence. She barely registered Rebecca's announcement of the creation of a new committee for the department, which was the diversity committee. There was a moment of great cognitive dissonance as Rebecca stressed the importance of valuing differences in the department and the role that such a committee would play in developing and implementing practices to promote diversity. Every time the word *diversity* was said, Andrea longed for Rebecca to clarify and incorporate social justice issues. Rallying herself to the potential to do good, Andrea grasped at the announcement as if it were a buoy thrown into the sea of despair in which she was beginning to drown. She volunteered to be part of the committee. Maybe there was still work that could be done and a reason for hope. She gathered her things and went home.

Act II: Setting a Different Tone?

In preparation for the individual meeting that Rebecca required for all department faculty, Andrea had made a list of ideas about changes and practices she would like to implement in the department. This time she was nervous, after the initial department meeting. Her misgivings were deeper this time and harder to dismiss. It would be the first official meeting since Rebecca became chair of the department and the semester had begun officially. Because it was taking place in the first month of the fall semester, it would make sense, Andrea thought, for them to jointly place some frame around the controversy that had rocked the department and Andrea's role in it. Andrea hoped that Rebecca would seek out her side of the story to give her a chance to lay out her perspective. It was a fervent wish that she would have the opportunity to declare her innocence on accusations of being belligerent. Thus far all the upheaval had taken place behind the scenes with no effort to achieve détente. Different parties were talking only to each other and about those on the other side. Andrea felt that everyone was talking about her, and no one was talking to her. It was a lonely feeling. With Rebecca becoming the chairperson, she hoped at least that these hostilities could be laid to rest.

"Good afternoon!" Andrea said as she walked into Rebecca's office and extended her hand for a handshake.

"How are you?" Rebecca asked, as she shook Andrea's hand.

"Really well. I am getting accustomed to having James in college."

"Can you believe they are now both college freshmen?"

"Where is your daughter going to college?" Andrea asked.

"She is attending Davidson College. She is studying music."

As they continued the exchange about their children, Andrea experienced the out-of-body sensation of both participating in the conversation and watching herself doing so. Her son was a precious part of her personal life, and it felt unsafe to be playing around there with someone whom she was beginning to mistrust in her new role. However, it seemed natural to do with Rebecca, but did she really know Rebecca that well? While she was committed to a level of openness that their present relationship did not warrant, force of habit compelled her to participate in seemingly mutual disclosures.

Rebecca asked, "So what kind of architecture is James studying?"

"He is doing architecture proper."

"Not urban planning?"

"Not as far as I know, Rebecca."

Andrea hated this clarification that followed disclosures about her son's major. It typically indicated that the listener was having trouble coming to terms with a young Black man pursuing this field. It was surprising how predictable this response was.

Rebecca began again, "So the purpose of this meeting is to get a sense of what your interests are in teaching and to have you share any ideas that you have about how to make this department better. What course do you typically teach, Andrea?" Rebecca had her pen and paper poised, it seemed.

"I teach courses in cultural policy studies and social foundations. These are typically the undergraduate licensure courses in the department."

Rebecca wrote carefully but quickly on her notepad, seemingly eager to capture the details.

"I have been told that faculty get stuck teaching the same thing multiple times. Does this repetition of the same course each semester get boring?"

Andrea offered some response to argue that she pursued much variability in her courses, even for those classes that she taught multiple times. But she was beginning to wonder whether their prior relationship would translate into a professional setting that offered her equal hearing. Andrea decided to take a risk and broach the subject of the racially charged climate of the department.

Andrea began, "Your coming to our department is a hopeful development. I am so optimistic that we can get back to doing the important work of promoting socially just education."

Rebecca ceased her notetaking and made eye contact with Andrea, who forged on.

"Given the conflicts and divide that exists in the department, it occurred to me that perhaps we could engage in a book study." If the notetaking was meant to signal that the comment was significant, Andrea was making no progress.

"The book I have in mind is an interdisciplinary work about philosophical frameworks for social science research." There was still no movement of the pen on the paper.

"The premise of the book is that Aristotle's idea of judgment as *phronesis* holds great prospect for a theory-to-practice pathway between social science and educational practice." The pen remained still.

"This kind of book study would go a long way toward engendering a different department culture that does not generate such tensions."

Rebecca looked down at her paper. "Yes. I have been told about the reactions that you have. We have to do something about diminishing these kinds of intense and reactionary behaviors from you," Rebecca said.

Andrea was unable to muster a response in the moment. What did Rebecca mean? What did she know about Andrea's reactions to the departmental conflict, and who had told her? Clearly, she seemed to be placing some blame squarely at Andrea's feet for being "intense" and "reactionary."

Rebecca was still looking down at her paper and the lack of eye contact spoke volumes. Andrea did not know how to tread in this space. What could she say? Feeling disempowered by the simple weight of perception, she hurried to close the conversation and leave this unwelcoming space that had become the office of her former family friend.

"Yes. Well," Andrea said, "it has been a difficult few years. Thanks for your time."

Two weeks later, she and Rebecca stood in the early-morning chill for the annual homecoming parade and the participation of the education student group in the two-mile walk/run. It could be a heady time of good, old-fashioned fun as students, faculty, and community members engaged in all-around silliness to celebrate the university.

Tired from the long morning activity, the group gathered at the top of the hill, having completed the parade. Andrea stood with a group of students and faculty.

Before she was aware of what instigated it, Andrea was confronted by Rebecca, who looked at her, a look of grim determination on her face, and said, "I don't think that Black women experience more hardships than any other racial groups!" Andrea simply stared back at Rebecca with incredulity. The statement made no sense to her, and this setting was not the place to engage the conversation. Andrea smiled and walked away. Later, as they gathered for lunch, Rebecca sauntered over to Andrea with another White female colleague to reiterate her point. "White women in general suffer more oppression than Black women!" Rebecca said and Ann nodded in agreement. Next to Andrea, her old friend protectively interrupted them to assert that the time and place were not right for this kind of conversation.

The following week, the diversity committee convened for its first meeting, and Andrea had determined that she would not nominate herself for the position of chairperson. Everything that she had seen about Rebecca had caused Andrea to seriously doubt that Rebecca was an ally. If she was right, then the diversity committee would merely be a front to suggest that things in the department had changed but there would not be serious reform.

As everyone waited for the meeting to convene, Andrea, feeling annoyed at the stunt that Rebecca had pulled over the weekend, decided to engage in a simple experiment. It was already clear that their former relationship had little bearing on their current professional one. More important, it seemed that Andrea had attributed more broad-mindedness to Rebecca than she possessed. As they chitchatted, Andrea injected,

"As long as I have known Rebecca, she has always been skilled at bringing various constituencies together. We go way back! In fact, her daughter had a serious crush on my son in middle school!"

Rebecca visibly shook her shoulders and Andrea had the satisfaction of confirming what she had suspected. The stakes were different now from when they were parents of children in middle school watching them grow up and find their way in the world. Now Rebecca's daughter was a beautiful White woman and Andrea's son was a handsome but tall, dark man.

Rebecca then convened the meeting and opened by highlighting the fact that the department had had no such committee previously. She then asked the faculty gathered to self-nominate for chairperson. Andrea remained silent and a contract faculty member volunteered. Rebecca, again not making eye contact, commented that contract faculty members were not obliged to take on committee memberships. Doing so was the responsibility of tenured or tenure-track faculty. Andrea made no response. Of course, it was expected that she lead the diversity committee; but such a position was not her idea of concrete steps toward promoting a more racially tolerant climate.

The new chairperson was given the chance to begin facilitating the meeting. Andrea immediately suggested that the name of the committee be changed to "Diversity and Inclusion." The new committee decided on the date for the next meeting and then disbanded.

Act III: The Meeting

The email seemed to come out of nowhere just one-third of the way into the semester. Rebecca wanted to meet with Andrea, and the meeting was to take place not in her office but at the library café. Andrea wondered what the nature of such a meeting could possibly be. One week later, she sat in the café as the clock showed that it was 10:20, twenty minutes past the time that Rebecca said she wanted to meet.

However, seconds later she saw her come through the door. And although Andrea looked her way, Rebecca made no eye contact. Beginning to understand these signals, Andrea's heart skipped a beat, and she took a deep breath.

"How is James?" Dear Lord, Andrea thought, I cannot muster any kind of protection against this woman if she insists on bringing my son into the conversation.

"He is doing well . . . ," Andrea started, and once again she had the sensation that her mind had detached from her body and was observing the movements of her lips as they made statements that, though they strung together in sentences, required no thought.

Once Andrea had finished speaking about her son, Rebecca said, "I wanted to meet you here to let you know that Jezzie is feeling threatened by your presence. Confidentially, she shared with me that she is fearing for her life because of you."

Rebecca paused, but Andrea did not speak. She could not speak. A world of hurt descended on her like a landslide. It crushed her and terrorized her dignity. In that moment she felt that she was the uncouth being that would have been capable of generating such a demeaning characterization from a colleague. And she was ashamed because it was delivered by her department chairperson as if there were a modicum of truth to it. The world outside the library café seemed covered in dusk. Andrea realized that the faint murmuring sound she heard was Rebecca still talking, eyes looking somewhere just beyond her shoulder. Andrea mustered her attention and focused on Rebecca's curled lips so that she could hear.

"You should not talk to Jezzie under any circumstances. When you see her coming down the hallway, look down and button your lips. Do not walk by her office unless it is necessary." Rebecca moved her hands to her mouth to simulate a locking motion. "I had to do something similar in my department when a colleague hated me. I could not even walk past his door, which was near the bathroom. To pee I had to go to floor above or below."

"Why don't you ask her to do the same? Her office is adjacent to the copy room and the mailboxes; there is no way to avoid it," Andrea managed to get out, afraid of herself and how angry she was.

"I know, and she did have the option to place her office in a better location, and I have told her to avoid you as well."

Rebecca then moved on to offer Andrea the opportunity to work on a grant to develop the diversity component of a university initiative. It would involve a course buyout. Andrea listened in a noncommittal way and was skeptical that any such opportunity would be realized. They parted company, and as Andrea walked back to the college, she wondered how no one could see that the world had just be shaken.

Three weeks later, as Andrea was on her way to her office on the department floor of the college, the department secretary, who was an African American woman, waved Rebecca into the stairway to tell her that Jezzie's request for a panic button had been submitted to Rebecca but that she had not approved it.

As the fall semester moved in pre-Thanksgiving mode, Andrea came from the elevator after her morning class to find a technician standing on a ladder with wires going from the ceiling into Jezzie's office. Bolder than usual, Andrea exchanged pleasantries with the technician. Then she asked, "So, what are you up to?"

"Oh, I am just fulfilling the request for a panic button to be placed in that office." He gestured to Jezzie's office.

"I see. Have a good day."

Andrea calmly checked university policy about panic buttons and happened upon the police department statement that a single panic button is allowed on each floor of the college and for some buildings, one is required in total. Under no circumstances ar individuals permitted to have them in their office.

She pulled herself together. In a single flash, she imagined a scenario where she was alone on the department floor in the building, as is sometimes the case. Because Jezzie's office was at a L-shape, ninety-degree angle to the door to the copy room, it was not inconceivable that Andrea's walking to the mailroom could contribute to a situation where Jezzie felt threatened as Andrea advanced up the hallway towards the copy room. If Jezzie pressed the panic button, what defense would Andrea have?

She emailed the dean and assistant provost to express her objections and copied Rebecca.

Act IV: Trial by Fire

The remainder of the academic year did not decrease the micro- and macroaggressions that Andrea confronted. The installation of the panic button was eventually prevented, but Rebecca's covert attacks continued. Where possible, she intercepted university opportunities that were rightfully Andrea's and redirected them to the people whom she believed deserved them. She contributed to a narrative that depicted Andrea as unprofessional and taciturn. All of this Andrea would discover not through subterfuge but through the serendipity of conversations with third parties. Gradually she would piece together a picture of Rebecca as anything but an ally.

Act V: The Book Club

On the first day of the book group, Rebecca did not attend. Indeed, it was not until one year into the meetings that she would appear in the small party of about eight people. That day, Andrea could hardly speak. The room was filled with White women who had gathered to talk about the lives of Black young women. They had no business being here, she thought, except to give a nod to each other that they were the right kind of academic. However, Andrea knew that they were occupying space that should have been filled by those who understood the hate that can be directed at the Black female body. Then again, they did understand, because they were the very ones doing so. I did not return after Rebecca's visit. The club carried on its performance and its director received the university's diversity award in the following fall convocation.

Conclusion: Potentiated Critique and Hope

In keeping with the womanist worldview, the foregoing narrative details long-standing sources of oppression directed at demeaning Black women's lives. The narrator confronts racial microaggressions that invade important areas of her professional life, and she is challenged to categorize her colleague's treatment as acts of racism, given their prior relationship as friends. She draws on multiple epistemological and interpretive resources as buffers against the onslaught of subjugation. For example, the narrator tests her intuitions, follows up with requests for clarification, and plans her course of action based on the facts before her.

There is a long and rich historical precedent that points to multiple exemplars of the womanist subject as ontologically whole, and the narrator clings to this understanding; therefore, she maintains a cognizance of that which she can dictate and control, which is the enactment of her professional identity. Scholars have performed ongoing and recursive excavation of the meaning of embodiment as a critical and analytic tool that uses the prevailing culture (e.g., media, readings, artifacts) as its text. Several have also acknowledged the structural impediments to full and equal personhood that are posed by the objectification of Black bodies and the bodies of other minoritized identity groups.

In *Black Looks*, hooks (1992, p. 129) is concerned with "the White supremacist capitalist imperialist dominating 'gaze'" inflicted on Black people, especially Black women. Afro-pessimism proposes that the extent of escape available is through the imaginary, where one can conceptualize refusal. Lewis Gordon (Soka University of America, 2021) argues that theorists should draw on Afro-pessimism not as a regulative ideal but as potentiated critique. In this vein, womanists draw on a psyche of transcendental freedom emanating from a divine awareness that transcends history, time, and space to question the intractability of anti-Blackness. Womanist thinking offers this alternative view because, as Maparyan (2012) describes, it offers a spirituality that presupposes extra human sources for healing and moral fortitude and provides a pathway to act in hope. The term *luxocracy* encapsulates this notion of acknowledgment of the relationship to the divine that views all people as being its unique manifestations. Similar to theocracy, it is spiritualized and spiritually centered; but it rests on the noncorporal, internal, and personal notions of spirituality rather than on the external rituals of organized religion.

Womanist theological ethics presented a heterodox theology to locate Black women's experiences as a necessary site for biblical interpretation and revelation. In doing so, there is the possibility of countering this ontological crisis in an ethic of freedom that discursively emanates from deep within the Black female experience in light of her positionality. While the White normative gaze has the motive of a "dehumanization that has accrued historically and symbolically to Black women's bodies" to disrupt the formation and exercise of agency that arises in the Black consciousness (Fraser-Burgess, et al., p. 506), the recognition of a transcendent divine gaze invokes a higher moral law. Therefore, engaging in subject formation and the cultivation of agency is an antidote to its dehumanization.

Through repositioning herself beyond the social strictures of her White colleagues, Andrea continued to both maintain her teaching obligations under the duress of Rebecca's leadership and to act opportunistically in hope. Not always sure of the outcome, she sought professional pathways to academic promotion, always means testing the capacity of academic systems to sustain Black faculty member participation. For instance, she proposed a research project with a subset of faculty members from the book club and co-created an association for the Black faculty and staff. Also, she seized the opportunity to submit the first fully electronic portfolio for promotion to full professor in her college. While there was a dearth of mentoring and support, she submitted her name for consideration for program director and other positions of leadership. For all these accomplishments, by the end of Rebecca's three-year tenure, the toll of the experience was unmistakable in Andrea's deteriorating mental and physical well-being. After being promoted to full professor, Andrea did take a medical leave of reduced professional responsibilities; but even this act was a testament of faith in the capacity of her mind, body, and soul to be healed and restored. They were. She carries on.

REFERENCES

Cannon, K. G. (2006). *Black womanist ethics*. Wipf and Stock. Original work published 1988.

Collins, P. H. (1996). WHAT'S IN A NAME? Womanism, Black Feminism, and Beyond. *The Black Scholar*, 26(1), 9–17. http://www.jstor.org/stable/41068619.

Constantine, M. G., Smith, L., Redington, R. M., & Owens, D. (2008). Racial microaggressions against black counseling and counseling psychology faculty: A central challenge in the multicultural counseling movement. *Journal of Counseling and Development*, 86(3), 348–355. https://doi.org/10.1002/j.1556-6678 .2008.tb00519.x.

Cooper, A.J. (2022). *Voice from the south*. General Press. Original work published 1896.

Dancy, T. E., Edwards, K., & Davis, J. E. (2018). Historically White universities and plantation politics: Anti-Blackness and higher education in the Black Lives Matter era. *Urban Education*, 53(2), 176–195.

Dumas, M. J. (2016). Against the dark: Antiblackness in education policy and discourse. *Theory into Practice*, 55(1), 11–19. https://doi.org/10.1080/00405841 .2016.1116852.

Fraser-Burgess, S. A., Warren-Gordon, K., Humphrey Jr, D. L., & Lowery, K. (2021). Scholars of color turn to womanism: Countering dehumanization in the academy. *Educational Philosophy and Theory*, 53(5), 505–522. https://doi.org/10 .1080/00131857.2020.1750364

Goodall, H. L., Jr. (2009). *Writing qualitative inquiry: Self, stories, and academic life*. Left Coast.

Grant, C. A., Woodson, A., & Dumas, M. (Eds.). (2020). *The future is black: Afropessimism, fugitivity, and Radical Hope in education*. Routledge.

Harris, J. C., Snider, J. C., Anderson, J. L., & Griffin, K. A. (2021). Multiracial faculty members' experiences with multiracial microaggressions. *American Journal of Education, 127*(4), 531-561. https://doi.org/10.1086/715004.

hooks, b. (1992). *Black looks: Race and representation*. South End.

Howe, L. (2003). Ontology and refusal in subaltern ethics. *Administrative Theory & Praxis, 25*(2), 277-298.

Jones, A. (2021). Conflicted: How Black women negotiate their responses to racial microaggressions at a historically White institution. *Race Ethnicity and Education, 25*(5), 738-753. https://doi.org/10.1080/13613324.2021.1924136.

Maparyan, L. (2012). *The womanist idea*. Routledge. Kindle edition.

McCabe, J. (2009). Racial and gender microaggressions on a predominantly-White campus: Experiences of Black, Latina/O and White undergraduates. *Race, Gender & Class, 16*(1-2), 133-151. https://www.jstor.org/stable/41658864.

Midgette, A. J., & Mulvey, K. L. (2022). White American students' recognition of racial microaggressions in higher education. *Journal of Diversity in Higher Education.* Advance online publication. http://dx.doi.org/10.1037/dhe0000391.

Morris, M. (2016). *Pushout: The criminalization of Black girls in school*. New Press.

Mustaffa, J. B. (2017). Mapping violence, naming life: A history of anti-Black oppression in the higher education system. *International Journal of Qualitative Studies in Education, 30*(8), 711-727. https://doi.org/10.1080/09518398.2017 .1350299.

Peters, M. A., & Tesar, M. (2016). The critical ontology of ourselves: Lessons from the philosophy of the subject. In M. A. Peters & M. Tesar (Eds.), *Beyond the philosophy of the subject: An EPAT post-structuralist reader* (pp. vii-xvii). Routledge. https://www.academia.edu/35495503/The_Critical_Ontology_of _Ourselves_Lessons_from_the_Philosophy_of_the_Subject.

Pittman, C. T. (2012). Racial microaggressions: The narratives of African American faculty at a predominantly White university. *Journal of Negro Education, 81*(1), 82-92. https://doi.org/10.7709/jnegroeducation.81.1.0082.

ross, k. m. (2020). On Black education: Anti-Blackness, refusal, and resistance. In C. A. Grant, A. Woodson, & M. Dumas (Eds.), *The future is Black: Afropessi- mism, fugitivity, and radical hope in education* (pp. 7-15). Routledge.

Rossini, G. (2021). *Self and wisdom in arts-based contemplative inquiry in education: Narrative, aesthetic and the dialogical presence of Thomas Merton*. Routledge.

Sanders, C. J., Gilkes, C. T., Cannon, K. G., Townes, E. M., Copeland, M. S., & Hooks, B. (1989). Roundtable discussion: Christian ethics and theology in womanist perspective. *Journal of Feminist Studies in Religion, 5*(2), 83-112. http://www.jstor .org/stable/25002114.

Smith, W., Mustaffa, J. B., Jones, C., Curry, T., & Allen, W. (2016). "You make me wanna holler and throw up both my hands!": Campus culture, Black misandric microaggressions, and racial battle fatigue, *International Journal of Qualitative Studies in Education, 29*(9), 1189-1209. https://doi.org/10.1080/09518398.2016 .1214296.

Soka University of America. (2021). Afropessimism and its others: A discussion between Hortense J. Spillers and Lewis R. Gordon. YouTube, May 4, 2021. https://youtu.be/Z-s-Ltuo6NI.

Sue, D. W., Capodilupo, C. M., Torino, G. C., Bucceri, J. M., Holder, A. M., Nadal, K. L., Esquilin, M. (2007). Racial microaggressions in everyday life: Implications for clinical practice. *American Psychology*, 62(4), 271–286. https://doi.org/10.1037/0003-066X.62.4.271.

Walker, A. (1983). *In search of our mothers' gardens*. Harcourt Brace Jovanovich.

Wilderson, F. (2020). *Afropessimism*. Liveright.

8

Let Me Tell You How to Teach

Students as Purveyors of Racial Violence against
Black Faculty in Canadian Institutions of Higher Learning

BEVERLY-JEAN M. DANIEL

The videos and images of the murder of George Floyd on May 25, 2020, crossed the borders into Canadian society and spaces within the academy, where many people expressed shock and disbelief. To most Black people, the responses appeared to be feigned and disingenuous given that the actuality of anti-Black racism has been identified and studied for decades. The confluence of events—the killing of Floyd and the early months of the COVID-19 pandemic, which forced people to remain in their homes transfixed by their televisions—exposed the continued brutalization of Black bodies. Black pain was becoming increasingly palpable with each passing day, as evidenced by the marches and protests. White academics and leaders prided themselves on the false assumption that the academy bore no similarity to the larger society that ravaged Black bodies on the streets. The brutal murder of Floyd unmasked the abject brutality of White violence, and the professions of care and facile acts of contrition remained superficial in most settings. The familiar tactics of feigned superiority, intelligence, and exceptionalism were unleashed in an attempt to uncouple the ivory tower from the unfolding social epidemic of racial violence being levied against Black bodies. However, the sentiments of those predominantly White leaders contradict the truth of the everyday experiences of Black faculty, particularly at the hands of students.

This chapter will examine the ways in which academic institutions and their leaders reinforce, condone, and legitimize racialized violence against Black faculty, through the failure to attend to issues of incivility (Cortina et al., 2001; Lim et al., 2008) among students that are based on race, which I will term *racial incivility*. Drawing primarily from critical race and anti-Black racism theories, the work will provide a discussion of the experiences of Black Canadian faculty members and a brief examination of racism in Canadian societies. Although I remain cognizant of the differences in experiences of Black faculty members that are mediated by gender—as I have discussed elsewhere (Daniel, 2018; 2019)—and sexuality (Bracho & Hayes, 2020), this chapter highlights the role of racial markers. Based on a content analysis, I will critically analyze the discrimination, harassment, and student code of conduct policies to determine whether they specifically address issues of racism and whether there are any direct references to addressing racism by students toward faculty or the attendant responses to student misconduct.

The chapter will explore the racialized dynamics of the interactions that students have with Black faculty, and argue that the institutional failure to address the racial incivility of students who target Black faculty is indicative of the continuation of anti-Black racism within Canadian institutions. Workplace incivility has been defined as "low-intensity deviant behavior with ambiguous intent to harm the target, in violation of workplace norms of mutual respect [that is] . . . characteristically rude and discourteous" (Andersson & Pearson, 1999, p. 457). Turnipseed and Landay (2018) use the term *academic incivility* to describe behaviors that disrupt and distract from classroom routines and can be aimed at students and the professor, including impolite language or interruptions, annoyances, and complaints. I would like to propose the concept of racial incivility to factor in varying forms of uncivil and negative behaviors that draw on racist stereotypes and attitudes, that are directed at Black people and other people of color, that negatively affect the targets, and that have the potential to disrupt the classroom environment. The final section will expand the theory of anti-Black racism and develop a model aimed at eliminating it that moves beyond its identification. The section will also discuss strategies and interventions to address racism aimed at Black faculty members.

Containing and Erasing the Black Body in Canada

Canada has a history of anti-Blackness that needs to be acknowledged and reckoned with. Canadian history is littered with stories of oppression against First Nations peoples, Jewish people, and Chinese and South Asian migrants, however much of that history remains liminal fragments, of an almost ephemeral nature, rather than central to the Canadian story. Similarly, Black people have been enslaved on Canadian soil for over two hundred years, but their histories continue to be erased along with the ongoing manifestations of anti-Blackness that have pervaded Black communities for generations since slavery officially ended (Austin, 2010; Cooper, 2007). Canadians also centralize the history of the Underground Railroad, a series of routes that Black Americans traveled toward freedom, under the stewardship of abolitionists such as Harriet Tubman (Reese, 2011). In 1793, as part of the Act to Limit Slavery, it was legislated that Black people who entered Canada would be considered free people in Canada, and this became a path to freedom for enslaved American Black people (N. Henry, 2023). However, the extreme levels of racism that Black people experienced in Canada, which "evolved mostly by practice, not law" (Reese, 2011, p. 215), were quite untenable, and many Black people returned to America, particularly after slavery was abolished (Canadian Museum of Immigration at Pier 21, n.d.; June, 2003). In 1971, the late prime minister Pierre Elliot Trudeau implemented the policy on multiculturalism, which became an official legal act in 1988. The legal document, the first of its kind in the world, was designed to "recognize and promote the understanding that multiculturalism is a fundamental characteristic of the Canadian heritage and identity" and "promote the full and equitable participation of individuals and communities of all origins in the continuing evolution and shaping of all aspects of Canadian society and assist them in the elimination of any barrier to that participation" (Berry, 2020).

The official credo that is embedded in narratives of multiculturalism has been central to the contemporary Canadian ethos. Armed with this ideology that was enshrined in law, the general Canadian populace employs the ethic of multiculturalism as both a basis for justifying social inclusion and the prima facie foundation for the denial of exclusionary practices—particularly race-based exclusion. Americans have a longer history of conducting research and discussions on race, but Canadians often adopt the ideology of displacement—"not here in Canada" (Solomon & Daniel, 2007; Solomon et al., 2005)—or color blindness (Berman et al., 2017; Swindler Boutte, 2008) while remaining abjectly aware of the fallacy of these propositions. Thus, the collection and disaggregation of race-based research remains limited, and although the power based remains unchanged, the visual landscape of bodies of color provides the illusion of equitable options for all Canadians irrespective of their various identity markers. As humans we tend to believe what we see, often at the expense of a critical analysis of conditions below the surface, which limits real dialogue regarding racism and its attendant outcomes.

Sighted human beings rely significantly on visual cues to makes sense of and frame their communication. What we see helps us to construct and conceptualize information and influences the language that informs what we communicate. The unfortunate reality is that most of the information that we receive about Blackness is framed through highly negative, problematic, and stereotypical perceptions (Evans, 2021; Fries-Britt & Griffin, 2007; Rogers & Way, 2016). Blackness is seldom paired with notions of intellectual capacity (Dei, 2018; Donnor, 2016; McGee & Martin, 2011; Wright, 2007); rather, that pairing is more often conceptualized as a rarity, and those who possess it are described as a credit to their race. Therefore, students enter classrooms armed with decades of misinformation that encloses Black bodies in limited roles, which, in Canada, are typically those of caregivers, sports figures, immigrants, and criminals. When students see Black bodies, their conceptions are informed by these pervasive ideologies of Blackness. These ideas are also underscored by the rejection of a holistic conception of Blackness and a regurgitation of the myth of color blindness, which is deployed as a pretext to minimize the impact of anti-Black racism.

The over two-hundred-year history of enslavement of Black people in Canada (1600s–1834) has essentially been erased from our history books. This strategic erasure has had several primary functions. First, it positions Black people as permanent outsiders within the Canadian context, thereby limiting any potential claims to historicity and citizenship (Austin, 2010). Second, this erasure permits a production and invention of Blackness within a uniquely Canadian vortex, structured as devoid of the historical stains associated with enslavement. The invention of the partial Underground Railroad narrative has pervaded the attitude of Canadian citizens, positioning them as being absolved of any responsibility for the experiences of Black people today. Third, Blackness emerges in a Canadian space as a contemporary invention that is linked to the licensed migration of Black bodies, which is positioned as a pathway to access economic stability and integration through immigration policies such as the domestic worker program (Calliste, 1993). However, the exclusion of Black males within this program, and the more contemporary seasonal agriculture program (Government of Canada, 2022), which allows Black males temporary work permits, produced a situation that led to the economic destabilization of Black communities and the construction of Black people as permanent outsiders (Calliste, 1993; England & Stiell, 1997).

Under the domestic worker program, Black women who were deemed to be single could apply to enter Canada as domestic workers or nannies. It is interesting to note that while on the one hand Canada professes its innocence in relation to the containment of Black bodies, the only avenue for Black people to migrate to Canada replicated the stereotypical image of Black women as the caretakers and wet nurses for White children and families, a replication of the "mammy" narrative (Sewell, 2013) produced during slavery. The domestic worker program resulted in the separation of Caribbean families—the removal of Black males and fathers as the bread earners in the family, the separation of children from their mothers, and the severing of intergenerational connections, all of which are carbon copies of the intentionally destructive patterns developed during enslavement that aimed at destabilizing and destroying Black families and communities. This immigration policy was built on a history of anti-Black racism already firmly entrenched in Canadian society.

Anti-Black Racism in Canada

The discourse of anti-Black racism has been central to highlighting the specificities of anti-Blackness in multiple contexts. The emergence of the terminology, which was first introduced by Akua Benjamin (2011), has allowed for a critically nuanced interrogation of the term *racism* by highlighting the fact that the historical tragedies of different racialized groups result in unique outcomes. Further, the term *racism*, in its generic usage, is applied in an essentialist manner that fails to extricate the forms of oppression that affect Black people versus other racialized groups.

Anti-Black racism has been defined as "policies and practices embedded in Canadian institutions that reflect and reinforce beliefs, attitudes, prejudice, stereotyping and/or discrimination that is directed at people of African descent and is rooted in their unique history and experience of enslavement and colonization here in Canada" (City of Toronto, 2017, p. 1). Benjamin's (2011) work underscores the importance of pinpointing interventions that are context specific and informed by the racial realities of the groups in question. The term *anti-Black* challenges the approach to the term *racism*, which is deemed to encompass and explain the multiple racisms experienced by varied groups in society. Benjamin argues, however, that the term *racism* is typically analyzed along a Black-White binary but fails to capture the multilayered complexities of anti-Blackness, which flourishes within other racialized communities.

There is a tendency on the part of marginalized communities to deploy Blackness as a way of highlighting the challenges that they experience with the all too familiar phrase, "It's just like being a Black person." Whether this statement is used as a referential marker of oppression or as an outcry that one could be treated with the level of contempt that has been specifically reserved for Black bodies, the statement foregrounds the notion that these communities are aware of the pervasiveness and perverseness of anti-Black racism. These racialized groups, including South Asian, Chinese (Atkin & Ahn, 2022; Yellow Horse et al., 2021), Hispanic, and Indigenous communities, deploy very clear forms of anti-Black racism, although there is a resistance to examining its manifestations among their group members. Benjamin (2011) argues, therefore, that an anti-Black racism framework allows for an examination of these issues within differing contexts, with a referential pattern that replicates dominant-subordinate narratives, which position Black bodies at the bottom of the social hierarchy. These non-Black racialized groups often seek to position themselves in proximity to Whiteness and its attendant benefits, but there is limited research or dialogues on intergroup oppressive dynamics and the ways in which they are linked to racial capitalism.

A panel titled "Brown Complicity in Anti-Blackness" was convened in 2020 by a group of South Asian academics in Toronto, Canada, after the murder of George Floyd. The discussants explored the ways in which anti-Black racism is evidenced within South Asian communities, with one of the panelists stating, "We shift towards Blackness when it's cool, when it demonstrates some sort of street cred or street smarts and then we shift right back to whiteness when we need to maintain access or mobility within the system. . . . We're chameleons" (York University, 2020). Bhutani & Tenneti (2020) further argue that as South Asians increase their economic and political influence, one must consider the ways in which they are and will be positioned in relation to a capitalist agenda that is inherently racist. These authors and academics also question the silence of these communities in the face of anti-Black racism, recognizing that appropriating Black culture as a site of resistance is not equivalent to directly addressing anti-Black racism (Patel, 2016).

The reality is that the caste system within continental South Asian communities intersects with colorism, and that practice is replicated in Canada as they migrate to the country (Patel, 2016). Thus, Black people are positioned in the Brown imagination as the Canadian equivalent of the Dalits (Modood & Sealy, 2022), the lowest social class in the community. The failure of Canadian society more generally to conduct a comprehensive examination of the manner in which the caste system intersects with skin color, career, social position, and economic options leaves a significant blind spot in addressing anti-Blackness more broadly and continues to place Black bodies squarely in the cross hairs of these different immigrant groups that simultaneously replicate their cultural traditions while also aligning with and maintaining the borders of White supremacy.

These groups are positioning themselves as the new power brokers in the nation (Patel, 2016), and the failure of Canadian society to examine the implications of anti-Black racism among racialized groups runs the risk of simply replacing one aggressor with another. Modood and Sealy (2022) argue that there needs to be a more nuanced approach to these conversations on racialization that recognizes the role of biological and cultural markers of racial oppression. Further, they speak to the need to center the context of the racialization while exploring mechanisms beyond the Black-White binary, to interrogate these practices when the racialization is not solely about the presence of White bodies (Modood & Sealy, 2022). Within the Canadian context, these patterns of anti-Blackness have also been evidenced among Chinese Canadian communities, even with the rise and recognition of anti-Asian racism (Zhou, 2020). The positioning of South Asians and Chinese as the model minorities (Dutt-Ballerstadt, 2020; Patel, 2016) reifies existing racial hierarchies that are framed by racial, cultural, economic, and broader power bases. These shifting racial and power dynamics highlight the need for more nuanced analyses of anti-

Blackness, particularly when these racialized groups also directly contribute to or remain silent in the targeting of Black faculty members.

Experiences of Black Faculty in the Canadian Ivory Tower

Anti-Black racism is evidenced in many ways in the academy—in the simultaneous absence of Black bodies, the stereotypical and problematic representations of Blackness, institutional policies that fail to protect Black bodies, and processes that fail to acknowledge the unique nature of the experiences of Black people and other racialized faculty (Dua & Bhanji, 2017). According to a 2018 Canadian Association of University Teachers report, although Black people make up 3.6% of the overall population, they only make up 2.1% of university instructors, while they have a higher unemployment rate (10.7%) than White faculty (4.4%). In addition, Black faculty earn approximately 11% less than their White counterparts, a gap that continues to increase. The statistical absence of Black faculty renders real change impossible, thus limiting the possibility of improving the treatment and experiences of Black faculty members.

Black faculty in predominantly White institutions, a category that encompasses all Canadian institutions of higher learning, teach in departments where their representation is limited. This is evident among the leadership, among faculty members, and even among the students who populate their classrooms. Unlike in the American context, there are no historically Black colleges and universities in Canada, so Black academics who choose to remain in Canada are all in White institutions, departments, and schools. In most departments and schools, there are seldom more than two or three Black pretenure-track faculty, and even fewer who are tenured or full professors. Therefore, it is quite common for Black faculty members to find themselves being the only one, often deemed to be an equity hire, and with limited options for exploring the ways in which their experiences in the classrooms, in the hallways, and among their peers are heavily racialized. Typically, their systems of support emerge from the hushed conversations they have with other faculty members who are spread across the country, in which they exchange stories about their experiences, often in search of some strategy to address, minimize, or avoid the negative interactions that infiltrate their everyday lives. I have often made the argument that having a PhD has never been a source of protection for me as a Black woman in the ivory tower, neither from my coworkers nor from my students. In addition, we have to navigate problematic conversations with senior faculty who make comments that are obviously racist. We must also set boundaries without being deemed hypersensitive, while trying to maintain some degree of balance between the demands of our academic and personal lives. In addition to trying to manage the violence that populates the academic landscape, Black faculty are tasked with supporting Black students in navigating the ever-present minefield of racial injustice. Black women are returned to the role of caretaker destined to serve, but with few spaces of escape and care.

Black faculty in Canadian academies of higher learning have lamented the ways in which they experience anti-Blackness on campus in interactions with their peers, the leaders in their institutions, and the students (Daniel, 2018; Hampton, 2020; Henry, A., 2015). In a previous work (Daniel, 2018), I spoke of the ongoing challenges of dealing specifically with White female colleagues, who have become the contemporary gatekeepers in the academy. For some of our White female colleagues who have migrated from the United States, the advancements they have gained because of the US civil rights movement, affirmative action, and, in Canada, the more recent diversity initiatives (Wrenn and Lutz, 2016) have not led to the emergence of the mythical sisterhood that they trumpeted to gain our partnership and labor within the various stages of the feminist movements. Many White feminists have learned to parrot the phrases of Black academics, place gifts at the altar of intersectionality, and speak with fervor about the ways in which they incorporate equity, diversity, and inclusion narratives in their classrooms. However, the flaccid claims of allyship are strategically aimed at using Black bodies on the front lines as the foot soldiers who will once again absorb brutality while other groups, including non-Black racialized groups, reap the benefits. An interesting example of this is the speed with which the Canadian government recognized and adopted the usage of the term *anti-Asian racism* in response to the targeting of Asian communities during the COVID-19 pandemic, when decades-long protests by Black groups have only led to some tacit acknowledgment of anti-Black racism in some sectors. In addition, the designation of Asian Heritage Month has occurred with similar ease and with limited claims of segregation, though the process of designating Black History Month has taken over a century and its observance is not mandated in Canadian schools. These differences are highlighted to underscore the specificity of anti-Blackness and the ways in which White power continues to rupture and limit Black lives.

I have worked with many White women who have provided unquestionable support to advance possibilities for racialized faculty. Sadly, I have encountered fewer committed supporters than I have colleagues who make claims to investing in addressing anti-Black racism while simultaneously engaging in practices that epitomize the roots, branches, and fruits of anti-Blackness. I have seen "leaders" implement staff initiatives supposedly aimed at addressing anti-Black racism, staffing the programs with virulent and toxic activists who were definitely not "kin" folk and who were more likely to lead Black bodies to a lynch mob than spirit them safely through the ravaging woods of racism. These scenarios have resulted in varying levels of chaos in the schools, often moving the change agenda further from the goal post. The damage done by these activists and their presumptive allies inevitably cements the glass ceiling (Reynolds-Dobbs et al., 2008) for Black female faculty.

Beyond the role that White women have played, White males have also continued to wield power in the academy, typically occupying the most high-ranking positions and authorizing university policies, hiring practices, and the overall direction of institutions (Dua & Bhanji, 2017), many of which also align with business interests (Hampton, 2020). Those in power are the gatekeepers in the academy and buttress oppressive and exclusionary institutional practices. Partially in response to the murder of Floyd, there has been a recent movement within several Canadian institutions to conduct cluster hires of Black faculty and to include a commitment to hiring visible minorities (James, 2017) as a strategy to redress their historical exclusions. However, Black faculty members on the hiring committees have been dismissed, minimized, silenced (F. Henry & Kobayashi, 2017; James, 2017), and expected to justify the need for intentional processes aimed at redressing the exclusion of Black people. Inevitably, the competency of the candidates is challenged and devalued (Settles et al., 2022), although Statistics Canada (2019; 2020) reports have indicated that Black females are some of the most educated members of society. According to Settles et al. (2022, p. 45), "Even when women and faculty of color work within disciplinary norms, gender and racial biases will still cause them to be seen as illegitimate scholars and their scholarship to be viewed as outside of the mainstream."

If, therefore, White males and females are simultaneously positioned as the ones who sanction access to the academy, tasked with protecting White supremacy, and also expected to be less oppressive and more inclusive, they are ultimately caught in a significant psychic conflict. How can they be charged with dismantling the system they are trying to preserve? And for Black faculty who are caught in the cross hairs of this conflict, what protections could they realistically expect, particularly when the attackers are predominantly the offspring of said White males and females, who police, maintain, and defend the boundaries of power? Further, is it realistic to expect that Whites would design, implement, and uphold policies that will improve the experiences of Black faculty and reframe the thinking of White students?

Classroom-level engagements between Black faculty and White students have the potential to expose the historical and contemporary patterns of oppression, destabilize White supremacy, and reveal the intergenerational fallacies of inherent White exceptionality. One can argue that the multiple attacks aimed at limiting conversations related to critical race theory are the most blatant examples of Whiteness reformulating itself to protect its power. We have not witnessed the same level of furor in discussions of diversity and race here in Canada, in part, one may argue, because of the presumptions of niceness and politeness among Canadians. However, the targeting of Black faculty in the classroom is a microcosm of the broader structural, institutional, and social machinations designed to protect Whiteness and its varying sites of investment. If Whites regard themselves as the presumptive owners of the land, the academy is also regarded as a White space. Therefore, White students are positioned on the front lines of the battle to preserve the self-proclaimed Canadian settler nation, and the deployment of anti-Black racist practices in the academy becomes an indispensable weapon in the maintenance of White supremacy.

Students on the Front Lines of the Attack

Postsecondary classrooms have emerged as the contemporary battleground for power, a phenomenon that is playing out in the American context, bringing to mind the various revolutions that resulted in the banning, censorship, and burning of books and the imprisonment and eventual killing of the critical thinkers of the society. The legal attacks against the teaching of critical race theory (Delgado & Stefanic, 2001, 2017) and the push to protect the emotions of Whites highlight the positioning of Whiteness as simultaneously fragile and brutal, which builds on the notion of White innocence (McClure, 2016; Ross, 1997; Solomon & Daniel, 2007). The next generation of power gatekeepers is being prepared in the classroom, and White students in particular are being trained to be oblivious to the violent history of Whiteness and how it will continue to manifest. In addition, the growing threat, or perhaps acceptance, of White nationalist groups, which are very openly populated by young White males (Jokic, 2020), is evidenced on Canadian campuses (Martis, 2020). Although the issue has not become a legal entanglement in the Canadian context, it is not uncommon for public officials, journalists, and politicians to deploy the term *woke* as a way of critiquing social activism and the demands for equitable inclusion and representation from marginalized groups (Kaufmann, 2022). The general sentiment being expressed is that such calls for inclusion essentially represent a destruction of what is truly Canadian culture (Morgan, 2022), which is understood to be a vanguard of Whiteness. Jokic (2020) argues that these calls to White nationalism are inherently tied to the belief that White men are the natural owners of the land, individually, economically, and politically, and that discussions of equitable inclusion or access are regarded as a threat to their ownership of the "settler whitespace" (p. 3), thus eliciting White rage. Consequently, within the academy, students, who are positioned within the classroom and some within right-wing movements, play a pivotal role in steering the outcomes of these dialogues (Martis, 2020). Therefore, Black faculty who include in their curriculum discussions of anti-oppression broadly are also positioned as a challenge to the status quo and can become the targets of "white rage" that is "baked into Canadian law and institutions" and has "a tendency to erupt . . . on a personal and political level" (Jokic, 2022, p. 3). And it is this rage that enters the classrooms with all too many White students.

In my work as an instructor in postsecondary institutions for over thirty years, although my experiences of blatant racism from students have been limited, I have been privy to conversations with many Black friends and colleagues who have discussed the nature of their interactions with students. It is these anecdotal incidents that connect to create a picture of the broader thematic patterns of racism that affect us in the classrooms of our nation's most elite spaces of intellectual advancement. In one incident, a student sent me an email in which she stated that she did not like the way I addressed a particular social justice issue and proceeded to provide suggestions on strategies I could adopt to improve classroom engagement, along with a list of readings that she thought were relevant to the topic. This second-year undergraduate student underscored her imposition by stating that she was *"not trying to tell [me] how to teach,"* but she believed that there were ways in which I could have engaged the class more in the discussion topic, which was relevant to her and her community. These types of interactions highlight the ideologies of Blackness with which students enter our classrooms—Black faculty are less competent and need to learn how to teach.

Colleagues have discussed incidents where students have shouted at them, wrote disparaging emails, and, as indicated in the title of this chapter, sought to undermine their capacity as teachers. In addition to the aggressions that have been encountered in the classroom, which have been documented (Gordon & Niles, 2011; Kohli, 2012; van Beinum, 2005), Black faculty have email exchanges with students that contain varying layers of violence and levels of toxicity that we are expected to respond to. Students question their grades (B.A.L., 2017; Delgado Bernal & Villalpando, 2002), ask for their papers to be regraded, and complain about the difficulty of tests, arguing that if they were practitioners, there would be limited need for them to engage in critical thinking in the field. Turnipseed and Landay (2018) frame these as varying levels of incivility and identify these challenges as a form of "terrorism in the classroom" (p. 286). Existing research and publications that speak to the experiences of Black female teachers, particularly in the United States (Moore & Toliver, 2010), describe tensions between White students and Black female faculty, but within the Canadian context there is an added layer that often emerges that demonstrates the expansive nature of anti-Blackness among non-White groups. In the previous section, I discussed the manner in which South Asian and Chinese communities reinforce and deploy anti-Blackness, and these narratives also play out in the classroom.

To assume that students across all identity groups have not been exposed to highly stereotypical manifestations of Blackness is at best delusional. Black faculty must contend with negative interactions with students from other racialized groups who adopt many of the same problematic attitudes and stereotypes evidenced through the oppressive lenses that are imposed on Black bodies. Faculty members have also had interactions with racialized students, including Black students, who challenge and devalue their competence and credentials (Settles et al., 2022) and expect them to prove their "intellectual prowess" (Thomas, 2020). Black faculty members are being targeted on multiple fronts, and this can increase the level of racial trauma they experience (Moise, 2021; Porcher, 2020), which Dotson (2012) frames as a form of epistemic violence.

Garriott et al.'s (2008) research supports the findings of Kivel (1996), which indicated that White students who express anti-Black racist sentiments have lowered self-esteem and socio-emotional regulation and difficulty adjusting to the college environment. In essence, the racial narratives that they perpetuate may in fact be an attempt to enhance their own sense of competence and may also be indicative of personality disruptions (Turnipseed & Landay, 2018). Although there is limited research on these issues in relation to racialized students, Garriott et al.'s and Kivel's work provides an interesting analytical frame for exploring students' engagement with Black professors.

The nature of teaching is such that the professor is expected to provide a relatively safe space in which students can explore ideas that at times conflict. Some of the ideas may challenge their foundational knowledge, which can be challenging. The classroom should be a dialectical space where students are supported in challenging long-accepted concepts, critiquing assumed truths, and developing new knowledge that can propel them into the future. However, in order to maintain the power and privilege embedded within and essential to White supremacy, White students are trained to adhere to the historicized narratives of Whiteness that have enabled their ancestors to gain power through the colonial enterprise and maintain intergenerational control through the use of laws and varying manifestations of direct and indirect violence (Jokic, 2020). The maintenance of power within institutions requires unquestioned adherence to White supremacist narratives and practices, including the minimization of Black and racialized bodies. One may argue that this diminution of Blackness is the central organizing principle of Whiteness and racialized capitalism; thus, White and non-Black racialized students who are jockeying to position themselves in relation to power regard this practice as a power play, and higher education classrooms have become the playing field.

Exploring the Efficacy of Existing Policies
in Addressing Anti-Black Racism

There are twenty-two public universities in Ontario, Canada, and each institution has a range of harassment, discrimination, and student code of conduct policies and procedures that are designed to regulate the way members of the school community engage with each other. For the purposes of this analysis, I examined the statements of the ten largest institutions, which are also typically representative of the most diverse student bodies. The content analyses of the policy documents revealed that each institution provides a generic statement that includes the multiple sites of identity as stated in the Ontario and Canadian human rights codes. However, "the policies often exist without the force of concrete action to achieve their goals" (Dua & Bhanji, 2017, p. 208), and there are few that include a specific category that clearly articulates the role of racism or refers to anti-Black racism. Although there have been concerted efforts to address the needs of Canada's Indigenous populations, which have been a result of the completion of the Truth and Reconciliation Commission of Canada (2015) report, these efforts are often disconnected and inconsistent. The report outlined specific recommendations that institutions are expected to adhere to. For example, most public institutions, including schools, have included a land acknowledgment that highlights and recognizes the presence of Indigenous populations as the original caretakers of the lands in Canada. Along with the acknowledgments, there have been attempts to develop Indigenous studies programs and centers and to articulate the actions that will be taken to address the historical and ongoing colonization of Indigenous peoples. However, many have argued that these measures are predominantly performative (Dua & Bhanji, 2017), given that there has been little change in the overall experiences of Indigenous populations in Canada.

Similarly, although there has been an increase in the acknowledgment of the existence of anti-Black racism within the broader Canadian context, and universities have attempted to pursue cluster hires of Black academics, the spaces remain unwelcoming and dangerous. Specific policies, practices, and procedures to ensure the safety of Black faculty, staff, and students have not materialized. In fact, my personal experiences have shown me that while leaders use terminology that emerges as a form of virtue signaling (Miles-Hercules & Muwwakkil, 2021), the actual investment in change is at best superficial or evidence of what Dua and Bhanji (2017) refer to as the "performativity of ineffectiveness."

The general language that is contained in university equity policy documents often aligns with the spirit of the Canadian Human Rights Code. Similarly, discrimination and harassment policies are framed as commitments rather than including action-oriented language aimed at eliminating problematic behaviors. For example, the University of Toronto (2019) policy states, "No person shall engage in a course of vexatious conduct that is directed at one or more specific individuals, and that is based on the race, ancestry, place of origin, colour, ethnic origin, citizenship, sex, sexual orientation, gender identity, gender expression, age, marital status, family status, or disability." The policy of Ryerson University (now renamed Toronto Metropolitan University) identifies the list of protected grounds and speaks specifically about discrimination, but it does not mention racism. In addition, there is a Workplace Civility and Respect Policy that addresses student nonacademic conduct, which includes the various processes and procedural outcomes that guide students' involvement in problematic activities, including discrimination. This policy was updated in the fall of 2021, but there is no mention of problematic student behavior in relation to their engagement with faculty, nor is there any specific mention of racism. In 2020, the university conducted an anti-Black racism climate review, and the report identified some of the challenges that contract and tenure-track faculty face (Ryerson University, 2020). The contract faculty members were constrained by their precarious status and believed that their attempts to foster change in the system were minimized. Tenured and tenure-seeking faculty spoke of the added responsibility of mentoring Black students, while dealing with their own experiences of racism, and being concerned about the potential backlash if they challenged the system. As a subtext to the ideas outlined in the report, one can assume that the fear of reporting racism would include reporting racist student interactions.

According to Dua and Bhanji (2017), the vast majority of racialized faculty do not report racist incidents, because of the required burden of proof, fear of reprisals, and high rates of dismissal (80%) of race-based complaints. Further, the authors argue that the procedures for addressing these claims are ineffective and do not address structural issues. Although Ryerson University established an office to address equity and inclusion, while I was writing this chapter, the head of that division, a Black woman, resigned from her post in part because of the limits to her ability to effect change and the ongoing interference and undermining of her abilities from White women in positions of authority. A vice president of equity at another university discussed, in a personal communication, the challenges this division head endured in her position and the ongoing impact on her health. These types of incidents underscore the extent of the anti-Black racism at play in the system.

Wilfrid Laurier University, in Ontario, updated its policy on the prevention of harassment and discrimination in 2021, which included statements that align with the Ontario Human Rights Code. They included specific references to race and racial discrimination, recognizing the systemic nature of these practices; however, there is no mention specifically of anti-Black racism. The student code of conduct clearly states that the person who is being accused must be afforded procedural fairness and that there must be proof of their misconduct, thereby placing the onus on the victim to prove the incident occurred. Racist acts can often occur without there being specific proof of the incidents, particularly when they involve microaggressions in students' interactions with professors. The code additionally states that the sanctions must be "developmentally and educationally based outcomes that repairs identified harm(s)" (Wilfrid Laurier University, 2021). The phraseology in the document clearly focuses on the outcomes for students, which, although important, sends a message that the students' needs and well-being will be central. The code does not address student conduct with faculty. The words *race* and *racism* are not used, nor are any derivatives of them, but the code includes reference to destruction of property, hazing, and the use of alcohol and drugs. This exclusion sends a powerful message about the limited value placed on the lives of Black faculty—the destruction of property and the use of drugs are more important than the lives, safety, and security of Black faculty members. Although the university's inclusion of race and racism as specific and distinct categories in its harassment policies constitutes a move in the right direction, there continues to be a need to highlight the specificities of anti-Black racism, particularly in relation to student codes of conduct.

In 2021, a group of Black faculty representing several Canadian institutions collectively developed a report titled *The Scarborough Charter on Anti-Black Racism and Black Inclusion in Canadian Higher Education: Principles, Actions, and Accountabilities: National Dialogues and Action for Inclusive Higher Education and Communities*. The charter is based on the need to acknowledge and respond to the ongoing manifestation of anti-Black racism in postsecondary education and to establish a set of priorities aimed at redressing the inequalities experienced by Black people in mainstream spaces. The charter focuses on the goals of Black flourishing, inclusive excellence, mutuality, and accountability. Recognizing, however, that each institution is informed by its own unique context, the charter provides a set of guiding principles that institutions can adopt. Each institution determines whether it will sign the charter, which actions it will implement, its own accountability structure, and the level of resources it will use to implement those actions. Therefore, although the intent that undergirds the charter is important and a significant step forward, there is no official body that will hold the institutions accountable. An intentional strategy must be implemented to address the needs of Black faculty members that moves beyond hollow commitments, particularly since those have been wholly ineffective.

Theoretical Model to Eliminate Anti-Black Racism

Lopez and Jean-Marie (2021) argue that addressing anti-Black racism requires an engagement with other theoretical formulations such as critical race theory and anticolonial theory. The authors further propose a model for addressing anti-Black racism in the context of education that involves four stages—*name, own, frame,* and *sustain*—arguing that it is important to name the issue of anti-Black racism and articulate one's stance in addressing it. They stress the importance of having educators intentionally engage in practices to challenge anti-Black racism and sustain them at all levels of schooling. However, based on the ongoing work to challenge anti-Black racism at all levels of society in Canada, I would like to propose an action-oriented model that focuses on incorporating behavior changes in addition to the needed analytical components.

Eliminating anti-Black racism requires an intentional approach, which can be found in the four stages of the proposed model—*history, impact, intervention,* and *maintenance.* The first stage involves providing the *history* and context of anti-Black racism while highlighting the connections between the historical and contemporary policies, laws, practices, and attitudes pertaining to it. The second stage examines the *impacts* of anti-Black racism at the individual, community, institutional, and societal levels. The third stage must include a set of specific *interventions* at various levels in the system, designed to ameliorate the negative impacts of anti-Blackness. The final stage identifies ways to *maintain* the identified interventions, which requires an investment in embedding the interventions that are identified in stage 3 within an accountability framework.

Stage 1 is built on the premise that much of the schooling that people have been exposed to in the North American context provides an antiseptic version of history that positions Whites as benevolent saviors, rather that providing a balanced and comprehensive version that also examines the impact of the colonial project on Indigenous and African populations. Within the Canadian context, as discussed earlier, the history of over two hundred years of enslavement of Africans and the ongoing dehumanization that remained after emancipation has largely been omitted. For example, Canadian history textbooks lack coverage of the various laws on immigration that were implemented to prevent Black people from migrating to Canada, the segregated schools that were legal as late as 1983, or the policies that prevented Black people from attending postsecondary institutions, including medical schools.

Therefore, any attempt to eliminate anti-Black racism requires a rewriting of history so that people are acutely aware that these events are not just anecdotes based on people's individual experiences. Historical analysis is a central foundation for underscoring the connections between anti-Blackness and systemic and institutional policies, all of which were intentionally designed to dispossess and limit the development of Black people and to resist any attempts to accord them full humanity and citizenship, which were erased through hundreds of years of legally sanctioned enslavement.

The first stage of eliminating anti-Black racism also requires engaging in an analysis of and drawing connections between the historical artifacts of enslavement and the contemporary manifestations of anti-Blackness. There is often the tacit assumption that the experiences of Black people remain an artifact of the past that was resolved when Canada implemented the multiculturalism policies. This stage requires a critical analysis of existing systems of power, Whiteness, and White supremacy that structure outcomes for Black and Indigenous communities in Canada.

Stage 2 of eliminating anti-Black racism requires an intentional focus on the *impact* of harms that continue to affect Black communities. Engaging with a range of theoretical approaches at this critical juncture allows for an explication of the ways in which, by employing a critical race theory lens, for example, one is able to examine how anti-Black racism has been embedded in historical laws, policies, and procedures. For instance, this could be accomplished if one were to examine the laws that were imposed to justify the enslavement of Black people across the globe, which essentially rendered Black bodies as property and consequently eliminated all of their rights as human beings, and then engage in an analysis of the legal and economic impacts of those laws. Additionally, examining the laws that preceded the end of slavery, which denied Black people access to schooling, housing, and career opportunities, can facilitate an understanding of the ways in which the legal system has divested Black individuals of their rights as citizens. Although the vast majority of those laws have been removed from the books, there continue to be policies and practices today that particularly disadvantage Black communities. Anti-racism theories more effectively facilitate an examination of those policies within the modern context.

In the context of this discussion, the failure of policies within academic institutions to specifically articulate how racism structures inequitable outcomes for racialized populations is an example of the ways in which policies today are structured based on acts of omission. As indicated earlier, such policies highlight varying forms or sites of oppression and discrimination that members of the university community need to recognize and respect. The failure to address racism is an indication that race is not regarded as a valid site of examination, thus condoning racist behaviors while simultaneously erasing any opportunities to identify or address the ongoing impacts of racism. Although Canada's multiculturalism policy indicates that people shall not be discriminated against based on categories such as race, gender, and religion, and although the Human Rights Code also bans discrimination based on those and many other social and identity categories, the failure of institutions to specifically articulate their responses to race and racism creates few opportunities to recognize racism's impact, address incidents, or seek any clear form of redress.

A further challenge of these policies is the expectation that those who are the victims of racism must prove not only that the incidents occurred but also that race was a primary factor in them. Therefore, if the victim lacks clear evidence of this, it is almost impossible to prove that racism has occurred. In the context of our society and in the classroom, when students have learned to use racially coded language, proving racism becomes an almost impossible feat, thus leaving Black faculty unprotected and with few courses of action for prevention or redress.

Stage 3, interventions, is a central aspect of eliminating anti-Black racism. The murder of Floyd resulted in many organizations posting statements in support of the Black Lives Matter movement. However, most of the statements were hollow missives that provided no plan of action or specific interventions that would result in improvements in Black communities. This phase of eliminating anti-Black racism is central to enhancing outcomes for Black individuals and communities because it highlights the importance of intentional, concrete, actionable policies. In strategies to eliminate anti-Black racism in education, terms such as *racism* and *anti-Black racism* need to be identified as specific areas of oppression. The language should also include mention of direct and indirect acts of racism, including microaggressions and racial incivility, that will be considered under broader harassment policies, thus reducing the burden to prove racism. Further, there needs to be a central process for reporting incidents, including inappropriate emails, to ensure that faculty members are not tasked with dealing with these issues. The policy also needs to clearly identify repercussions, such as having the student removed from the class as a penalty for racist or racially coded behaviors that are indicative of racial incivility.

Stage 4, maintenance, is a core aspect of this work. Historically, programs that have been designed and implemented to improve outcomes for Black communities have been tied to the party that was in power or to a specific organizational leader. Unfortunately, once that political party changes or the leader retires, resigns, or moves on to a different organization, the intended projects and activities are often shelved. In order to ensure that these activities continue to be implemented in ways that are beneficial to Black communities, there has to be a clearly outlined implementation strategy built around notions of sustainability and accountability. Institutions must ensure that there is an oversight body, linked to the central reporting body, that conducts audits to determine the number, types, severity, and outcomes of the incidents so that interventions can be targeted and the institution can report on its progress toward eliminating anti-Black racism.

Conclusion

This chapter sought to provide context for understanding the experiences of anti-Black racism among Black faculty in Canadian institutions of higher education. The discussion focused on the erasure of Black history in Canada and the resulting denial of citizenship through the construction of Black people as permanent immigrants and outsiders. Although slavery did not occur on the scale it did in America, Canada had legalized slavery for over two hundred years; and though the Underground Railroad, which stretched into Canada, is often touted as a pathway to freedom, the dominant account of that historical journey fails to highlight the contributions of Black people to the development of Canada or the brutal segregation to which Black people were and continue to be subjected. The chapter also argued that Black Canadians are subjected to anti-Black racism by other racialized groups and provided examples of this, including the failure of Asian communities to challenge systemic anti-Blackness, while positioning themselves as model minorities and aligning with Whiteness as a strategy for achieving economic and political power.

An analysis of the discrimination policies and codes of conduct of select higher education institutions revealed that these policies are very general in the terminology that is used, and the term *race* is simply included as an aspect of the broader protected identity groups in Canada, which aligns with the Ontario and Canadian human rights codes. In large part, however, there is limited reference to racism as requiring specific intervention and no mention of anti-Black racism as a distinct category of oppression.

The chapter also discussed the ways in which professors experience anti-Black racism in the classroom and proposed that the threshold that is required to prove that an act of racism has occurred is often difficult to meet, given that many of the behaviors of students are not direct acts of racism. Most people today, including students, have developed a level of savvy in committing public racist acts, and the victim is thus left trying to prove racism, which becomes an added burden. The chapter explored the possibility of engaging with the notion of *racial incivility*, which allows for an analysis of student behaviors through a racialized lens that can be layered onto existing notions of incivility. The concept of incivility speaks to behaviors and attitudes that are intended to cause discomfort, and I have argued that when students question our abilities and credentials, send inappropriate emails, and so on, these are all forms of incivility and violence that target racialized faculty members. Further, these acts draw on highly stereotypical notions of Black people and are deployed as a strategy of containment. Students are uniquely positioned in the academy to engage in these acts, because they are afforded the option of challenging our intellectual capacities, which becomes an effective strategy for policing and protecting the power of Whiteness.

Policies, if effectively developed with clear guidelines that outline the issues and the resulting penalties, can play a significant role in addressing anti-Black racism and racial incivilities, which continue to plague Black academics in Canada. As a starting point, policies must emphasize that race-based discrimination cannot be conflated with other forms of discrimination and oppression, and addressing anti-Black racism requires that the specificity of the experience be acknowledged. I have also proposed that institutions explore the possibility of including racial incivility as a site of discrimination, because it has the potential to provide some form of redress and there can be specific penalties or interventions outlined in the policies. Students should also be made aware that they will be held to account for such targeted violence.

The chapter further introduced a new model for eliminating anti-Black racism that is action oriented and moves beyond the virtue signaling that is prevalent in Canadian academies. I developed this model based on my work with institutions that have had results in addressing anti-Black racism. The four-stage model involves, first, examining the *history* and historical contexts that give rise to anti-Blackness and, second, studying the *impact*, in both historical and contemporary contexts, and drawing connections to broader social and economic outcomes. The third stage focuses on *interventions*, which need to be action oriented and developed as a series of attainable goals with clearly outlined activities and outcomes. The final stage, *maintenance*, is a core aspect of the model because it needs to be embedded in the policies and guidelines of the broader institutional mandates and strategic planning to ensure that the interventions are not susceptible to the changing whims of organizational leaders.

Black Canadian academics are positioned with multiple intersectional identities and continue to experience varying forms of marginalization and oppression in the ivory tower from leaders, colleagues, and students. The experiences require an analytical lens that, while recognizing Black faculty's multiple identities, must also center race as a primary site of violence. Institutions, if they are truly invested in benefiting from the knowledge and competencies of this faculty group, beyond making promises of inclusion, must engage in intentional and targeted interventions to ensure that these intellectuals are accorded the right to a safe, racism-free work environment.

REFERENCES

Ally, N., & Ally, S. (2008). Critical intellectualism: The role of Black consciousness in reconfiguring the race-class problematic in South Africa. In A. Mngxitama, A. Alexander, & N. C. Gibson (Eds.), *Biko lives! Contesting the legacies of Steve Biko* (pp. 171–188). Palgrave Macmillan. https://doi.org/10.1057/9780230613379_10.

Andersson, L. M., & Pearson, C. M. (1999). Tit for tat? The spiraling effect of incivility in the workplace. *Academy of Management Review, 24*(3), 452–471.

Atkin, A. L., & Ahn, L. H. (2022). Profiles of racial socialization messages from mothers and fathers and the colorblind and anti-Black attitudes of Asian American adolescents. *Journal of Youth and Adolescence, 51*, 1048–1061. https://doi.org/10.1007/s10964-022-01597-2.

Austin, D. (2010). Narratives of power: Historical mythologies in contemporary Québec and Canada. *Race & Class, 52*(1), 19–32. https://doi.org/10.1177/0306396810371759.

B.A.L. (2017). The hidden costs of serving our community: Women faculty of color, racist sexism, and false security in a Hispanic-serving institution. *Feminist Teacher, 27*(2-3), 176–195. https://doi.org/10.5406/femteacher.27.2-3.0176.

Benjamin, A. (2011). Afterword: Doing anti-oppressive social work: The importance of resistance, history, and strategy. In D. Baines (Ed.), *Doing anti-oppressive practice: Social justice social work* (pp. 290–297). Fernwood.

Berman, R., Butler, A., Daniel, B. M., McNevin, M., & Royer, N. (2017). Nothing, or almost nothing, to report: Early childhood educators and discursive constructions of colorblindness. *International Critical Childhood Policy Studies, 6*(1), 52–65.

Bernal, D. D., & Villalpando, O. (2002). An apartheid of knowledge in academia: The struggle over the "legitimate" knowledge of faculty of color. *Equity & Excellence in Education, 35*(2), 169–180. https://doi.org/10.1080/713845282.

Berry, D. (2020). Canadian Multiculturalism Act. *The Canadian encyclopedia.* https://www.thecanadianencyclopedia.ca/en/article/canadian-multiculturalism -act.

Bhutani, A., & Tenneti, A. (2020). Addressing racism in South Asian Canadian communities. https://nationalinterest.org/blog/reboot/addressing-racism -south-asian-canadian-communities-167220.

Bracho, C. A., & Hayes, C. (2020). Gay voices without intersectionality is White supremacy: Narratives of gay and lesbian teachers of color on teaching and learning. *International Journal of Qualitative Studies in Education, 33*(6), 583–592. https://doi.org/10.1080/09518398.2020.1751897.

Calliste, A. (1993). Race, gender and Canadian immigration policy: Black people from the Caribbean, 1900–1932. *Journal of Caribbean Studies, 28*(4), 131–148.

Canadian Association of University Teachers. (2018). *Underrepresented and underpaid: Diversity and equity among Canada's post-secondary education teachers.* https://www.caut.ca/sites/default/files/caut_equity_report_2018-04final.pdf.

Canadian Museum of Immigration at Pier 21. (n.d.) To Canada and back again: Immigration from the United States on the Underground Railroad (1840–1860). https://pier21.ca/research/immigration- history/ immigration-from-united-states-on-underground-railroad.

City of Toronto. (2017). The Toronto action plan to confront anti-Black racism. https://www.toronto.ca/legdocs/mmis/2017/ex/bgrd/backgroundfile-109126.pdf.

Cooper, A. (2007). Acts of resistance: Black men and women engage slavery in upper Canada, 1793–1803. *Ontario History, 99*(1), 5–17, 134. https://www.proquest .com/scholarly-journals/acts-resistance-black-men-women-engage-slavery /docview/208522811/se-2.

Cortina, L. M., Magley, V. J., Williams, J. H., & Langhout, R. D. (2001). Incivility in the workplace: Incidence and impact. *Journal of Occupational Health Psychology,* 6, 64–80.

Daniel, B.M. (2018). Knowing the self and the reason for being: Navigating racism in the academy. *Canadian Woman Studies: Sexual and Gender Violence in Education,* 32(1–2), 59–66. https://search-proquest-com.ezproxy.lib.ryerson.ca /docview/2226331921?pq- origsite=summon.

Daniel, B. M. (2019). Teaching while Black: Racial dynamics, evaluations, and the role of White females in the Canadian academy in carrying the racism torch. *Race Ethnicity and Education, 22*(1), 21–37. https://10.1080/13613324.2018.1468745.

Dei, G. J. S. (2018). "Black like me": Reframing Blackness for decolonial politics. *Educational Studies, 54*(2), 117–142. https://doi.org/10.1080/00131946.2018.1427586.

Delgado, B. D., & Villalpando, O. (2002) An apartheid of knowledge in academia: the struggle over the "legitimate" knowledge of faculty of color. *Equity & Excellence in Education, 35*(2), 169–180. https://doi.org/10.1080/713845282.

Delgado, R. A., & Stefancic, J. (2001). *Critical race theory: An introduction.* New York University Press.

Delgado, R. A., & Stefancic, J. (2017). *Critical race theory: An introduction* (3rd ed.). New York University Press.

Donnor, J. K. (2016). Lies, myths, stock stories, and other tropes: Understanding race and whites' policy preferences in education. *Urban Education, 51*(3), 343–360. https://doi.org/10.1177/0042085916628613.

Dotson, K. (2012). A cautionary tale: On limiting epistemic oppression. *Frontiers: A Journal of Women Studies, 33*(1), 24–47. https://doi.org/10.5250/fronjwomestud.33 .1.0024.

Dua, E., & Bhanji, N. (2017). Mechanisms to address inequities in Canadian universities: The performativity of ineffectiveness. In F. Henry, E. Dua, C. James, A. Kobayashi, P. Li, H. Ramos, & M. Smith (Eds.), *The equity myth: Racialization and indigeneity at Canadian universities* (pp. 206–238). University of British Columbia Press.

Dutt-Ballerstadt, R. (2020). Colonized loyalty: Asian American Anti-Blackness and complicity. Faculty Publications Published Version. Submission 78. https:// digitalcommons.linfield.edu/englfac_pubs/78.

England, K., & Stiell, B. (1997). "They think you're as stupid as your English is": Constructing foreign domestic workers in Toronto. *Environment and Planning A: Economy and Space, 29*(2), 195–215. https://doi.org/10.1068/a290195.

Evans, S. A. (2021). "I wanted diversity, but not so much": Middle-class white parents, school choice, and the persistence of anti-black stereotypes. *Urban Education.* https://doi.org/10.1177/00420859211031952.

Fries-Britt, S., & Griffin, K. A. (2007). The Black box: How high-achieving Blacks resist stereotypes about Black Americans. *Journal of College Student Development, 48*(5), 509–524.

Garriott, P. O., Love, K. M., & Tyler, K. M. (2008). Anti-Black racism, self-esteem, and the adjustment of White students in higher education. *Journal of Diversity in Higher Education, 1*(1), 45–58. https://doi.org/10.1037/1938-8926.1.1.45.

Gordon, N. S., & Niles, M. N. (2011). *Still searching for our mothers' gardens: Experiences of new, tenure-track women of color at "majority" institutions.* University Press of America.

Government of Canada. (2022). Hire a temporary worker through the Seasonal Agricultural Worker Program: Overview. https://www.canada.ca/en /employment-social-development/services/foreign-workers/agricultural /seasonal-agricultural.html.

Hampton, R. (2020). *Black racialization and resistance at an elite university.* University of Toronto Press.

Henry, A. (2015). "We especially welcome applications from members of visible minority groups": Reflections on race, gender and life at three universities. *Race, Ethnicity and Education, 18*(5), 589–610. https://doi.org/10.1080/13613324 .2015.1023787.

Henry, F., & Kobayashi, A. (2017). The everyday world of racialized and Indigenous faculty members in Canadian universities. In F. Henry, E. Dua, C. James, A. Kobayashi, P. Li, H. Ramos, & M. Smith (Eds.), *The equity myth: Racialization and indigeneity at Canadian universities* (pp. 115–154). University of British Columbia Press.

Henry, N. (2023). Underground Railroad. *The Canadian encyclopedia.* https://www
.thecanadianencyclopedia.ca/en/article/underground-railroad.

James, C. (2017). "You know why you were hired don't you?" Expectations and
challenges in university appointments. In F. Henry, E. Dua, C. James, A. Kobayashi, P. Li, H. Ramos, & M. Smith (Eds.), *The equity myth: Racialization and
indigeneity at Canadian universities* (pp. 155–170). University of British Columbia
Press.

Jokic, D. (2020). Cultivating the soil of White nationalism: Settler violence and
Whiteness as territory. *Journal of Critical Race Inquiry, 7*(2), 1–21. https://doi.org
/10.24908/jcri.v7i2.13537.

Junne, G.H. (2003). *The history of Blacks in Canada: A selectively annotated bibliography.* Greenwood.

Kaufmann, E. (2022). Justin Trudeau's woke agenda is tearing Canadian society
apart. *Telegraph* (UK), January 31, 2022. https://www.manhattan-institute.org
/justin-trudeaus-woke-agenda-tearing-canadian-society-apart.

Kivel, P. (1996). *Uprooting racism: How White people can work for racial justice.* New
Society.

Kohli, R. (2012). Racial pedagogy of the oppressed: Critical interracial dialogue for
teachers of color. *Equity & Excellence in Education, 45,* 181–196.

Lim, S., Cortina, L. M., & Magley, V. J. (2008). Personal and workgroup incivility:
Impact on work and health outcomes. *Journal of Applied Psychology, 93*(1), 95–107.
https://doi.org/10.1037/0021-9010.93.1.95.

Lopez, A. E., & Jean-Marie, G. (2021). Challenging anti-Black racism in everyday
teaching, learning, and leading: From theory to practice. *Journal of School
Leadership, 31*(1–2), 50–65. https://doi.org/10.1177/1052684621993115.

Martis, E. (2020). *They said this would be fun: Race, campus life, and growing up.*
McClelland and Stewart.

McClure, D. R. (2016). Possessing history and American innocence: James Baldwin,
William F. Buckley, Jr., and the 1965 Cambridge debate. *James Baldwin Review, 2,*
49–74.

McGee, E. O., & Martin, D. B. (2011). "You would not believe what i have to go
through to prove my intellectual value!" Stereotype management among
academically successful Black mathematics and engineering students. *American
Educational Research Journal, 48*(6), 1347–1389. https://doi.org/10.3102
/0002831211423972.

Miles-Hercules, D., & Muwwakkil, J. (2021). Virtue signaling and the linguistic
repertoire of anti-Blackness: or, "I would have voted for Obama for a third term."
Journal of Linguistic Anthropology, 31(2), 267–270. https://doi.org/10.1111/jola.12320.

Modood, T., & Sealy, T. (2022). Beyond Euro-Americancentric forms of racism and
anti-racism. *Political Quarterly, 93*(3), 433–441. https://doi.org/10.1111/1467-923X
.13138.

Moise, E. C. (2021). *Teaching while Black: Navigating emotional labor and the White
waters of academia* (Publication No. 28717314). Doctoral dissertation, University
of Washington. ProQuest Dissertations and Theses A&I; ProQuest Dissertations
and Theses Global.

Moore, P. J., & Toliver, S. D. (2010). Intraracial dynamics of Black professors' and Black students' communication in traditionally White colleges and universities. *Journal of Black Studies, 40*(5), 932–945. https://doi.org/10.1177/0021934708321107.

Morgan, C. (2022). MORGAN: Trudeau and the woke are paving the path to the end of confederation. *Western Standard* (Calgary), June 26, 2022. https://www.westernstandard.news/opinion/morgan-trudeau-and-the-woke-are-paving-the-path-to-the-end-of-confederation/article_1540b028-f3f9-11ec-ad46-2b5076ffbf61.html.

Patel, S. (2016). Complicating the tale of "Two Indians": Mapping "South Asian" complicity in White settler colonialism along the axis of caste and anti-Blackness. *Theory & Event, 19*(4), https://www.muse.jhu.edu/article/633278.

Porcher, K. (2020). Teaching while Black: Best practices for engaging White pre-service teachers in discourse focused on individual and cultural diversity in urban schools. *Journal of Urban Learning, Teaching and Research, 15*(1), 116–134.

Reese, R. (2011). Canada: The promised land for U.S. Slaves. *Western Journal of Black Studies, 35*(3), 208–217. https://www.proquest.com/scholarly-journals/canada-promised-land-u-s-slaves/docview/1018080495/se-2.

Reynolds-Dobbs, W., Thomas, K. M., & Harrison, M. S. (2008). From mammy to superwoman: Images that hinder Black women's career development. *Journal of Career Development, 35*(2), 129–150. https://doi.org/10.1177/0894845308325645.

Rogers, L. O., & Way, N. (2016). "I have goals to prove all those people wrong and not fit into any one of those boxes": Paths of resistance to stereotypes among black adolescent males. *Journal of Adolescent Research, 31*(3), 263–298. https://doi.org/10.1177/0743558415600071.

Ross, T. (1997). White innocence, Black abstraction. In R. Delgado & J. Stefanic (Eds.), *Critical White studies: Looking behind the mirror* (pp. 262–266). Temple University Press.

Ryerson University. (2020). *Anti-Black racism campus climate review report.* https://www.ryerson.ca/confronting-anti-black-racism/pdfs/anti-black-racism-campus-climate-review-report-july-2020.pdf.

Settles, I. H., Jones, M. K., Buchanan, N. T., & Brassel, S. T. (2022). Epistemic exclusion of women faculty and faculty of color: Understanding scholar(ly) devaluation as a predictor of turnover intentions. *Journal of Higher Education, 93*(1), 31–55. https://doi.org/10.1080/00221546.2021.1914494.

Sewell, C. J. P. (2013). Mammies and matriarchs: Tracing images of the Black female in popular culture 1950s to present. *Journal of African American Studies, 17*, 308–326. https://doi.org/10.1007/s12111-012-9238-x.

Solomon, R. P., & Daniel, B. M. (2007). Discourses on race and "White privilege" in the next generation of teachers. In P. R. Carr & D. E. Lund (Eds.), *The great White north? Exploring Whiteness, privilege and identity in education* (pp. 161–172). Sense Publishers.

Solomon, R. P., Portelli, J., Daniel, B. M., & Campbell, A. (2005). The discourse of denial: How White teacher candidates construct race, racism and "White privilege." *Race Ethnicity and Education, 8*, 147–169.

Statistics Canada. (2019). Diversity of the Black population in Canada: An overview. https://www150.statcan.gc.ca/n1/pub/89-657-x/89-657-x2019002-eng.htm.

Statistics Canada. (2020). Canada's Black population: Education, labour and resilience. https://www150.statcan.gc.ca/n1/pub/89-657-x/89-657-x2020002 -eng.htm.

Swindler Boutte, G. (2008). Beyond the illusion of diversity: How early childhood teachers can promote social justice. *Social Studies*, July/August, 165–173.

The Scarborough Charter on Anti-Black Racism and Black Inclusion in Canadian Higher Education: Principles, Actions, and Accountabilities. National Dialogues and Action for Inclusive Higher Education and Communities. (2021). https://www.utsc.utoronto.ca/principal/sites/utsc.utoronto.ca.principal/files/docs /Scarborough_Charter_EN_Nov2022.pdf.

Thomas, V. (2020). "How dare you!" African American faculty and the power struggle with White students. *Journal of Cases in Educational Leadership*, 23(4), p. 115–126. https://doi.org/10.1177/1555458920945762.

Truth and Reconciliation Commission of Canada. (2015). *Honoring the truth, reconciling for the future: Summary of the final report of the Truth and Reconciliation Commission of Canada.* https://ehprnh2mwo3.exactdn.com/wp-content /uploads/2021/01/Executive_Summary_English_Web.pdf.

Turnipseed, D. L., & Landay, K. (2018). The role of the dark triad in perceptions of academic incivility. *Personality and Individual Differences*, 135(1), 286–291.

University of Toronto. (2019). Code of student conduct. Governing Council, December 13, 2019. https://governingcouncil.utoronto.ca/secretariat/policies /code-student-conduct-december-13-2019.

van Beinum, A. L. (2005). *Black teacher, White spaces: Negotiating identity across the classroom.* Master's thesis, University of Toronto.

Wilfrid Laurier University. (2021). Non-academic student code of conduct. June 3, 2021. https://www.wlu.ca/about/governance/assets/resources/12.3-non -academic-student-code-of-conduct.html.

Wrenn, C. L., & Lutz, M. (2016). White women wanted? An analysis of gender diversity in social justice magazines. *Societies*, 6(2), article 12. https://www .wellbeingintlstudiesrepository.org/divsmov/2/.

Wright, W. D. (2007). *Crisis of the Black intellectual.* Third World Press.

Yellow Horse, A. J., Kuo, K., Seaton, E. K., & Vargas, E. D. (2021). Asian Americans' indifference to Black Lives Matter: The role of nativity, belonging and acknowledgment of anti-Black racism. *Social Sciences*, 10(5), article 168. https://doi.org /10.3390/socsci10050168.

York University. (2020). Brown complicity in White supremacy. July 3, 2020. https://www.yorku.ca/edu/2020/07/03/brown-complicity-in-white-supremacy/.

Zhou, S. (2020). "Why don't they just work harder?" This kind of anti-Blackness is prevalent in Chinese-Canadian communities. It's time to address it. *Toronto Star*, July 23, 2020. https://www.thestar.com/opinion/contributors/2020/07/23 /why-dont-they-just-work-harder-this-kind-of-anti-blackness-is-prevalent-in -chinese-canadian-communities-its-time-to-address-it.html.

PART III

Pathways for Black Faculty to Succeed in the Academy

9

Exploring Black Faculty Narratives
through Three Theoretical Frameworks

FRED A. BONNER II, STELLA L. SMITH, AND ARETHA F. MARBLEY

Sojourner Truth's moving speech, "Ain't I a Woman?", delivered before
the assembled masses at the 1851 Women's Rights Convention held in
Akron, Ohio, galvanized the hearts and minds of women across myriad generations—especially Black women who sought to find some
sense of agency in a racist and sexist America. Just as Truth's speech
captured the plight of women and African Americans in their pursuit
of freedom and liberation from a hostile society, so too are her words
a poignant rallying cry to frame the extant experiences of diverse faculty who teach in predominantly White institutions (PWIs).

According to Bonner et al. (2014) and Stanley (2006), a litany of
phrases have been used to describe the engagements and experiences
of diverse faculty in PWI settings: multiple marginality; multiple oppression; otherness; living in two worlds; academe's new cast; silenced
voices; ivy halls and glass walls; survivors; transformers; from border
to center; visible and invisible barriers; the color of teaching; and navigating between two worlds. Each phrase in some nuanced capacity
contributes not only to how faculty of color frame their experiences

in the academy but also how they go about establishing some sense of identity.

For diverse faculty in general and Black faculty in particular, "fitting in" means developing a professional identity that is congruent with the mores, values, and traditions of the academy, one that is often at odds with the cultural, social, and personal identities that these faculty members bring to the academy (Bonner et al., 2014; Fries-Britt & Kelly, 2005; Higgins, 2004; Patitu & Hinton, 2003; Stanley, 2006; Thompson et al., 2016; Thompson & Louque, 2005; Tuitt et al., 2009; Turner et al., 2008). According to Turner and Myers (2000) and Turner et al. (2008), the academy's recalcitrance to modify traditional practices and policies, accentuated by both covert and overt acts found detrimental to the success of Blacks and other groups of color at PWIs, continues to reify the "chilly climate" that faculty of color often identify in these contexts.

We have selected three critical frameworks (critical race theory [CRT], intersectionality, and liminality) to serve as the scaffolds on which we present our respective narratives. Each one of our narratives is unpacked using scholarly personal narrative as both an analytical and discursive tool. We invite the reader to join us on this journey as we reflect on our past and contemporary experiences, foregrounding our scholarship as Black scholars and scholar-practitioners in the White academy.

The first frame, CRT, is illuminated through Stella Smith's scholarly personal narrative, titled "Tempered, Radical, and Tenacious: One Black Woman's Experience in White Academic Spaces." Stella narrates her experiences moving in and through a PWI, a research-intensive enclave located in the South. She talks about how she matriculated from undergraduate to graduate school in an academic space that at times she viewed as foreign and unwelcoming. The title of Stella's narrative is taken from her dissertation, *African American Females in Senior-Level Executive Roles Navigating Predominately White Institutions: Experiences, Challenges and Strategies for Success*, which focused on the experiences of African American women in leadership at PWIs. Her narrative begins with a brief overview of CRT. She continues by sharing how the tenets of CRT influenced her scholarly personal narrative. She concludes with advice from her journey for colleagues at PWIs.

In the second frame, intersectionality is illuminated through aretha marbley's scholarly personal narrative, titled "Protecting Black Women Faculty from the Unchecked Abuse of Power of Student Evaluations that Publicly Blame and Shame." After defining the concept of intersectionality, aretha provides vivid detail in her narrative, chronicling her movements in higher education as a Black woman counselor educator in rural West Texas. Following her narrative, she provides critical takeaways for diverse faculty in the academy.

The third frame, liminality, is foregrounded through Fred A. Bonner II's scholarly personal narrative, titled "'Mascu'sectionality: Creating a Black Male Scholar Identity in the Liminal Space." In his narrative, he explores how intersectionality as a theoretical framework has been used in profound ways to bring into focus the engagements of Black women, notwithstanding their experiences in the academy. However, he takes a point of departure to unpack how intersectionality, with its derivational ties to Black feminist thought, feminism, and womanism, has often left Black men outside the margins in their attempts to operationalize this theory in ways that are emblematic of their identity construction and development. What Bonner offers is not a diminution of the powerful analytical and heuristic utility of intersectionality but rather an alternative frame—namely, liminality—to explore how he has grappled with developing his identity as a Black scholar in White academe. Liminality serves as a key theoretical tool that has allowed him to craft his identity as a Black, male scholar who views himself as not being confined to any one of those respective identities but rather as the sum total, the holistic rendering, of all of these identity vectors at the same time. After defining the concept of liminality, he offers his scholarly personal narrative. He then provides a number of critical takeaways for diverse faculty in the academy—especially Black males who are grappling with their own identity development and formation.

Critical Race Theory

Illuminating the Theoretical Frame

"Critical race theory (CRT) movement is a collection of activists and scholars engaged in studying and transforming the relationship among race, racism and power" (Delgado & Stefanic, 2017, p. 3). Emerging from legal studies in the 1970s, seminal scholars such as Derrick Bell, Alan Freeman, and Richard Delgado sought to develop theories and strategies for legal application to support the progress gained during the civil rights movement (Crenshaw, 2010; Delgado & Stefancic, 1993). Today, CRT has been applied to many other fields. For example, researchers in education apply CRT principles to understand educational issues including affirmative action and bilingual and multicultural education (Collins, 2021; Ladson-Billings, 2016). CRT is a useful framework to theoretically and methodologically consider diverse faculty experiences because it underscores the role that racism plays in US education and works toward its elimination (Ladson-Billings, 1999; Solórzano et al., 2000; Tate, 1997).

In the tradition of CRT, the authors in this chapter will interweave personal counternarratives that depict creative interpretations of their lived experiences as diverse faculty in PWIs. According to Ladson-Billings (1999), personal narratives and stories are important in truly understanding lived experiences and how those experiences may represent confirmation or counter-knowledge of the way society works. She contends that stories are used to analyze the myths, presuppositions, and received wisdoms that make up the common culture about race. To that end, in this chapter the counternarratives will explore and utilize shared and individual experiences of race, gender, imagination, status, language, and sexuality in education (Solórzano, 1997; Yosso, 2002).

The tenets of CRT are that racism is ordinary, not aberrational; progress toward racial equality only occurs when the interests of those in power converge with the interests of marginalized groups; race is a social construction; different racial groups are subjected to different forms of racial oppression; and the experiences and perspectives of people of color must be valued and included in discussions about race and racism (Delgado & Stefancic, 2017). The overarching goal is to provide higher education in general and PWIs in particular with viable recommendations and insights to influence best practices and policy decisions that lead to the success of these critical faculty cohorts (Sleeter & Delgado Bernal, 2003).

Tempered, Radical, and Tenacious: One Black Woman's Experience in White Academic Spaces

I grew up in the 1980s and early 1990s, making me part of a generation of students that, in some respects, was trained to be comfortable in spaces that were not designed for us. I benefited from the protests and unrest of the 1960s and 1970s as well as the scholarship of accomplished Black women (Collins, 1989; Giovanni, 1993; hooks, 1989; Lorde, 1984; Walker, 1983). My apprehension and fear about predominantly White spaces was less about being allowed entry and more about how I would perform in those spaces. I was the smart girl . . . the smart Black girl, and often the *only* one who occupied most of those White spaces that I entered. As I consider my educational and professional trajectory through a CRT lens, it is clear how the philosophy of CRT has influenced my experience within academe. This narrative demonstrates not only the systemic impact of CRT but its ubiquitous application.

What I came to understand is my counternarrative is my *only* narrative. This professional space that I called home for more than twenty years functioned to increase equity and opportunity for underrepresented minorities in higher education. Hindsight reveals that not only were the principles of CRT foundational to the mission and vision of my workplace, but they had been essential even, to providing me access. In addition, my undergraduate experience as a microbiology major further exposed me to academic experiences that were at the intersection of many of the tenets of CRT. I felt isolated and like an imposter, and the place that I had once felt safe in high school, the classroom, now felt foreign. My saving grace was having had the opportunity to work in enclaves at the institution that were bastions of social justice and equity on campus.

As a student, I was working with African American professional staff members who held titles with distinction and esteem well respected within the institution. My role models fought the traditional norms of higher education to provide pathways for other underrepresented minorities to have access to the resources of the institution in new and innovative ways. They modeled for me behavior that was supportive of an institutional structure, but also disruptive. As a scholar, I now know that those staff members operated through a *tempered radical* perspective where they were committed to the institution in which we worked but were also committed to making changes within the institution (Meyerson, 2003). They saw their position as an opportunity to make purposeful, influential, and systemic changes within the institution.

Once I graduated with my undergraduate degree, I knew that science was not my path, as I was inspired to make a difference as an administrator within higher education. Diverse faculty and administrators mentored me and provided me with the skills that are the bedrock of my professional skill set. They also modeled strategies to work within the institution to make systemic and visible changes toward more equitable and accessible practices for all faculty, staff, students, and administrators.

Although not explicitly stated in the positions that I held, the tenets of CRT were guideposts for my work. Moreover, my work in an administrative role helped me to understand that in higher education all aspects of the institution (administrators, faculty, staff, and students) must work in concert to support equity and diversity within the institution. CRT provided a foundation for how we operationalized the work that we did and how we approached increasing diversity, equity, and inclusion within areas of campus. The work we did to push the envelope was innovative and exemplified the importance of diversity, equity, and inclusion as an institutional priority. We made a business case for the need for equitable spaces and opportunities.

When I transitioned to a position as a scholar and researcher at a historically Black college and university (HBCU), I realized that CRT is applicable here as well. Although I am at a HBCU, this institution functions and operates within a larger higher education system that was built on systemic racism. Our campus's institutional mission and vision support the equitable access and academic success of underrepresented populations, but we still face systemic challenges to achieving these goals.

Takeaways: Advice for Black Scholars in the Academy

As I think back on my journey, there are a few key takeaways that I wish I would have realized as a student (undergraduate and graduate) as well as a young professional working at a PWI. Understanding these lessons would have helped me recognize how key aspects of my professional journey, including both the opportunities received and challenges I encountered, were influenced by CRT principles.

Takeaway 1: CRT Influences Our Journeys Regardless of Whether We Acknowledge It

I never considered myself to be a critical race scholar. If anything, I purposefully avoided the term because in the environment in which I worked, labeling myself as a critical race scholar would foreclose opportunities that would allow me to make change at the institution. I thought and hoped that by focusing on the diversity, equity, inclusion, belonging, and social justice in my work, research, and teaching, I would be able to effect a change on the campus that would enrich the experience of all students. I now understand as a scholar and faculty member that much of the confusion around CRT is related to a lack of understanding of the concept and a reaction to the words *critical race*. I also understand that CRT is a systemic argument that affects our experiences whether we name it or not. Our actions to promote a more just and equitable society occur within a racist system. As diverse faculty we must recognize and adjust for these systemic challenges that would thwart our efforts.

Takeaway 2: The Challenges of CRT Occur at All Types of Institutions
Given that many researchers and scholars misunderstand the tenets of CRT, there might be some notion that the challenges of CRT are more prevalent or pervasive at a PWI. My narrative provides a counterpoint to this assertion. CRT focuses on systemic imbalances of power. All higher education institutions are susceptible to inequity, inequality, racism, and bias, regardless of their designation (e.g., PWI, minority-serving institution, religious institution, women's college). The various levels of racism (internal, interpersonal, cultural, institutional, and systemic) have a multiplicative effect on the experiences of diverse faculty as well as our production and impact in an educational capacity. As diverse faculty shift among institutional types, they should keep in mind that there is no panacea of racial justice in the higher education system.

Takeaway 3: Achieving Work-Life Harmony Is Critical
Regardless of the institution type, position, or role that diverse faculty have *earned*, it is essential that they prioritize time to focus on their vital needs. In my professional roles, I found that as a woman, and specifically an African American woman, there was an expectation that I support my colleagues to ensure they were successful, sometimes to my own detriment. Not wanting to disappoint anyone, I fulfilled this obligation, suspending my own needs (e.g., professional progression, health, and wellness). As diverse faculty, we often juggle more competing interests than our White colleagues. The cultural tax that we pay as diverse faculty at PWIs can cause us to reevaluate our other priorities (e.g., research, teaching, service, family, relationships, health, and rest). Diverse faculty should consider seeking to achieve harmony as they pursue these goals. Rather than striving for a work-life balance, which implies that the priorities in one's life are in opposition to each other, I propose that diverse faculty seek a state of harmony. As the chords of one's favorite song align in harmony, so too can one's (life and work) priorities become a consonant melody. This work is hard, and diverse faculty will make many sacrifices if they stay the course. Their self-care and vital needs should not be among them.

Intersectionality

Illuminating the Theoretical Frame

I sit and sew—a useless task it seems,
My hands grown tired, my head weighed down with dreams.
The panoply of war, the martial tread of men,
It stifles me—God, must I sit and sew?
—ALICE MOORE DUNBAR-NELSON (1988)

Simply put, intersectionality is the interconnection of socially and psychologically constructed identities (privileged and oppressed) such as those pertaining to race, class, age, sexuality, and gender, on which established systems of power and domination and systems of discrimination and disadvantages stand. Intersectionality holds that people can exist at the intersections of their identities. Black feminist legal scholar Kimberlé Crenshaw (1989) formulated the term to describe the employment discrimination Black women experienced that Black men and White women did not. As she explained, at the intersection of gender and race, Black women had become invisible. Indeed, being a Black person and a woman means frequently experiencing intersecting patterns of racism and sexism and gender and racial biases at the intersections.

The concept of understanding Black women through the lens of their multiple identities—specifically, as doubly oppressed as Black and female—has a long history with deep roots. It can be traced back decades before Crenshaw coined the term *intersectionality*—for example, to Sojourner Truth's famous "Ain't I a Woman?" speech at the Women's Convention in Akron, Ohio, in 1851 and the work of other Black female feminist abolitionists. Civil rights, social, community, and political activists; poets, essayists, playwrights, and authors; and scholars, Black feminists, womanists, and Africana feminists contributed to the concept of intersectionality before it was named, women like Anna Julia Cooper writing in 1892, Georgia Douglass Johnson writing in 1918, Angela Davis (1981), June Jordan (2021), Gerda Lerner

(1972), Audre Lorde (1984), Ntozake Shange (1977). Black women scholars and activists and feminists of the past fifty years have also contributed to the scholarship on intersectionality—Akasha Gloria Hull, Patricia Bell-Scott, Barbara Smith, Patricia Hill-Collins, bell hooks, Clenora Hudson-Weems, Alice Walker, Carmen Wiggins, and Marsha Williams.

Through an intersectional lens, my positionality on domination is projected from my intersecting identities of being Black and female and comes from an insider perspective as an African American female and now as a graying academic counselor. Hegemony for other African American women and me is double, if not triple, jeopardy— that is, as Anna Julia Cooper (1988, p. 45) wrote in 1892, "when and where I enter, in the quiet undisputed dignity of my womanhood, without violence and without suing or special patronage, then and there the whole *Negro race enters with me*" (emphasis in original). My race, color, gender, and age enter with me.

Historically, the Black and White feminist movements and scholarship have not fully represented the experiences of Black women living at the intersection of race and gender, particularly within the discourse of either feminism or antiracism. Because of their multiple and intersectional racial and gendered identities, Black women are expected to respond to each other. So they and other women of color are marginalized within feminism and antiracism.

Black feminist and feminist and womanist scholars must guard against a repeat of what happened during the first, second, and third waves of feminism, in the civil rights and Black Power movements of the 1960s and 1970s, and more recently the Black Lives Matter movement, where Black women were forced to choose either their gender or racial identity.

As Alice Moore Dunbar wrote in her poem about Black women who spend a lot of their time sitting and sewing, I will attempt to sit and sew together the narrative of my personal and professional experiences as a Black woman faculty member in a PWI. My narrative is one example of the marginalization of Black female faculty. It presents a tapestry of my experience, revealing the intersectional experience in which my racial, cultural, gender, ethnic, and aging identities are rendered invisible, not only at the intersection of these many identities but also by academia and higher education.

Protecting Black Women Faculty from the Unchecked Abuse of Power of Student Evaluations That Publicly Blame and Shame

Being in academia has had a damaging impact on my sense of ethnic, cultural, gender, and racial identity. As individuals living at the intersections, Black women faculty are speaking out about the particular challenges we encounter in higher education institutions in general and PWIs specifically, where we are constantly made to feel we do not belong. Many terms have been used to describe the atmosphere for women and people of color in these academic settings: chilly; unwelcoming; isolating; wracked with racism, sexism, and microaggressions; and silencing. To belong, I must develop an identity congruent with the academy's culture, mores, values, and traditions, and this means leaving behind parts of myself.

Earlier in my career, a former dean immediately convened a task force to investigate when White faculty teaching online courses complained that student evaluations centered on the technology rather than their teaching skills. Yet no committee was ever convened to investigate when faculty of color complained about receiving low evaluations because of our ethnic or racial background or when both women of color complained about low evaluations because of our gender and race.

For me, these incidents encouraged the question, does a legitimate space in the academy of higher education exist for my concerns and for those of others who are Black and female like me? As an African American female professor at a PWI, specifically in the professoriate, am I in a place to be heard? Nothing existed in our operating policies, our handbooks, or even the nation's laws to ensure I would be.

Twenty years later, in the spring semester, student comments on my courses reflected a pattern of criticism that I know my counterparts would not have experienced. One student wrote, "Professor seemed to [have] a bit of paranoia about students talking about her outside of class"; "Cohort frequently received public blame and shame"; "I ended up paying for a semester of unchecked abuse"; and "It boils down more to a lack of confidence in ultimately the university's system to protect its students." These comments leaped out of the page and landed inside me, flipping me upside down, a signal of dire distress and extreme danger. My heart and soul felt shredded. The comment that stood out the most was, "The other thing that is disappointing is the University probably won't do anything about this."

It took me a few years to bury the hurt and shame and pain from the comments and attacks on my credibility, character, and ethics. But I can now reflect on the irony of the words. Being accused of being unethical and callous, of violating the Family Educational Rights and Privacy Act of 1974, of blaming and shaming students, and of having abused my power left me shattered and stunned. Ironically, those same comments captured my thirty years of experience as a Black professor and as a female professor in a PWI classroom and within the halls of the academy. It was me, in that classroom and many others, who had experienced unchecked power and abuse.

The comments were so hurtful and damaging that I considered leaving academia, filing an official complaint, and seeking legal counsel. Massive and compelling evidence-based research shows that student evaluations of instructors are biased against women and women of color. Up and down the halls of the academy, we have discussed the negative impact of student evaluations on women and faculty of color. I also knew firsthand how that kind of bias can affect an instructor's employment and academic career directly. Yet all of the discussions failed to bring any change.

After reading the comments, I met with colleagues, administration at all levels, and legal counsel to discuss how to address what I perceived as the students' attack on my credibility and personhood. Some colleagues questioned my intent. They felt that questioning the value of student evaluations was a personal attack on them. They would ask me *why* I thought students said what they said, implicitly ignoring the fact that I knew that my race and gender were the reasons.

One colleague made a statement about noticing that I always talk about what happened to me in the classroom and not the students' experiences, claiming that I do not take responsibility for what happens in my classroom and instead blame it on something else. My statements about the evidence-based research on student bias against women faculty of color fell on deaf ears. Others said I sounded defensive. Sadly, for me, as an African American female instructor with nearly three decades in the professoriate, tenure and promotion to full professor did not confer respect and credibility.

Takeaways: Advice for Black Scholars in the Academy

I have less power in and outside the classroom compared with both Black male faculty and White female faculty. I am attacked more than they are and am more vulnerable because of my intersecting identities. Being a Black and female professor in a PWI is detrimental to my career and well-being.

In essence, the comments from my student evaluation mirrored the microassaults, microinsults, and microinvalidations Black women faculty and other women faculty of color experience daily in the academy.

Being at the intersections of color, gender, and aging, this dynamic interplay among my multiple identities requires an alternate framework for understanding the impact of PWI environments on me; my intersecting identities, and ultimately my professional identities as a counselor educator and Black feminist and womanist activist scholar; my professional integrity; and my mental health.

In recent years, growing scholarship has called for reform of student evaluations of teaching. However, reform is not enough. Without an alternative framework and a major overhaul of student evaluations, African American women faculty, like me, will remain invisible and unprotected at the intersections of race and gender. The need is urgent, if we are to end the dynamics of public blame and shame.

Takeaway 1: Living at the intersection, I was invisible. Unfortunately, as an African American and female instructor, tenure and promotion to full professor had not earned me respect, nor had my three decades in the academy.

Takeaway 2: I knew firsthand of the many articles that had been written, studies conducted, and conversations held up and down the halls of the academy about the negative impact of student evaluations on women and faculty of color. Nonetheless, I was powerless to block the power of such bias on my employment and academic career.

Takeaway 3: Nothing exists in our operating policies or handbooks to help us address concerns about student instructor evaluations.

Takeaway 4: Black feminist scholars and activists, whose contributions explore multiple forms of oppression by targeting topics such as racism, oppression, family, work, and sexuality, still go virtually unnoticed and garner little support.

Advice: Be a leader who fights to eliminate all forms of oppression. To eliminate racial and gender discrimination, biases must be extricated from the unconscious, even the dormant ones, and be brought to form by many Black, male, and female scholars and leaders.

Conclusion: The good news is that at my institution, the administration in my program, college, and institution is tackling the issue of bias in student evaluations head-on. Multiple pockets of colleagues, including White women and men and males and females of color, as well as some student groups, are invested in this process. My campus is taking major steps to create an environment of inclusivity, equity, diversity, and belonging. Yet, as a nation and as a global community, we have made little progress in eliminating racism, sexism, and other oppressions.

Implicit biases and insidious forms of oppression lie dormant in the unconscious. Carl Jung believed that a leader is a person who brings to form that which has been in the collective consciousness of a people. Thus, it is incumbent upon antiracist and other anti-oppression activist scholars to be the leaders who bring to form these unconscious biases as tool to eliminate them.

The work of Black feminist scholars and activists still goes virtually unnoticed. I am almost rendered invisible, as are other women who look like me, and age like me. It is no roseate dream, says Alice

Moore Dunbar Nelson, "that beckons me—This pretty futile seam / It stifles me—God, must I sit and sew?"

Liminality

Illuminating the Theoretical Frame

According to Victor Turner (cited in Bigger, 2009), liminality is a concept borrowed from the Belgian folklorist Arnold van Gennep. Van Gennep observed rites of passage across different cultures. What he found is that "three analytically distinctive phases" occur in which individuals undergo transitions from one social status to another (Wels et al., 2011, p. 1). These phases include separation, margin (*limen*), and aggregation. In essence, the transition in rites of passage involves pulling away from the known (e.g., family, friends, and community); searching for the self in a sea of choice and confusion; and ultimately establishing connections with a new community—congruous with the individual's newfound identity. To further illustrate this theory, Beech (2011, p. 286) proffered, "The notion of liminality, meaning 'betwixt and between,' has been developed in social anthropology (Turner, 1967) and has been adopted by some organizational researchers (Tempest and Starkey, 2004; Sturdy et. al., 2006)."

In "Honoring Liminality: Teaching Critical and Race-Gendered Approaches in Doctoral Social Work Education," Joyce et al. (2021, p. 3) notes, "Coming from anthropology and specifically ethnography (Adorno et al., 2015), liminality refers to a degree of maturation in which an individual's current state changes. In other words, a previously fixed and stable condition is uprooted by entering a place of ambiguity and unknowing." Perhaps most salient to my scholarly personal narrative is the definitional aspect of liminality, and the ritual process of rites of passage, which illuminates the interstitial space—undefined space in between fixed polarities that allows for unfettered cogitation and the imagining of realities that are not stayed and fixed but transitory and fluid. Wels et al. (2011, p. 1) state, "During the middle phase of such a process the individuals involved are understood to be 'no longer' and simultaneously also 'not yet.'"

"Mascu"sectionality: Creating a Black Male Scholar Identity in the Liminal Space

So much of the person I have become is tethered to my formative years growing up in rural East Texas. I am an amalgamation of the southern Black Baptist church, HBCU-trained public school teachers, and the wise counsel of community griots who shared stories of challenge and triumph they secured in a society that assured them their separate circumstances would somehow yield equal outcomes. Yet what I remember most vividly are the "coming of age" lessons learned at the feet of the Black men like my father (a.k.a. Uncle Sonny), Uncle Crock, Uncle June, Uncle Snake, Daddy Cutt, Uncle Ennis—for me their names connoted essence before existence. I interfaced in both proximal and distal spaces with these men, these towering figures who taught me the importance of being caring, compassionate, determined, empathic, and hardworking.

What I learned from these men is that who I was and who I would become was a collection of *all* of these identity vectors. It was their wholeness that made them such towering figures in my mind. As a young Black male, this collection of Black men embodied what it meant to be somebody, somebody who was accomplished, Black, male, and strong—what I saw in them was not representations of singularity but holistic renderings of what it meant to be a Black man. In essence, these men were real-life representations of the ideal that I could strive to be *both and*, as opposed to settling for the *either-or* designation that the world seemed to surreptitiously ascribe to Black males.

Flash-forward to contemporary times, in my capacity as a college professor, it makes me chuckle when I find what I call the "egg head" explanation for my everyday experiences and thoughts. Kimberlé Crenshaw (1989), more than two decades ago in a paper titled "Demarginalizing the Intersection of Race and Sex: A Black Feminist Critique of Antidiscrimination Doctrine, Feminist Theory and Antiracist Politics," proposed the term *intersectionality* to describe the experiences of Black women. Crenshaw stated, "I will center Black women in this analysis in order to contrast the multidimensionality of Black women's experience with the single-axis analysis that distorts these experiences" (p. 139). What she illuminated for Black women was a new way to frame their experiences and ultimately their identity. They began to see themselves as the product of the intersection of an array of identity vectors; who these Black women are is at the center of all of their respective identities—Black, daughter, lesbian, mother, professional, and woman. Intersectionality as a theoretical frame was illuminating in that it brought to light that Black women did not have to choose or ignore any aspect of their being but could sit comfortably in the seat of their collective identities.

As a Black man and researcher, discovering intersectionality as a conceptual frame that I could use to examine my experiences—especially those related to my identity as Black, male, a researcher, a scholar, and a professor—was, in my estimation, nothing short of divine. I had my hammer, so I was now ready to go out and find the nails. In very short order my new playhouse was torn down—*completely*.

What started off as a national conference presentation later resulted in my efforts to reframe the conference presentation as a fundable grant project. "'Mascu'sectionality: Theorizing a Black Masculinity Framework" was the tentative title for the conference session and subsequent grant proposal. My intent was ultimately to develop a new theoretical framework that would speak to Black masculine identity and identity development. Like Crenshaw, I wanted to offer a frame that was explanatory and transgressive for Black men. I thought that Black men, too, needed a heuristic tool that gave them an extended range of motion to explore their multiple and layered identities. However, I discovered that the surface-level review of literature that I had previously conducted fell far short of the detailed analysis of the extant literature that I needed to perform in order to develop the theoretical sensitivity to approach this critical topic.

My deep dive into the literature on masculinity introduced me to authors who included Eric Anderson (2010), R.W. Connell (2005), and

Michael S. Kimmel et al. (2004). However, when I added the filter "Black" to my search for literature on masculinity, the search engine unearthed a new vanguard of intellectuals and scholars—Marianne Cooper (2000), Tommy Curry (2017), David Jackson (2015), Dante Pelzer (2016), and Gilman Whiting (2008). After exploring much of the scholarship advanced by these intellectuals, it was a quote by Curry (2017, p. 208), who happened to be a former colleague and friend, that captured my attention, "The exact disadvantages men of color—specifically, heterosexual Black males—confront seems [sic] largely absent in intersectionality theory. Some intersectionality thinkers assert that Black males have privilege and advantages over Black women because they are male." He also says, "Scholars use intersectionality to suggest Black males share the same proclivities as white males, or patriarchs" (p. 209). And perhaps the statement that most caused me to question the *goodness of fit* of intersectionality as an analytical frame for Black masculinity was the following: "While Crenshaw has acknowledged the non-universality of categories such as *woman*, she fails to inquire into the limits that such a category imposes on the normative operation of *man* within the theory" (p. 210).

I thought, what now? What other door could I open, what container is left on the shelf that might have contents that I could use to unpack who I was as a Black male? The last time I could remember speaking to the topic of Black masculinity was when my colleague J. Luke Wood, at the time editor of the *Journal of African American Males in Education*, asked me to pen the prefatory remarks for one of the journal issues. "Negotiating the 'In-Between': Liminality and the Construction of Racial Identity among African American Male Collegians" (Bonner 2011) is where I talked about the importance of Black men, especially Black men in the halls of the academy, having an unfettered space—a quiet place to ruminate on who they were. This place that I envisioned was not a place at all, it was *interstitial space* where they did not have to lock into any one identity vector—not Black, male, cis, trans, brother, son, father, or any other identity. The beauty of this interstitial space is that it is a region where it would be okay for these men to be "almost" but "not quite yet."

I discovered that this middle space that I dreamed of was actually a real concept, a theoretical frame called *liminality*. In explaining what happens to individuals in this middle space when engaging in rites of passage, Turner (1980, p. 45), a key architect of this frame, observed, "These individuals find themselves thrust into what is known as *the liminal space*—the 'precarious in-between' place that bridges 'what is' and 'what can or will be.'" So there it was, liminality—a theoretical framework that gave me breathing room and the opportunity to undo the shackles that connected me to the weight of all these identities that I felt I had to carry around. Now I could freely choose what identity items I wanted to pack and what I could leave behind as I prepared for my identity development voyage. Harking back to my scholar brother Curry's scholarship, and the promise that this shiny new theoretical tool provided, I now felt the earth shifting me toward a stable position, a place in which I could be self-affirmed, self-defined, self-directed, and self-motivated. As the idiomatic expression goes, find a way to cut out the middleman. Yet the middleman, or the man I would craft in this middle space, would be precisely the man I needed to cut *in*. My Black masculinity and manhood, freed from the prescriptive identity constructions that existed at each one of the identity poles, could be jettisoned for this middle place of contemplative thought. What did it mean for me as a Black man to define myself for myself, not looking at my masculinity through a dim glass or from what I referred to as the "Secret" theoretical framework—a reference to the iconic tag line for the Secret deodorant commercial, "Secret, strong enough for a man, but made for a woman." As a Black man and as a Black male scholar in the academy, finding the authentic space as well as the proper tools to hone, refine, and develop my identity has been rewarding.

Takeaways: Advice for Black Scholars in the Academy

It is my hope that my scholarly personal narrative created for the reader what one of my favorite comedians, Arsenio Hall, would refer to during his weekly show as "something to make you go hum." Diverse faculty who find themselves navigating the variegated higher education terrain must find critical venues to share narratives chronicling their challenges and triumphs, as well as their everyday experiences—especially as they relate to finding their authentic selves. For me, my coming of age and discovering who I was as a man—a Black man—superseded my search for my identity as a professor, researcher, and scholar.

Takeaway 1: If the Frame Doesn't Fit, Change the Frame, Don't Change the Picture

The search for the self and attempt to find our true identities is a long and arduous process. Many times, just when you feel as if that revelatory moment has arrived, the moment when you think you have it all figured out—this is who I am—you discover that when the context changes or the environment shifts, you are thrown right back into an abyss of self-doubt. I see these contextual movements as frames. At times, if the frame is too small, it will only capture a portion or section of the picture. Yet the picture, the authentic rendering, is no less complete simply because the frame only is able to capture a portion. Would we cut away part of a Picasso or Van Gogh because the frame was too small? Yet we are willing to make the decision to truncate a part of our identity because the frame (perspective) of who we are and who we are destined to be is too narrow. We must learn to change the frame (i.e., department, institution, peer group) as opposed to making the costly decision to lose a part of ourselves.

Takeaway 2: Find Conceptual and Theoretical Approaches That Foreground Both Accomplishment and Liberation

What is the use of conceptual and theoretical approaches that force the individual into circumstances that cause them to shave off or let go of critical aspects of their identity? As I contemplated a career move years ago, a mentor shared with me, "It appears that you have your hand in the candy jar, and when you try to retrieve it holding the candy, your hand gets stuck." She then went on to say, "Now, my dear, you must decide: What's the candy?" From her lesson parable, I was forced into thinking about what *mattered*, what was *important*, what I would *gain*, what I would *lose*, and what was the better *circumstance* (candy). So the takeaway for Black scholars in the academy is to assess each situation in turn and make informed decisions in light of what will be accomplished as well as what might be left behind. These contemplative moments should always have some focus on what identity negotiation and positionality maneuverings will be required to be happy and successful. Engagements, experiences, and spaces that move Black faculty away from identity liberation to identity confinement should be problematized.

Takeaway 3: Avoid Getting the E's Twisted: Clarifying Emic and Etic Perspectives

In the rush to find a panacea to cure our conceptual and theoretical ills, it is all too often the practice to use what worked for one community and population as the elixir for others. What we know from anthropology and sociology is that there are perspectival lenses through which we view the communities around us. And depending on the context, we have an insider (emic) perspective or outsider (etic) perspective. Said differently, as a Black male, my emic perspective related to my research on academically gifted African American males provides me with key insider insights. Yet much of the extant research about diverse communities in the academy, especially Black scholars, has been crafted by individuals outside the Black diaspora. Thus, the etic perspectives of White scholars have in many instances taken center stage in examinations of the Black scholar experience. The same thing has happened for Black males and the extant discussions about Black masculinity. While some of the discord has been due to emic/etic wire crossing related to the Black-White binary, much of it has arisen from translation across the gender divide—that is, Black masculinity through a Black feminist lens. Whether concerning race or gender, the takeaway is what I alluded to in my *Diverse: Issues in Higher Education* op-ed, "Code-Switching to Code Stitching: Theorizing an Alternative Framework" (Pegram & Bonner, 2021): while an etic perspective might serve as a welcomed opinion, it should never occupy a place of dominion over the "authentic" voice and perspective.

Conclusion

Each of these counternarratives illuminates the impact of theories on the experiences of Black faculty at PWIs. The authors share key lessons that helped them be successful both within their organizations and within academe. Together, their stories demonstrate that diverse faculty should claim their narratives and use them to chart their experiences in higher education.

REFERENCES

Anderson, E. (2010). *Inclusive masculinity: The changing nature of masculinities.* Routledge.

Beech, N. (2011). Liminality and the practices of identity reconstruction. *Human Relations, 64*(2), 285-302.

Bigger, S. (2009). Victor Turner, liminality, and cultural performance. *Journal of Beliefs & Values, 30*(2), 209-212.

Bonner, F. A. (2011). Negotiating the 'in-between:' Liminality and the construction of racial identity among African American male collegians. *Journal of African American Males in Education* (JAAME), 2(2), 146-149.

Bonner, F. A., II, marbley, a. f., Tuitt, F., Robinson, P. A., Banda, R. M., & Hughes, R. L. (Eds.). (2014). *Black faculty in the academy: Narratives for negotiating identity and achieving career success.* Routledge.

Collins, P. H. (1989). The social construction of Black feminist thought. *Signs, 14*(4), 745-773.

Collins, P. H. (2021). Critical race theory. In G. Delanty & S. P. Turner (Eds.), *Routledge international handbook of contemporary social and political theory* (pp. 84-94). Routledge.

Connell, R. (2005). *Masculinities* (2nd ed.). Routledge. https://doi.org/10.4324/9781003116479.

Cooper, A. J. (1988). *A voice from the South.* Oxford University Press.

Cooper, M. (2000). Being the "go-to guy": Fatherhood, masculinity, and the organization of work in Silicon Valley. *Qualitative Sociology, 23*, 379-405. https://doi.org/10.1023/A:1005522707921.

Crenshaw, K. (1989). Demarginalizing the intersection of race and sex: A Black feminist critique of antidiscrimination doctrine, feminist theory and antiracist politics. *University of Chicago Legal Forum, 14*, 139-167.

Crenshaw, K. W. (2010). Twenty years of critical race theory: Looking back to move forward. *Connecticut Law Review, 43*(5), 1253-1352.

Curry, T. J. (2017). *The man-not: Race, class, genre, and the dilemmas of Black manhood.* Temple University Press.

Davis, A. Y. (1981). Reflections on the Black woman's role in the community of slaves. *The Black Scholar, 12*(6), 2–15. http://doi.org/10.1080/00064246.1981.11414214.

Delgado, R., & Stefancic, J. (1993). Critical race theory: An annotated bibliography. *Virginia Law Review, 79*(2), 461–516.

Delgado, R., & Stefancic, J. (2017). *Critical race theory: An introduction* (3rd ed.). New York University Press.

Dunbar-Nelson, A. M. (1988). I sit and I sew. In *The Works of Alice Dunbar-Nelson: Vol. 2* (pp. 972–975). Oxford University Press on Demand.

Fries-Britt, S., & Kelly, B. T. (2005). Retaining each other: Narratives of two African American women in the academy. *The Urban Review, 37*(3), 221–242. https://doi.org/10.1007/s11256-005-0006-2

Higgins, E. T. (2004). Making a theory useful: Lessons handed down. *Personality and Social Psychology Review, 8*(2), 138–145. https://doi.org/10.1207/s15327957pspr0802_7.

hooks, b. (1989). *Talking back: Thinking feminist, thinking Black.* South End Press.

Jackson, D. (2015). *Unmasking Masculinity: A Critical Autobiography.* Routledge. Original work published 1990.

Johnson, G. D. C. (1918). *The heart of a woman.* Comhill.

Jordan, J. (2021). *The essential June Jordan.* Copper Canyon Press.

Joyce, P. A., Quiros, L., & Waller, B. (2021). Honoring liminality: Teaching critical and race-gendered approaches in doctoral social work education. *Social Work Education.* Advance online publication. https://doi.org/10.1080/02615479.2021.1908986.

Kimmel, M. S., Hearn, J., & Connell, R. W. (Eds.). (2004). *Handbook of studies on men and masculinities.* Sage Publications.

Ladson-Billings, G. J. (1999). Preparing teachers for diverse student populations: A critical race theory perspective. *Review of Research in Education, 24*(1), 211–247.

Ladson-Billings, G. (with Tate, W. F.). (2016). Toward a critical race theory of education. In *Critical race theory in education* (pp. 10–31). Routledge.

Lerner, G. (Ed.). (1972). Black women speak of womanhood. In G. Lerner (Ed.), *Black women in White America: A documentary history.* Vintage Books.

Lorde, A. (1984). *Sister outsider: Essays and speeches.* Crossing Press.

Meyerson, D. (2003). *Tempered radicals: How everyday leaders inspire change at work.* Rutgers University Press.

Ntozake, S. (1977). *For colored girls who have considered suicide, when the rainbow is enuf: A choreopoem.* Book club ed. New York, MacMillan.

Patitu, C. L., & Hinton, K. G. (2003). The experiences of African American women faculty and administrators in higher education: Has anything changed? *New Directions for Student Services 2003*(104), 79–93.

Pegram, B., & Bonner, F. A. (2021, September 8). Code-switching to code stitching: Theorizing an alternative framework. *Diverse Issues in Higher Education.* https://www.diverseeducation.com/opinion/a rticle/15114454/codeswitching-tocodestitching-theorizing-analternativeframework.

Pelzer, D. L. (2016). Creating a new narrative: Reframing black masculinity for college men. *The Journal of Negro Education, 85*(1), 16-27.

Sleeter, C. E., & Delgado Bernal, D. (2003). Critical pedagogy, critical race theory, and antiracist education. In D. J. Flinders & S. J. Thornton (Eds.), *The curriculum studies reader* (3rd ed., pp. 298-311). Routledge. .

Solorzano, D. G. (1997). Images and words that wound: Critical race theory, racial stereotyping, and teacher education. *Teacher Education Quarterly, 24*(3), 5-19.

Solórzano, D., Ceja, M., & Yosso, T. (2000). Critical race theory, racial microaggressions, and campus racial climate: The experiences of African American college students. *Journal of Negro Education, 69*(1/2), 60-73.

Stanley, C. A. (2006). Coloring the academic landscape: Faculty of color breaking the silence in predominantly White colleges and universities. *American Educational Research Journal, 43*(4), 701-736.

Tate IV, W. F. (1997). Critical race theory and education: History, theory, and implications. *Review of Research in Education, 22*(1), 195-247.

Thompson, A. A., Peteraf, M. A., Gamble, J. E., Strickland, A. J. (2016). *Crafting and executing strategy : The quest for competitive advantage concepts and cases* (20th ed.). McGraw Hill.

Thompson, G. L., & Louque, A. (2005). *Exposing the "culture of arrogance" in the academy: A blueprint for increasing Black faculty satisfaction in higher education.* Stylus.

Tuitt, F., Hanna, M., Martinez, L. M., Salazar, M., & Griffin, R. (2009). Teaching in the line of fire: Faculty of color in the academy. *Thought & Action, 25*, 65-74.

Turner, C. S., & Myers Jr., S. L., (2000). *Faculty of color in academe: Bittersweet success.* Allyn & Bacon.

Turner, R. N., Hewstone, M., Voci, A., & Vonofakou, C. (2008). A test of the extended intergroup contact hypothesis: The mediating role of intergroup anxiety, perceived ingroup and outgroup norms, and inclusion of the outgroup in the self. *Journal of Personality and Social Psychology, 95*(4), 843-860. https://doi .org/10.1037/a0011434.

Turner, V. (1980). Social dramas and stories about them. *Critical inquiry, 7*(1), 141-168.

Walker, A. (1983). *In search of our mothers' gardens: Womanist prose.* Harcourt Brace Jovanovich.

Wels, H., Van der Waal, K., Spiegel, A., & Kamsteeg, F. (2011). Victor Turner and liminality: An introduction. *Anthropology Southern Africa, 34*(1-2), 1-4.

Whiting, G. W., & Lewis, T. (2008). On manliness: Black masculinity revisited. *AmeriQuests, 6*(1). https://doi.org/10.15695/amqst.v6i1.153.

Yosso, T. J. (2002). Toward a critical race curriculum. *Equity & Excellence in Education, 35*(2), 93-107.

10

Navigating the Tenure Track, Anti-CRT Rhetoric, and Red-State America

LARRY J. WALKER

Since 2019, we have witnessed the continued attack of Black scholars by conservative media and an influx of cases concerning the unfair treatment of Black scholars during the tenure and promotion process (Watson, 2020). Despite these recent challenges, Black academicians for decades have fought for, and received, tenure at predominantly White institutions (PWIs) of varying sizes (Arnold et al., 2021). While celebrating the accomplishments of Black scholars is important, they are frequently scarred by a process that can be unforgiving and littered with unwritten rules. Gaining tenure at PWIs is particularly problematic during a pandemic, insurrection, and racial reckoning. Some of the Black scholars seeking tenure apply concepts from critical race theory (CRT) in their work. CRT began as critical legal studies developed by legal scholars such as Derrick Bell and Richard Delgado. Other legal scholars, including Kimberlé Crenshaw (1989), expanded the concept by highlighting the impact the system has on Black women and others.

Exploring the lived experiences of a Black male professor during this turbulent time is critical. Currently, only 6% of professors are

Black; the number is evenly split between Black women (3%) and Black men (3%; US Department of Education, National Center for Education Statistics, 2020). The lower number in comparison to the overall US Black population (13%) highlights why the tenure-earning process can feel like navigating a maze. Black scholars have also had to confront some administrators, alumni, faculty, and students regarding critical issues inside and outside the ivory tower. Adams (2021, p. 184) asserts, "As Black scholars, we are more willing than most to move students to critically discuss how violence on Black men and boys is reproduced within academic and social spaces." Feeling responsible for initiating conversations regarding racism, maintaining relationships with faculty with different lived experiences, and meeting tenure guidelines can be difficult. Nonetheless, Black faculty face these issues while fighting against racial hostilities. For instance, we must advocate for causes on campus such as racial profiling while fending off social media attacks (Finley et al., 2018).

This chapter focuses on a red state because they are ideologically conservative states, they vote Republican in most elections, and they are at the center of the right-wing culture war. Not all red states are monoliths. For example, there are issues that occur in blue states that cause problems for Black faculty. However, two of the largest red states are led by individuals with extreme views. For instance, the governors of Florida (Rick DeSantis) and Texas (Greg Abbott) have sought national media attention by making public health decisions that are inconsistent with science, shutting down the US-Mexican border and sending migrants to Massachusetts, and making it difficult to discuss racism in educational settings. The decision by Florida to pass HB 7, known as the Stop WOKE Act, has made it challenging for Black scholars to discuss issues related to racism.

In this chapter, I will unpack red-state perceptions, attitudes, and political interference; examine extant literature to discuss anti-Blackness and CRT; utilize autoethnographic vignettes to investigate my lived experiences as a Black faculty member at a PWI in Florida; and conclude with implications for practice and policy. Overall, the chapter addresses vital issues and provides postsecondary institutions and researchers with solutions for retaining more Black male faculty members.

Literature Review

Red-State Perceptions, Attitudes, and Political Interference

Over the last several years the nation has been forced to reckon with how the lived experiences of the Black community differ from those of Whites. This includes the murders of Breonna Taylor and George Floyd, among others. Frequently their murders have galvanized civil rights organizations in the United States and led to large international protests. However, the fight to live a fear-free life by the Black community has been met with apprehension from some Whites.

For instance, a study of more than two thousand participants found that White conservative older men were likely to oppose movements like Black Lives Matter (Updegrove et al., 2020). This point is vital considering I currently teach in Florida, a red state with a large older population that voted for Donald Trump in the most recent presidential election. Often Florida's right-leaning politics have caused a national stir. For example, throughout his tenure, DeSantis has placed himself in the middle of typical red-state positions, including deemphasizing the importance of the COVID-19 vaccine and signing a bill that undermines local jurisdictions' ability to require masks (Krieg, 2021). Additionally, the state considered a bill that would allow college students to record professors to prevent political bias (Luscombe, 2021). Sponsors of the bill asserted that this was necessary to prevent professors from indoctrinating students.

Recently, several professors from the University of Florida sued the university because they were not allowed to testify in court against a voting bill passed by the state. The interference, the move to record professors, and steps to demonize CRT place me and others in a difficult position. I must worry about unfair political interference and criticism that could lead to the denial of tenure, online harassment, and in some cases threats. These challenges are unique to red states. Moreover,

I must publish, teach, and meet service requirements while navigating anti-Blackness.

Anti-Blackness and Higher Education

Recently researchers have considered how anti-Blackness permeates higher education. Dancy et al. (2018, p. 180) determined that "anti-Blackness names the ways in which the technologies and imaginations that allow a social recognition of the humanness of others systematically excludes this possibility for Black people." Specifically, the authors argue there is a connection between Blackness and property. They continue, "Anti-Blackness holds that the Black is not a relational being but is always already property" (p. 180). This concept of the ownership of Black bodies has endured for centuries. For example, after the Civil War, states in the South targeted formerly enslaved Africans with Black codes. The punitive policies forced African Americans into low-paying labor contracts, or they risked arrest. The labor data on pay equity between African Americans and Whites in higher education indicate that these compensation disparities persist (Li, 2019). For this reason, we must consider whether, and how, higher education can be fixed to meet the needs of Black professors.

Mustaffa (2017) explores the concept of violence and higher education from a historical perspective. The author considers how anti-Black oppression was and is used as a tool against Black people. In addition, Mustaffa repurposes the words *higher education* and *violence* to develop new phrasing: "I coin the term education violence to describe how marginalized people both in and outside of formal systems of schooling have had their lives limited and ended due to white supremacy" (p. 711). This point is underscored by PreK–12, higher education, and policing literature that highlights that African Americans encounter violence and trauma consistently throughout the life span (Henderson et al., 2019; Walker, 2015, 2021). Furthermore, Black researchers have consistently raised concerns regarding their treatment at postsecondary institutions (Overstreet, 2019). I believe we must investigate the relationship between perceived ownership of Black bodies, violence, and higher education.

The idea that higher education institutions can serve as places where Black people can experience violence, neglect, or isolation may seem inconsistent with depictions on television and in the movies. For example, while Netflix's *The Chair* examines the experiences of one Black woman navigating the tenure track at a PWI, the show does not highlight some of the horrific treatment Black women experience, including being bombarded with hate mail and receiving death threats. The vitriol directed at Black women who study and discuss race has forced some to close their social media accounts and alter their daily and weekly patterns to avoid violence. Ignoring these challenges will embolden individuals throughout the nation to attack Black women, which contributes to racial stressors.

Deconstructing the lived experiences of Black professors at PWIs is vital considering the ongoing dialogue regarding racism, White supremacy, and privilege in America (Nelson, 2020). Further, universities must consider how places viewed as bastions of liberalism can be racially hostile. Mustaffa (2017, p. 712) argues, "Scholars in and outside the field of higher education argue college and universities are both a reflection and an engine of racial hierarchy wherein White supremacy is central." This idea that White supremacy is embedded in higher education has been discussed by various researchers, including Haynes (2017).

While confronting the belief that institutions do not reflect, or embrace, ideas that are not centered in Whiteness is challenging, higher education can no longer run away from the increased hostility directed at minoritized faculty (Dutt-Ballerstadt, 2018). During the pandemic, political pundits, think tanks, websites, and other platforms have sought to disrupt the work of Black scholars by directing supporters to harass them constantly. Threatening the lives of academicians seeking to have an honest dialogue about documented events is not consistent with a healthy democracy.

Currently, the hysteria over examining the nation's history of enslaving Africans and creating Jim Crow post-Reconstruction is in overdrive. Some Americans are choosing to latch onto the belief that Black scholars are attempting to rewrite US history. More importantly, they have continued to attend school board meetings, harass Black college professors, confront policy makers, and create misconceptions that CRT is anti-American.

Critical Race Theory

Since the nation's inception, African Americans have sought to dismantle Whiteness (Patton & Haynes, 2020). Frequently this included challenging the legal system to remedy years of racist policies. Examples include successfully winning the *Brown v. Board of Education* case. The NAACP's Legal Defense Fund chief counsel Thurgood Marshall, among others, litigated a decision that ended de jure segregation in public schools.

After other civil rights achievements, such as the Voting Rights Act of 1965, legal scholars continued to critique the system. This included reconceptualizing how racism affects the legal system. As a result, critical legal studies was developed by a variety of scholars including Derrick Bell (Roithmayr, 2019). Eventually critical legal studies evolved into CRT and LatCrit, among other frameworks (Pérez Huber, 2010). According to Dixson (2018, p. 233), "CRT emerged as a response to the limitations of the class-only analysis by Critical Legal Scholars (CLS), who engaged a Marxist critique of U.S. jurisprudence. While not abandoning class as an explanatory factor, CRT scholars believed that the law played a specific role in reifying (and was often responsible for) racial subordination and inequity."

CRT has become one tool that researchers can use to examine racism in America. Solórzano (1998, p. 122) defines CRT as follows: "Specially, a critical race theory in education challenges the dominant discourse on race and racism as they relate to education by examining how educational theory, policy, and practice are used to subordinate certain racial and ethnic groups."

Researchers who focus on higher education have considered how CRT applies to the field. Patton (2016) asserts that CRT can be used to disrupt White supremacy. Patton argues that higher education is not the great equalizer in a society filled with inequities. In fact, the author suggests that "U.S. higher education, from its genesis, has been a primary force in persistent inequities" (p. 318). This point is important considering recent data that determined that Black males were less likely to return to postsecondary institutions because of the pandemic (National Student Clearinghouse Research Center, 2020). While school leaders could argue that the reasons are beyond their control, colleges have failed for years to create supportive environments that are welcoming to Black males. Similarly, Black professors have highlighted that they are consistently mistreated by administrators, colleagues, and students (Davis et al., 2021).

Other researchers (Hughes & Giles, 2010; Patton et al., 2015; Solórzano & Villalpando, 1998) have considered how CRT can be used to investigate the challenges faced by Black and other minoritized students and faculty. Challenging systems of oppression in the academy is important considering the dearth of Black faculty and administrators. The need to upend higher education is more urgent that ever because schools appear to be unwilling to protect Black researchers' free speech. For this reason, next I share my lived experiences as a Black academic at a PWI navigating racial resentment in a red state.

Autoethnographic Vignettes

Autoethnography allows researchers from underserved and marginalized communities to share their lived experiences without being filtered. According to Ellis et al. (2011, p. 273), "Autoethnography is an approach to research and writing that seeks to describe and systematically analyze (graphy) personal experiences (auto) in order to understand cultural experiences." Increasingly, Black scholars including Goings (2015), among others (Walker, 2016, 2019), have used autoethnography as a tool to convey vital points.

Since beginning my tenure-track career at the University of Central Florida in 2019, I have maintained a log of my experiences. I reviewed my writings, placed them in chronological order, and sorted them into themes. Each theme reflects my experiences and thoughts about the tenure-earning process. While I have teaching experience at another PWI, those insights are not included in any of the themes.

Throughout my adolescence and adulthood, hip-hop has played an important role in my life. The rhythms of my life have been and will continue to be influenced by the genre. Consequently, I developed the following themes in this chapter based on songs from the album *Fear of a Black Planet* by Public Enemy (1990), which include "Brothers Gonna Work It Out" and "Power to the People." Each section opens with a quote from the song that reflects my thoughts.

Brothers Gonna Work It Out

History shouldn't be a mystery.
Our stories real history.
Not his story.
We gonna work it one day.
—Public Enemy (1990)

The fight over CRT in red states has been instigated by individuals who are not interested in the nation's history of creating a race-based caste system. This is particularly true in Florida, which has witnessed thousands of lives lost to COVID-19 but has shifted to criticizing CRT. The visceral reaction to CRT is a bait and switch. Politicians in Florida and conservative television networks have asserted that CRT is destroying America and are seeking to eliminate any discussion of racism in textbooks, classrooms, or other public places. According to a news report, during a three-month period, Fox News mentioned CRT almost 1,300 times (LaHut, 2021). The alarming rate is concerning and feeds the anti-CRT rhetoric. Florida, similar to other red states, has made it clear that anyone who studies or discusses CRT will face ramifications.

My work is centered on examining how racism affects the lives of Black people. Further, I have used CRT as a framework and cited CRT scholars. This means that I could become a target of local, state, and national pundits who view my work as anti-American. Since my arrival on campus, I have kept notes on this topic and wondered who would come to my defense. For example, in one journal entry I stated, "Over the last several weeks I have seen Black professors post on social media that they are being threatened because someone posted a comment on a website" (May 2020). The thought that we are experiencing modern-day McCarthyism is troubling.

Unfortunately, this is an ongoing problem that Black scholars throughout the country must face. A few months later I wondered what my future as a faculty member in a red state would look like long term. I asked, "Will my work be accepted, or will I have to fight off (on my own) a mob of ideologues that do not care about my research?" (August 2020). Despite the challenges, I believe in telling America's history. This belief could eventually cause researchers, Florida policy makers, and others to misinterpret my work and could endanger my career.

Earlier this year I considered what Black professors had to endure in the past. Specifically, I wondered, "What was it like to teach at a PWI in the 1960s and 1970s?" I continued, "They did not have access to social media or other support systems which could inspire people to rally around them" (January 2021). The fight over defining US history has reached a boiling point. This is particularly true in a red state like Florida that is seeking to ban CRT and prevent discussions about important events. Consequently, facts that most historians would view as clear, including what caused the Civil War, are no longer considered accurate. Now, we live in a society where phrases including "alternative facts" and "misinformation" have become commonplace.

In December 2020, I lamented what the future could look like for a country that denies its own history. "The fight to rewrite how Africans were enslaved and how Black people continue to be treated is enraging. What will happen when children believe that the country has always been fair to everyone?" Regrettably, we are already witnessing what misinformed Americans will believe. For instance, the infatuation with the Confederate flag points to how millions of people feel about Blackness. Further, if I continue to conduct research centered on Blackness, I could face resistance from school leaders who would prefer to avoid drawing the attention of the governor and other policy makers. However, changing my research agenda and ignoring US history is counter to my belief that the nation must redress years of violence aimed at Black people.

Power to the People

Had to kick it like that as we roll as one.
One under the sun, to all the cities and to the side.
Brothers and sister stateside and the whole wide world.
—PUBLIC ENEMY (1990)

The last few years have been difficult for Black scholars. Our work has been unfairly attacked, some have not received adequate support from their institutions, and others have encountered intense online harassment. While the period has been challenging, I feel fortunate to have support on and off campus from colleagues. For example, my department chair (a Black woman) made my transition to the university seamless. When I had questions or faced issues, she immediately identified solutions and offered support. I noted this point: "Whenever I need help or feedback Dr. Jones [pseudonym] has always been there for support" (May 2021).

While the support of the department chair has been important, I have encountered race-based stressors, such as when a colleague suggested (to me and another Black colleague) "there was a time when we would not be allowed" to talk in a room alone. The episode was surprising, and we both needed time to process the interaction. Sadly, I have experienced other incidents that would be considered microaggressions, but if you are Black and teach in higher education, these events can become commonplace.

Implications and Conclusion

The insights from my autoethnographic vignettes can help postsecondary institutions retain Black professors. However, they must be willing to undergo self-reflection, listen to Black faculty, improve the culture, and fund initiatives that identify talented individuals. In the first vignette, "Brothers Gonna Work It Out," I examined the challenges teaching in a red state that is openly hostile to CRT. Florida is one of a growing list of states that have adopted language that prevents CRT from being taught in PreK–12 schools. The mandate was signed by Ron DeSantis, although CRT has never been taught in Florida's public schools. I believe the new language is the first step to attacking Black professors, including me, who use CRT as a framework. The bill mirrors efforts by other red states to ban CRT.

Red states like Florida cannot expect to recruit Black male scholars to work in the state if there are rules and regulations focused on preventing a specific worldview. Institutions in Florida should consider collecting and reviewing campus climate data to determine whether Black faculty feel welcomed and valued. Additionally, schools must develop crisis-management plans that aim to support faculty when their research is under attack. Far too many schools have been unwilling or slow to respond to the increasingly hostile right-wing rhetoric.

In the second vignette, "Power to the People," I described the important role mentorship plays in my tenure journey, such as that of my department chair. However, I have encountered racism on campus. Overall, the university should ensure all administrators, faculty, and staff receive comprehensive training to properly interact with Black faculty.

I hope my thoughts lead to a shift in the way colleges retain Black male faculty members by funding programs focused on their short- and long-term needs and creating empowering places for them to engage in research uninhibited by larger political forces. Indeed, like other Americans, Black male professors have endured a difficult time in higher education and expect postsecondary institutions to be reflective and supportive.

REFERENCES

Adams, R. (2021). Teaching activism as a pre-tenured Black male faculty member in White academe. *Urban Social Work, 5*(3), 180–194.

Arnold, N., Osanloo, A. F., & Sherman Newcomb, W. (2021). Paying professional taxes for promotion and tenure: The costs of justice work for Black faculty. *Journal of Research on Leadership Education.* Advance online publication. https://doi.org/10.1177/19427751211002220.

Crenshaw, K. (1989). Demarginalizing the intersection of race and sex: A Black feminist critique of antidiscrimination doctrine, feminist theory and antiracist politics. *University of Chicago Legal Forum, 1989,* 139–167.

Dancy, T. E., Edwards, K. T., & Davis, E. J. (2018). Historically White universities and plantation politics: Anti-Blackness and higher education in the Black Lives Matter era. *Urban Education, 53*(2), 176–195.

Davis, C. H., Hilton, A., Hamrick, R., & Brooks, F. E. (2021). Black professorship: The beauty and the beast. In C. H. Davis, A. Hilton, R. Hamrick, & F. E. Brooks (Eds.), *The beauty and the burden of being a Black professor* (pp.1–6). Emerald.

Dixson, A. D. (2018). "What's going on?": A critical race theory perspective on Black Lives Matter and activism in education. *Urban Education, 53*(2), 231–247.

Dutt-Ballerstadt, R. (2018). Are you supporting White supremacy? *Inside Higher Education,* January 12, 2018. https://digitalcommons.linfield.edu/cgi /viewcontent.cgi?article=1075&context=englfac_pubs.

Ellis, C., Adams, T. E., & Bochner, A. P. (2011). Autoethnography: An overview. *Historical Social Research / Historische Sozialforschung, 36*(4), 273–290.

Finley, S. C., Gray, B. M., & Martin, L. L. (2018). "Affirming our values": Black scholars, White virtual mobs, and the complicity of White university adminis- trators. *AAUP Journal of Academic Freedom, 9,* 1–20.

Goings, R. B. (2015). The lion tells his side of the (counter) story: A Black male educator's autoethnographic account. *Journal of African American Males in Education, 6*(1), 91–105.

Haynes, C. (2017). Dismantling the White supremacy embedded in our classrooms: White faculty in pursuit of more equitable educational outcomes for racially minoritized students. *International Journal of Teaching and Learning in Higher Education, 29*(1), 87–107.

Henderson, D. X., Walker, L. J., Barnes, R., Lunsford, A., Edwards, C., & Clark, C. (2019). A framework for race related trauma in the public education system and implications for Black youth. *Journal of School Health, 89*(11), 926–933.

Hughes, R., & Giles, M. (2010). CRiT walking in higher education: Activating critical race theory in the academy. *Race Ethnicity and Education, 13*(1), 41–57.

Krieg, G. (2021). Ron DeSantis leans into mask mandate fights as COVID cases soar in Florida. CNN Politics, August 20, 2021. https://www.cnn.com/2021/08/20 /politics/ron-desantis-masks-florida-schools-covid-19/index.html.

LaHut, J. (2021). Fox news has mentioned "critical race theory" nearly 1300 times since March, according to watchdog study. *Business Insider,* June 15, 2021.

https://www.businessinsider.com/fox-news-critical-race-theory-mentions -thousand-study-2021-6.

Li, D. (2019). *Three essays on economics of higher education.* Doctoral dissertation, University of Missouri-Columbia.

Luscombe, R. (2021). Florida bill would allow students to record professors to show political bias. *Guardian,* April 25, 2021. https://www.theguardian.com/us-news /2021/apr/25/florida-bill-record-professors-universities.

Mustaffa, J. B. (2017). Mapping violence, naming life: A history of anti-Black oppression in the higher education system. *International Journal of Qualitative Studies in Education, 30*(8), 711-727.

National Student Clearinghouse Research Center. (2020). COVID-19: Stay informed with the latest enrollment information. https://nscresearchcenter.org/stay -informed/.

Nelson, C. (2020). *"They're protecting Whiteness and their fragility is showing": How feminist praxis disrupts White supremacy in neoliberal predominately White institutions.* Doctoral dissertation, University of Wisconsin-Milwaukee.

Overstreet, M. (2019). My first year in academia *or* the mythical Black woman superhero takes on the ivory tower. *Journal of Women and Gender in Higher Education, 12*(1), 18-34.

Patton, L. D. (2016). Disrupting postsecondary prose: Toward a critical race theory of higher education. *Urban Education, 51*(3), 315-342.

Patton, L. D., Harper, S. R., & Harris, J. (2015). Using critical race theory to (re)interpret widely studied topics related to students in US higher education. In A. M. Martínez-Alemán, B. Pusser, & E. M. Bensimon (Eds.) *Critical approaches to the study of higher education: A practical introduction* (pp. 193-219). Johns Hopkins University Press.

Patton, L. D., & Haynes, C. (2020). Dear White people: Reimagining Whiteness in the struggle for racial equity. *Change: The Magazine of Higher Learning, 52*(2), 41-45.

Pérez Huber, L. (2010). Using Latina/o critical race theory (LatCrit) and racist nativism to explore intersectionality in the educational experiences of undocumented Chicana college students. *Educational Foundations, 24,* 77-96.

Public Enemy. (1990). *Fear of a Black planet.* Def Jam Recordings.

Roithmayr, D. (2019). Introduction to critical race theory in educational research and praxis. In L. Parker, D. Deyhle, & S. Villenas (Eds.), *Race is . . . race isn't: Critical race theory and qualitative studies in education* (pp. 1-6). Routledge.

Solórzano, D. G. (1998). Critical race theory, race and gender microaggressions, and the experience of Chicana and Chicano scholars. *International Journal of Qualitative Studies in Education, 11*(1), 121-136.

Solórzano, D. G., & Villalpando, O. (1998). Critical race theory, marginality, and the experience of students of color in higher education. *Sociology of Education: Emerging Perspectives, 21,* 211-222.

Updegrove, A. H., Cooper, M. N., Orrick, E. A., & Piquero, A. R. (2020). Red states and Black lives: Applying the racial threat hypothesis to the Black Lives Matter movement. *Justice Quarterly, 37*(1), 85-108.

US Department of Education, National Center for Education Statistics. (2020). *The condition of education 2020*. NCES 2020-144. National Center for Education Statistics.

Walker, L. J. (2015). Trauma, environmental stressors, and the African-American college student: Research, practice, and HBCUs. Penn Center for Minority Serving Institutions, Philadelphia. https://cmsi.gse.rutgers.edu/sites/default /files/Walker%20Research%20Brief%20%28final%29.pdf.

Walker, L. J. (2016). Why are we all here? Reflections of an African-American male. *Illinois Schools Journal*, 95(2), 104–126.

Walker, L. J. (2019). Strengthening the Black male teacher pipeline at HBCUs: Recruitment, retention, and breaking down barriers. In C. Rinke & L. MaWhinney (Eds.), *Opportunities and challenges in teacher recruitment and retention: Teachers' voices across the pipeline*. Information Age.

Walker, L. J. (2021). Why don't you see me? Meeting the mental health needs of Black male students. *New Educator*, 17(3), 264–280. https://doi.org/10.1080 /1547688X.2021.1909788.

Watson, J. (2020). The peculiar tenure denial of Dr. Paul Harris. *Diverse Issues in Higher Education*, June 23, 2020. https://www.diverseeducation.com /demographics/african-american/article/15107155/the-peculiar-tenure-denial -of-dr-paul-harris.

11

A Double Minority in Higher Education

The Intersection of Blackness and a Stuttering
Disability on the Tenure Track

ANTONIO L. ELLIS

> There is no such thing as a single-issue struggle because we do
> not live single-issue lives.   —AUDRE LORDE

Kimberlé W. Crenshaw (1989) coined the term *intersectionality* to refer to the specific oppression Black women face. Intersectionality argues that Black women, on account of being both Black and women, face oppression at the intersection of those two things (Crenshaw, 1989). The way disability intersects with anti-Blackness is slightly different because it is much easier to make disability invisible and completely erase it from the narrative. The role that disability has played in the lives of many famous Black people, such as Harriet Tubman, Emmett Till, and Audre Lorde, is regularly ignored, which further deprives Black people of representation. For example, Till was a Black boy who was brutally murdered in 1955 for allegedly wolf-whistling at a White woman. However, his stuttering disability is an important piece of the story that is consistently left out. When he experienced dysfluency, he would whistle to relax and help control his breathing. In Till's case, anti-Blackness and racism cannot be separated from disability. Likewise, in this chapter, I attempt to uncover the ways anti-Blackness intersects with disability among African American males with stuttering disabilities while they pursue tenured professorships at colleges and universities. This chapter uses autoethnography to critically analyze the personal and professional life experiences of a Black male tenure-track professor. Autoethnography is a research method that uses personal experience to describe and interpret cultural text, beliefs, experiences, and practices (Bochner & Ellis, 2016, p. 111).

Anti-Blackness and Disabilities

Anti-Blackness is central to understanding the ongoing conditions of Black life in North America. Anti-Blackness manifests in the exclusion of Black people from humanity—exclusion that is foundational to the structure of the Euro-Western concept of Man (Wynter, 2003). The brutality and ubiquity of anti-Blackness endure in a myriad of ways, including "skewed life chances, limited access to health and education, premature death, incarceration, and impoverishment" (Hartman, 2007, p. 6). I argue that anti-Blackness cannot be detached from the intersecting life experiences of Black people with disabilities. These experiences are not an either-or but instead both-and, as they are inextricably intertwined.

Minority Populations and Tenure-Track Positions

The ability of institutions of higher education to remain accessible and relevant is largely dependent on the nation's faculty. As they serve in these institutions, faculty members juggle hefty workloads while contributing to the human stores of knowledge in ways that are applicable and vital to their communities (Boyer, 1990). Among the demands they face is the education of diverse populations of students. Boyer's (1990) definition of diversity for America's student body references race, ethnicity, and gender. In his definition, he also considers students who are dual language learners and those with physical disabilities. If higher education institutions are to remain committed to effectively meeting the needs of diverse student populations, it is incumbent on them to create welcoming spaces for qualified diverse faculty of all races, genders, ethnicities, and abilities. Arguably, fully embracing the diversity among tenure-track faculty applicants during the interview and hiring process is a means to this end.

In many instances, the pool of diverse tenure-track faculty is limited to faculty of color and women faculty. The benefits of an academic community that is inclusive of faculty of color and women faculty are well documented in scholarly research. Race and gender scholars have noted how faculty from these collective backgrounds contribute to the educational experience and environment for all students (Ellis et al., 2016; Hutchison, 2009; Turner, 2002). The common rationale for recruiting a diverse faculty pool in higher education institutions is its positive impact on minority student populations, and the breadth of expansive knowledge they embody (American Society for Higher Education, 2009; Turner, 2002). While colleges and universities continue to increase the enrollment of students of color and women, these students are continuously surrounded by faculty and administrators who are largely White or male.

Nevertheless, the presence of and interaction with faculty of color and women faculty helps students from similar backgrounds understand what is possible for their own aspirations. These faculty members also become mentors, confidants, and guides as students find their own way in an academic world that is substantially different from that of their White male peers (Pascarella & Terenzini, 1991). Service by minority faculty in this capacity provides students of color and women students various forms of social capital to support their success in the academy, and ultimately their success when navigating diverse environments and organizations upon graduation (Yosso, 2005). Moreover, faculty of color and women faculty contribute significantly to the traditional majority students' academic engagement and achievement. As society continues to evolve, it is important that students be able to navigate various cultures in order to maximize their success (American Society for Higher Education,

2009). As diversity among faculty increases, more students will be exposed to various realities that they most likely will encounter when they enter the workforce.

Not only do colleges and universities prepare students to become productive citizens in society, but they also serve as an incubator for showcasing the vast array of diversity within humanity. Intellectual growth happens when new research is developed by individuals with various perspectives and life experiences (Turner, 2002). Limiting the amount of diversity at colleges and universities will ultimately limit what can be known and the ways in which it can be known. When selected populations are not welcomed to serve as faculty at higher education institutions, this act of overt discrimination diminishes these institutions' ability to contribute in relevant ways to an evolving global society (American Society for Higher Education, 2009). In 1990, Boyer made a clarion call to colleges and universities to broaden their horizons regarding faculty recruitment, with the goal of strengthening relationships among students and faculty. Referring to the "intolerably small pool" of underrepresented faculty, Boyer described the current state of affairs as a "shocking weakness," if not an indictment, of American education (p. 66).

More than thirty years have passed since this call was issued. Boyer's (1990) challenge to higher education to diversify the tenure-track faculty pool was tenacious and courageous. If higher education institutions are to substantially respond to Boyer's call, they must first face the harsh reality behind what is keeping members of underrepresented communities from entering academia as faculty members. Beyond Boyer's interrogation of diversity and equity among faculty, employment discrimination toward potential faculty and faculty with disabilities is also a matter of regulatory importance (US Department of Justice, n.d.). While significant research exists that sheds light on insufficient representation and toxic environments for faculty of color and women faculty, their remains a lack of scholarship centering the absence of faculty with disabilities, as well as the work environments that often prohibit their growth and upward mobility when they are members of the faculty (Dancy et al., 2018; Trower & Chait, 2002). In this chapter, I argue that the tenure-track faculty interview process is biased and discriminatory toward people with a stuttering disability, with a laser focus on African American males who stutter.

Correcting the Individuals with Disabilities Education Act

The Individuals with Disabilities Education Act defined speech and language impairment as a "communication disorder, such as stuttering, impaired articulation, a language impairment, or voice impairment, that adversely affects a child's educational performance" (Ellis & Hartlep, 2017). The definition implies that people who are speech and language impaired are automatically adversely affected simply by having this disability. In other words, they have lost the game before they begin to play. However, I argue that being speech and language impaired alone does not result in adverse effects on a person's educational performance. The educational environment, social spaces, and discriminatory practices, paired with a lack of institutional tolerance and understanding, contribute to people's low self-esteem, self-worth, and expectations. These factors, therefore, adversely affect their ability to achieve at the level of their peers who are not speech and language impaired. Researchers suggest that people who find school uninviting are more likely to become academically disengaged (Anderman, 2003; Wesley & Ellis, 2017).

Furthermore, other studies (Zhang et al., 2007) contend that academic disengagement has a direct impact on dropout rates, delinquency, and poor adult outcomes. Strategies to address the needs of people who are speech impaired can help ameliorate these situations. Much of the existing research on speech and language impairments, particularly stuttering, does not focus directly on the African American male population. The lack of scholarly publications and knowledge about this population is particularly troubling.

The experiences of African American males with a stuttering disability as they seek tenure-track faculty positions have been largely unheard. Their experiences with racism, marginalization, and employment discrimination have the propensity to reinforce negative beliefs about higher education institutions. These beliefs have not been the focus of qualitative scholarship and are undertheorized. Therefore, this chapter focuses directly on the tenure-track job-interviewing experiences of African American males who have a stuttering disability. Understanding the lived experiences of this group of males can help higher education department chairs, deans, faculty search committees, and human resources specialists provide resources and create policies to level the playing field through equitable and fair employment practices.

History and Definitions of Stuttering

Stuttering has provoked thought by scholars for centuries. The primary documented reports of stuttering trace back to the Egyptian empire (2000 B.C.) and may be found in Egyptian hieroglyphics. Furthermore, Moses, in the Old Testament (1350–1200 B.C.) of the Bible (Shapiro, 1999), employed the coping strategy of having his brother verbally communicate for him. However, the cause of stuttering remains a mystery (Guitar, 2006, p. 5). For centuries, investigators attempted to fully understand the disability while searching for cures. Over the years, people who stutter have experienced depression, low self-esteem, impatience, negative reactions, and unflattering portrayals in television shows, music, theater, and society at large (Guitar 1998; Perkins, 1990). Scientists still investigate what causes stuttering and have several clues. These include familial histories and the discovery that stuttering typically begins in children between the ages of two and five (Guitar, 2006, p. 6).

The definition of stuttering varies because of the many variables that are part of this communication disorder. Traditionally, stuttering has been viewed as a disorder in which the "rhythm" or fluency of speech is impaired by interruptions or blockages (Bloodstein & Ratner, 2008, p. 1). It is a disorder with several possible subtypes (Yairi, 2007). People who stutter will have involuntary disruptions to the fluency of their speech, consisting largely of syllable repetitions, prolongations, blockage of sounds, substitutions, and avoidance of words (Craig & Hancock, 1996). Stuttering is also described as a multifactorial disorder having affective, behavioral, and cognitive components (Yaruss & Quesal, 2004).

Stuttering's Impact on Quality of Life

Several researchers suggest that ethnic, cultural, and racial factors have an impact on the life experiences of people who have a stuttering disability (Flynt & Morton, 2004; Matthews & Daniels, 2019). Disability studies indicate that, for students with disabilities, social experiences at school are different from those of students without disabilities (Chen et al., 2020; Israelite et al., 2002). However, rarely do studies include the combination of race and gender factors for people who stutter (Leigh & Mims, 1975; Ressa et al., 2021; Van Keulen et al., 1998).

The notion that society treats people differently based on their disability has direct implications within educational settings for students who stutter, as they interact with others who may exhibit biases through institutional stereotypes, policies, and practices. People who stutter are often susceptible to stereotypes, identity issues, and both internal and external conflicts. Cochran and Stewart (1998), for example, conducted a qualitative study that consisted of eight adult participants who stutter. They found that, "since the cause of stuttering was unknown, these participants were left without a legitimate explanation for its presence in their lives. Lacking an explanation, they blamed themselves and assumed the guilt of their stuttering" (p. 255).

Considering the lack of qualitative studies regarding Black culture and stuttering, one might conclude that stuttering is an issue that is kept silent in mainstream Black society. Further, regarding African American men who stutter, the literature is absent. Much of the current literature on Black men—while valuable in offering knowledge on race, academic achievement, and contemporary issues—often fails to examine the impact of communication disorders such as slurring, stammering, or stuttering.

Educational and Social Experience

Research has found that those who stutter are teased by peers (Blood & Blood, 2004, 2007; Ellis & Hartlep, 2017; Hugh-Jones & Smith, 1999). The literature suggests that bullying may be experienced by a substantial number of children who stutter during school-age years and adolescence at rates higher than those for children who do not stutter. For individuals who stutter, "negative reactions from others can be seen during communication interactions beginning even at preschool age and may persist throughout the child's future school experiences" (Blood et al., 2010). Langevin et al. (1998) obtained self-reported data from twenty-eight children who stutter and found that 57% were teased or bullied about their stuttering, and 81% self-reported that they were upset about being teased or bullied. Hugh-Jones and Smith (1999) surveyed 267 adults who stutter and found that 83% of the respondents reported being bullied when they were in school. Blood and Blood (2004) obtained data from fifty-three adolescents who stutter and fifty-three adolescents who do not stutter and found that 43% of the adolescents who stutter had experienced bullying in the previous week compared with only 11% of adolescents who do not stutter.

In a qualitative study of adolescents who stutter, Hearne et al. (2008) reported that only 15% of their sample reported being teased or mocked in association with stuttering. However, the data showed that participants experienced being teased more frequently in primary school. Logan et al. (2008) highlighted that students who stutter are reported to be victims of mean-spirited teasing, name calling, and demeaning remarks or bullying. Blood and Blood (2007) conducted a study of eighteen children who stuttered and eighteen children who did not stutter. Sixty-one percent of children who stutter were reported as having a significantly higher risk of experiencing bullying behavior than the children who did not stutter. Shames and Rubin (1986) reported that the most common attitudes expressed by stutterers were anxiety, helplessness, victimization, and low self-esteem. Victims of bullying in schools can also experience academic difficulties including decreased concentration and learning (Menesini & Salmivalli, 2017; Sharp & Smith, 1994), increased school failure, and higher school dropout rates (Flennaugh, 2016; Sharp, 1995).

They are also at increased risk for emotional and mental health problems such as depression and anxiety (Chen et al., 2020; Juvonen et al., 2003), poorer social skills, and lower self-esteem (Dahlbeck & Lightsey, 2008; Fox & Boulton, 2005). Hawker and Boulton (2000) reported that these negative social and emotional consequences experienced by victims at early ages often persist years after the actual bullying occurs. Anxiety disorders have been reported as more common in children with communication disorders (Beitchman et al., 2001). Furthermore, studies suggest that children and youths with anxiety disorders may be at higher risk for educational underachievement, depression, poorer social support networks, and increased family conflicts (Ameringen et al., 2003; Nail et al., 2015; Velting et al., 2004).

Firsthand Account: Intersecting My Blackness and Disability

The intrinsic realities and feelings of the vast majority of African American males who stutter are best conveyed by Pitts (2009). He states, "In a new environment without the comfort of people who knew me well, I slipped back into my pattern of silence to avoid the shame of stammering and stuttering" (p. 99).

As I reflect on my lived experiences as an African American male pursuing tenure-track faculty positions at colleges and universities, the power of the message behind those words reverberates within my consciousness. Given my position as an emerging scholar in the field of higher education and as one who aims to lay a new foundation within the academy, I am challenged to revisit my epistemological commencement as a way to evaluate my sources of knowledge, my perspectives on the world, and, more importantly, my experience-based beliefs about the discriminatory treatment of African American male faculty and potential faculty who are speech and language impaired, particularly those who stutter.

As a child who avoided verbal communication because of my stuttering disability, I carefully navigated school buildings in the urban communities in which I was raised. I recall being teased and bullied by teachers and students alike. Now, as an adult who is pursuing tenure at a university, I find myself navigating the tenure-track process the same way I went about surviving in the K–12 environment as a child. In addition, I also witness how stuttering directly affects other African American males' ability to obtain tenure-track faculty positions at colleges and universities. According to personal conversations I have had with my peers who stutter, the process of interviewing tenure-track faculty automatically places our population at a disadvantage for obtaining these positions. For example, the process typically requires candidates to give an hour-long research presentation, provide a sample lesson delivery, and participate in meetings with various stakeholders within a particular department and sometimes the larger university. In total, this interview process requires at least three to four hours of verbal communication. While accommodations are often made that allow people who are speech impaired to respond to interview questions through forms of writing, it stills creates feelings of abnormality during the interview process in undeniable ways.

As an African American male emerging scholar who is on the cusp of earning tenure at a university, I represent the potential embedded within my peers who are marginalized within various higher education spaces. As a result of having supportive peers and senior scholar mentors who, in my early academic development, recognized my potential abilities and nurtured my dreams and desires, I have been able to overcome barriers. My doctoral dissertation chair, for example, demanded that I never give up in the face of adversity and what I perceived to be hopelessness. Therefore, I am motivated by a fierce sense of self-empowerment, a desire to empower others who are marginalized, a passion for educational achievement, and a sense of responsibility to mobilize speech-impaired people who experience hopelessness and have lost the strength to advocate for themselves. The discriminatory tenure-track interview process played a significant role in my tenacity as a junior faculty member and created a passion within me to interrogate the interview process through my scholarship and public advocacy for my peers.

My desire to advocate for marginalized groups has a sturdy religious base. My first advanced degree is in theological studies. Besides my mentors within the academy, my other mentor is my pastor. I sought a theological degree hoping to gain a better understanding of my experiences as an African American male who stutters. During my matriculation in divinity school, I gained a deeper understanding of my experiences by studying the writings of contemporary authors such as Cain Hope Felder, Martin Luther King Jr., Marcus Garvey, Reinhold Niebuhr, and Fannie Lou Hamer. Regardless of their various perspectives, all of them dedicated their lives to standing proxy on behalf of minority groups who were marginalized by dominant cultures. Therefore, my spiritual, religious, and theological base represents an extensive number of social and Black nationalist movements that were dedicated to altering racism, dominance, sexism, ageism, and White supremacy within the US context.

It is my belief that one of the most influential tools for providing positive change in the life of disenfranchised populations is education and the acquisition of knowledge. However, there is a possibility that an educational structure embedded in fluency-dominated cultures, where the "gift of gab" is used to maintain social and economic power, can be seen as an advantage to the dominant culture. In the discriminatory tenure-track faculty interview process, having a terminal degree, admirable work ethic, robust research agenda, and reputable scholarly publications is often not adequate for a person with a stuttering disability. Instead, the ability to verbally promote yourself is often what impresses the search committee and ultimately leads to being offered the position. Those who are nonfluent often live in poverty and are positioned at the bottom of the social ladder due to the lack of reasonable accommodations, patience, and acceptance by those who are more fluent (Ellis & Hartlep, 2017). I argue that these adulthood experiences can be traced back to K–12 schools.

Educators in K–12 schools rarely highlight African American males who stutter and have excelled in various careers so that male students who stutter can gain inspiration. For example, throughout my educational journey in higher education, I never met a tenured professor with a stuttering disability. This indirectly lowered my confidence that becoming a tenured professor is possible. To only teach a child, particularly an African American male who stutters, the accomplishments and contributions of nonstutterers creates a sense of doubt and hopelessness that he cannot achieve his goals in life. Human beings tend to be motivated by what we can see, hear, taste, touch, and smell (Ignatow, 2007). The absence of mention lowers our expectations and diminishes our idea of possibilities. Therefore, I have been challenged to respond to a pressing question: What is the role of K–12 educators and higher education scholars in educating and supporting African American males who stutter?

This question has been instrumental in my decision to become a tenured professor, educational leader, and forerunner on behalf of people who stutter, focusing on African American males. My greatest accomplishment thus far has been my presence in urban school buildings, higher education classrooms, and academic conferences. As an educator and advocate, I am charged with motivating people who stutter who live the same realities that I did as a child and as an adult. My obligation is to assist them in developing strength and boldness to pursue their dreams in the face of multiple barriers, such as those presented during the tenure-track faculty interview process. I have had the privilege and honor of meeting some of the most talented, intelligent, and bright minds who are silent voices in society. They possess an undeniable glow that demands attention and validation, which I wholeheartedly give. While spending time with them in the classroom, I reflected on my own experiences and realities. It is because of my students that I realized the significance of my own life history, and I now embrace healing through advocating for those who face the same obstacles. It is for this reason that this chapter focuses on the life experiences of African American males who, like me, have endured educational, social, and environmental challenges in K–12 schools as students and in higher education as scholars who are on the tenure track.

I am deeply committed to uncovering the barriers within higher education institutions that prohibit African American male scholars from pursuing and obtaining tenure, with a focus on those with a stuttering disability. As previously mentioned, much of my success in higher education is a result of the mentorship of senior scholars and the unwavering support of my junior faculty peers. For example, senior scholars William Tate, Gloria Ladson-Billings, Robert T. Palmer, and Rich Milner, among several others, have actively supported my pursuit of becoming a tenured professor. On the other hand, junior scholars such as Nathaniel Bryan, Nicholas D. Hartlep, and Lisa Maria Grillo have been instrumental in keeping me encouraged. They provide positive role models for what empathy looks like within the academy. However, before encountering these mentors and supporters, my experiences with higher education faculty were the opposite, which led me to experience low self-esteem and a lack of self-worth. As a former K–12 teacher, and a current tenure-track professor, I realize that many African American males who stutter are in search of positive mentors and allies who are empathetic and serve as advocates.

The personal relationships that I developed with African American males who stutter through my work as a researcher, educator, and peer and my experiences as a person who stutters have been extremely rewarding. I have come to understand and embrace the significance of our lives and relationships. I realize that my interest in their perspectives is deeply ingrained in the fact that I am emotionally and culturally connected and personally invested in their lives and well-being. I was reared in communities that are similar to theirs. In addition, I understand and identify with their struggles, concerns, pains, and cultural codes. Using my personal stories, experiences, and humor, I work diligently to relate to their everyday lives.

Considering my upbringing as a student influenced by social and political movements like the civil rights movement and the Black Panther Party, I feel a fierce sense of urgency in eradicating systems of inequality, suppression, oppression, and marginalization like those seen within the tenure-track faculty interview process. Therefore, my intellectual contribution to the field of education will also be to give support to the expansion of novel, innovative, and critical theoretical frameworks. West (1993), in his article "The Dilemma of the Black Intellectual," refers to a new "regime of truth" that challenges scholars of color to analyze and critically examine the unique experiences of African Americans. I have developed a deep commitment to interrogating the tenure-track faculty hiring process so that more African American males who stutter will feel confident about pursuing such positions, without feeling automatically disadvantaged because of their race and disability.

It is critical that more scholarship is dedicated to developing systems of support that offers possibilities for helping African American males to be successful in higher education and in the larger society. An examination of these "possibilities for success" is meant to be a catalyst and prototype for disrupting discriminatory institutional practices in higher education with regard to the absence of this population within the ranks of tenure and tenure-track faculty. My goal is to deconstruct and challenge the status quo within higher education that has produced centuries of negative experiences for people who stutter and to identify fair and equitable systems and processes. Dillard (2000), Scheurich and Young (1997), and West (1993) all urge Black scholars to be bold enough to embrace their stance as African Americans within the academy and to deliberately focus on the mobility of Black people. Amid scholarship that gives direct attention to African American males who stutter, I hope that additional research paradigms and peer-reviewed scholarship will emerge to address and alleviate challenges while shedding light on the success stories of African American males who stutter and have achieved tenured professorships within higher education.

Embracing Diversity in Higher Education

The stuttering community has been largely ignored in academic research regarding obtaining tenure-track positions. While writing this chapter, I could not find a single scholarly or nonscholarly publication on this topic. In addition to focusing on the importance of ensuring that faculty of color and women faculty are within the ranks of tenured professors, I invite the higher education community to also create welcoming and affirming spaces for people with disabilities. It is critical to understand the issues and perspectives of other underrepresented communities regarding the tenure-track hiring process. In light of the lack of representation of African American males who stutter in tenure-track and tenured faculty roles, combined with the African American male students who stutter in the university setting, I encourage institutions to hire Black male tenure-track faculty who stutter to serve as role models for this population of students.

Valuing Black Scholars, Black Scholarship, and Intersectionality

Due to the centrality and all-encompassing nature of Whiteness as the standard in higher education, it can be extremely difficult for Black scholars to gain opportunities to pursue and earn tenure without modifying their research agenda to accommodate Whiteness. The normativity of White supremacy in higher education continues to serve as a barrier for Black tenure-track professors, as the faculty recruitment and tenure and promotion processes remain racially biased, especially with regard to Black scholarship. Over the last three decades, empirical research studies have shown that African American faculty members experience structural racial inequities that result in barriers to access, promotion, tenure, and retention within higher education institutions (Allen et al., 2000; Croom, 2017; Frazier, 2011). One of the leading barriers to tenure and promotion for aspiring Black faculty and current Black faculty is the devaluing of Black scholarship, particularly Black scholarship that focuses on uplifting Black and Brown communities.

For instance, my research largely focuses on the life experiences of Black males who stutter. I have been questioned about why I do not give any attention to White males who stutter, and I have been accused of being racially biased because I only focus on Black males. Such questions and accusations constantly increase my anxiety and stress level as I pursue tenure. My experiences are not new for Black scholars. Black faculty are prone to experience isolation, invisibility, marginalization, unequal treatment, and the devaluation of scholarly expertise by White colleagues, administrators, and students (Tuitt et al., 2009). I contend that the devaluation of Black scholarship is a tool of racial microaggression used to uphold Whiteness and to ensure that the voices of Black scholars are silenced within the literature as much as possible. From my perspective, it remains important to acknowledge racial microaggressions and racism within the academy, while also giving attention to ways Black people are further marginalized due to their disability, gender, sexual orientation, and other factors.

Recommendations for Future Research

Although this chapter provided new information regarding Black males who stutter, there are additional perspectives that can be captured. The following recommendations are offered for future studies on African American males who stutter, to expand the scope of this research.

- Develop a study using focus groups of Black males who stutter. This would allow participants to serve as sources of empowerment and advocacy for each other.
- Conduct a longitudinal study. This would allow the research scope to be expanded into the midlife experiences of this population while examining long-term outcomes of Black males with a stuttering disability who seek tenure-track professorships at predominantly White institutions.
- While my personal experiences are sufficient for this chapter, I recommend that future research include a larger sample size and broaden the age range of participants.
- Although the aim of this chapter is to highlight the intersection between Blackness and disability for an African American male

who stutters, I recommend that future research capture the voices of university department chairs, deans, professors, provosts, human resources managers, and other stakeholders who are responsible for equitable hiring practices.

- I encourage Black scholars and disability studies scholars to continue writing on issues related to racism and anti-Blackness, while also addressing race in connection with other factors such as disability, keeping in mind the quote by Audre Lorde that opens this chapter: "There is no such thing as a single-issue struggle because we do not live single-issue lives."

REFERENCES

Allen, W. R., Epps, E. G., Guilloy, E. A., & Bonous-Hammarth, M. (2000). The Black academic: Faculty status among African-Americans in U.S. higher education. *Journal of Negro Education, 69*(1), 112–127.

American Society for Higher Education. (2009). The changing landscape and the compelling need for diversity. *American Society for Higher Education Report, 35*(1), 1–26.

Ameringen, M. V., Mancini, C., & Farvolden, P. (2003). The impact of anxiety disorders on educational achievement. *Journal of Anxiety Disorders, 17*(5), 561–571.

Anderman, L. H. (2003). Academic and social perceptions as predictors of change in middle school students' sense of belonging. *Journal of Experimental Education, 72*(1), 5–22.

Beitchman, J. H., Wilson, B., Johnson, C. J., Atkinson, L., Young, A., & Adlar, E. (2001). Fourteen-year follow-up of speech/language impaired and control children: Psychiatric outcome. *Journal of the American Academy of Child and Adolescent Psychiatry, 40*(1), 75–82.

Blood, G. W., & Blood, I. M. (2004). Bullying in adolescents who stutter: Communicative competence and self-esteem. *Contemporary Issues in Communication Science and Disorders, 31*, 69–79.

Blood, G. W., & Blood, I. M. (2007). Preliminary study of self-reported experience of physical aggression and bullying of boys who stutter: Relation to increased anxiety. *Perceptual and Motor Skills, 104*(3, pt. 2), 1060–1066.

Blood, G. W., Boyle, M. P., Blood, I. M., & Nalesnik, G. R. (2010). Bullying in children who stutter: Speech-language pathologists' perceptions and intervention strategies. *Journal of Fluency Disorders, 35*(2), 92–109.

Bloodstein, N., & Ratner, B. (2008). *A handbook of stuttering* (6th ed.). Thomson Delmar Learning.

Bochner, A. P., & Ellis, C. (2016). *Evocative autoethnography: Writing lives and telling stories.* Left Coast.

Boyer, E. L. (1990). *Scholarship reconsidered: Priorities of the professoriate.* Carnegie Foundation for the Advancement of Teaching. Jossey-Bass.

Chen, F., Zheng, D., Liu, J., Gong, Y., Guan, Z., & Lou, D. (2020). Depression and anxiety among adolescents during COVID-19: A cross-sectional study. *Brain, Behavior, and Immunity, 88,* 36–38.

Cochran, J. A., & Stewart, M. (1998). Stories of stuttering: A qualitative analysis of interview narratives. *Journal of Fluency Disorders, 23*(4), 247–264.

Craig, A. R., & Hancock, K. (1996). Anxiety in children and young adolescents who stutter. *Australian Journal of Human Communication Disorders, 24*(1), 28–38.

Crenshaw, K. (1989). Demarginalizing the intersection of race and sex: Black feminist critique of antidiscrimination doctrine, feminist theory and antiracist politics. *University of Chicago Legal Forum, 1989,* 139–168.

Croom, N. N. (2017). Promotion beyond tenure: Unpacking racism and sexism in the experiences of Black womyn professors. *Review of Higher Education, 40*(4), 557–583.

Dahlbeck, D. T., & Lightsey, O. R., Jr. (2008). Generalized self-efficacy, coping, and self-esteem as predictors of psychological adjustment among children with disabilities or chronic illnesses. *Children's Health Care, 37*(4), 293–315.

Dancy, T. E., Edwards, K. T., & Earl Davis, J. (2018). Historically White universities and plantation politics: Anti-Blackness and higher education in the Black Lives Matter era. *Urban Education, 53*(2), 176–195.

Dillard, C. (2000). The substance of things hoped for, the evidence of things not seen: Examining an endarkened feminist epistemology in educational research and leadership. *Qualitative Studies in Education, 13*(6), 661–681.

Ellis, A. L., & Hartlep, N. D. (2017). Struggling in silence: A qualitative study of six African American male stutterers in educational settings. *Journal of Educational Foundations, 30*(1–4), 33–62.

Ellis, A. L., Smith, C. N., & Barnett, J. A. (2016). Graduate-level education at historically Black colleges and universities: A three-part qualitative exposition. In R. Palmer and L. Walker (Eds.), *Graduate Education at Historically Black Colleges and Universities (HBCUs): A Student Perspective.* Routledge.

Flennaugh, T. K. (2016). Black male high school students: (Un)accepted failure in U.S. schools. In S. R. Harper & J. L. Wood (Eds.), *Advancing Black male student success from preschool through Ph.D.* (pp. 61–75). Stylus.

Flynt, S. W., & Morton, R. C. (2004). Bullying and children with disabilities. *Journal of Instructional Psychology, 31*(4), 330–333.

Fox, C. L., & Boulton, M. J. (2005). The social skills problems of victims of bullying: Self, peer and teacher perceptions. *British Journal of Educational Psychology, 75*(2), 313–328.

Frazier, K. N. (2011). Academic bullying: A barrier to tenure and promotion for African-American faculty. *Florida Journal of Educational Administration and Policy, 5*(1), 1–13.

Guitar, B. (1998). *Stuttering: An integrated approach to its nature and treatment* (2nd ed.). Lippincott Williams & Watkins.

Guitar, B. (2006). *Stuttering: An integrated approach to its nature and treatment* (3rd ed.). Lippincott Williams & Watkins.

Hartman, S. V. (2007). *Lose your mother: A journey along the Atlantic slave route.* Farrar, Straus and Giroux.

Hawker, D. S. J., & Boulton, M. J. (2000). Twenty-two years' research on peer victimization and psychosocial maladjustment: A meta-analytic review of cross-sectional studies. *Journal of Child Psychology and Psychiatry and Allied Disciplines, 41*(4), 441–445.

Hearne, A., Packman, A., Onslow, M., & Quine, S. (2008). Stuttering and its treatment in adolescence: The perceptions of people who stutter. *Journal of Fluency Disorders, 32*(2), 81–98.

Hugh-Jones, S., & Smith, P. K. (1999). Self-reports of short and long-term effects of bullying on children who stammer. *British Journal of Educational Psychology, 69*(2), 141–158.

Hutchison, C. B. (2009). *What happens when students are in the minority.* Rowman & Littlefield Education.

Ignatow, G. (2007). Theories of embodied knowledge: New directions for cultural and cognitive sociology? *Journal for the Theory of Social Behavior, 37*(2), 115–135.

Israelite, N., Ower, J., & Goldstein, G. (2002). Hard-of-hearing adolescents and identity construction: Influences of school experiences, peers, and teachers. *Journal of Deaf Studies and Deaf Education, 7*(2), 134–148.

Juvonen, J., Graham, S., & Schuster, M. A. (2003). Bullying among adolescents: The strong, the weak and troubled. *Pediatrics, 112*(6, pt. 1), 1231–1237.

Langevin, M., Bortnick, K., Hammer, T., & Weibe, E. (1998). Teasing/bullying experienced by children who stutter: Towards development of a questionnaire. *Contemporary Issues in Communication Science and Disorders, 25,* 12–24.

Leigh, W. R., & Mims, H. A. (1975). Cultural influences in the development and treatment of stuttering: A preliminary report of the Black stutterer. *Journal of Speech and Hearing Disorders, 40*(4), 459–466.

Logan, K. J., Mullins, M. S., & Jones, K. M. (2008). The depiction of stuttering in contemporary juvenile fiction. *Psychology in Schools, 23*(1), 609–626.

Matthews, J. R., & Daniels, D. E. (2019). The gendered experiences of male students in a speech-language pathology graduate program: A multi-case study. *Teaching and Learning in Communication Sciences & Disorders, 3*(2), article 2.

Menesini, E., & Salmivalli, C. (2017). Bullying in schools: The state of knowledge and effective interventions. *Psychology, Health & Medicine, 22*(sup1), 240–253.

Nail, J. E., Christofferson, J., Ginsburg, G. S., Drake, K., Kendall, P. C., McCracken, J. T., Birmaher, B., Walkup, J. T., Compton, S. N., Keeton, C., & Sakolsky, D. (2015). Academic impairment and impact of treatments among youth with anxiety disorders. *Child & Youth Care Forum, 44*(3), 327–342.

Pascarella, E. T., & Terenzini, P. T. (1991). *How college affects students.* Jossey-Bass.

Perkins, W. H. (1990). What is stuttering? *Journal of Speech and Hearing Disorders, 55*(3), 370–382.

Pitts, B. (2009). *Stepping out on nothing: How faith and family helped me conquer life's challenges*. St. Martin's.

Ressa, T., Daniels, D. E., & Wells-Jensen, S. (2021). Time as a hidden curriculum: Qualitative study of challenges faced by students with mobility, speech, and visual disabilities in P-12 settings. *International Journal of Educational Research Review, 6*(3), 250–263.

Scheurich, J., & Young, M. (1997). Coloring epistemologies: Are our research epistemologies racially biased? *Educational Researcher, 26*(4), 4–16.

Shames, H., & Rubin, R. (1986). *Stuttering then and now*. Columbus, OH: Merrill Publishing Co.

Shapiro, D. A. (1999). *Stuttering intervention: A collaborative journey to fluency freedom*. PRO-ED.

Sharp, S. (1995). How much does bullying hurt? The effects of bullying on the personal well-being and educational progress of secondary aged students. *Educational and Child Psychology, 12*(2), 81–88.

Sharp, S., & Smith, P. (1994). *Tackling bullying in your school: A practical handbook for teachers*. Routledge.

Trower, C. A., & Chait, R. P. (2002). Faculty diversity: Too little for too long. *Change, 104*(4), 33–38.

Tuitt, F., Hanna, M., Martinez, L., Salazar, M., & Griffin, R. (2009). Faculty of color in the academy: Teaching in the line of fire. *Thought and Action, 23*(Fall), 65–74.

Turner, C. S. (2002). *Diversifying the faculty*. Association of American Colleges and Universities.

US Department of Justice. (n.d.). Americans with Disabilities Act homepage. Retrieved November 25, 2021. http://www.ada.gov.

Van Keulen, J. E., Weddington, G. T., & DeBose, C. E. (1998). *Speech, language, and learning and the African American child*. Allyn and Bacon.

Velting, O. N., Setzer, N. J., & Albano, A. M. (2004). Update on and advances in assessment and cognitive-behavioral treatment of anxiety disorders in children and adolescents. *Professional Psychology: Research and Practice, 35*(1), 42–54. https://doi.org/10.1037/0735-7028.35.1.42.

Wesley, L., & Ellis, A. L. (2017). Exclusionary discipline in preschool: Young Black boys' lives matter. *Journal of African American Males in Education, 8*(2), 22–29.

West, C. (1993). The dilemma of the Black intellectual. *Journal of Blacks in Higher Education, 2*, 59–67.

Wynter, S. (2003). Unsettling the coloniality of being/power/truth/freedom: Towards the human, after man, its overrepresentation—an argument. *CR: The New Centennial Review, 3*, 257–337.

Yairi, E. (2007). Subtyping stuttering I: A review. *Journal of Fluency Disorders, 32*(3), 165–196.

Yaruss, J. S., & Quesal, R. W. (2004). Stuttering and the International Classification of Functioning, Disability, and Health (ICF): An update. *Journal of Communication Disorders, 37*(1), 35–52.

Yosso, T. (2005). Whose culture has capital? A critical race theory of community cultural wealth. *Race, Ethnicity and Education, 8*(1), 69–91.

Zhang, D., Katsiyannis, A., Barrett, D., & Wilson, V. (2007). Truancy offenders in the juvenile justice system: Examinations of first and second referrals. *Remedial and Special Education, 28*(4), 244–256.

Conclusion

Recentering the Emergent Themes on the Theory of Anti-Blackness

Implications for Research and Practice

ALONZO M. FLOWERS III, SOSANYA JONES, ROBERT T. PALMER, KATRINA STRULOEFF, AND NICOLE JOHNSON

Anti-Blackness ideologies continue to persist in higher education, particularly as sentiments about critical race theory (CRT), antiracist pedagogy, and social justice, as evidenced by the increasingly polarized state of the political landscape. While a substantial amount of empirical and scholarly research has identified the importance of a racially and ethnically diverse faculty (Carey et al., 2018; Lee, 2010; Turner et al., 2008), predominantly White institutions (PWIs) of higher education have not sufficiently addressed the racial inequalities that continue to marginalize Black faculty (Carey et al., 2018; Sensoy & DiAngelo, 2017). Critical to the issues that Black faculty encounter are the various levels of institutional racism and anti-Blackness that are usually engrained in the institution's history and systemic processes for tenure and promotion. Academic research continues to reveal several situations within PWIs in which Black faculty feel overlooked by senior faculty; White colleagues often insist that Black faculty research does not align with their department or the discipline; or Black faculty's research abilities and intellectual acumen are called into question (Arnold et al., 2021; Ross, 2006;

Subbaraman, 2020). These micro and macro levels of anti-Blackness have affected the experiences of Black faculty as they attempt to navigate the institutional context of their universities (Carter & Craig, 2022). Even after years of scholarship and increasing calls for attention to this problem, the number of tenure-track Black faculty recruited to the academy is still very low, and the number of Black faculty who persist and achieve tenure at PWIs in particular has not increased (US Department of Education, National Center for Education Statistics, 2017; Zambrana et al., 2017). Moreover, while there is a growing body of literature that captures the unique experiences Black faculty encounter, as they navigate the tenure and promotion process within PWIs, untenured Black faculty are often in a precarious and vulnerable position that hinders their ability to disclose the full extent of their experiences. Black faculty members who are in the tenure process are less likely to be retained or receive tenure in comparison with their White and Asian counterparts (Campos et al., 2021; Jayakumar et al., 2009). Additionally, at many PWIs, research is the main priority and a major consideration for tenure and promotion, while teaching and service carry little weight (Bonner, 2006; Edwards & Ross, 2018). Black faculty seeking tenure and promotion must quickly learn how to balance their time in research, service, and teaching. As Orey (2006) notes, if faculty fail to learn how to do this, there could be negative repercussions when they submit their tenure dossier. However, some of the barriers to securing tenure and promotion within the academy have nothing to do with Black faculty's adjustment to expectations. In fact, several empirical studies prove that one of the major obstacles to the retention and advancement of Black faculty is the hidden politics related to the tenure and promotion process (Arnold et al., 2016, 2021; Griffin et al., 2013; Haynes et al., 2020).

Black faculty are more likely to lack access to social capital to help navigate institutions' policies regarding the tenure and promotion process (Williams & Williams, 2006; Zambrana et al., 2015). Too often in higher education, Black faculty are unfairly affected by added stressors such as the devaluation of racism in the classroom, as well as a disproportionate caseload of mentoring and advising work, that affect job satisfaction and longevity of employment. Furthermore, at most colleges and universities, while research productivity is one of the linchpins in a successful tenure and promotion case, Black faculty are more likely to be tasked with extra service activities such as committee and taskforce work related to diversity, which often detracts from the time available for research activities (Griffin et al., 2013; Zambrana et al., 2017). As noted in the introduction to this book, the tenure cases of both Paul Harris and Nikole Hannah-Jones illustrate the permanence of racism within the academy. Even though Black faculty's scholarship has changed the academic landscape and established critical ideologies as necessary frameworks for research within several fields, the tenure and promotion structure does not always reward the value of such diverse thought in scholarship (Haynes et al., 2020; Urrieta & Méndez Benavídez, 2007). Blackburn et al. (1994, p. 280) indicate that "higher education institutions need to focus on the experiences of Black faculty if we hope to understand the work environments needed to support creative talents." To be more specific, PWIs and the academy, as a whole, need to recommit to their diversity, equity, and inclusion values with actions that provide Black faculty with an institutional climate that is both professionally and mentally supportive of their needs. Even though the academy claims to offer tenure-track faculty members various opportunities for intellectual and personal growth, unfortunately, Black faculty are often not allotted the same opportunities as their White counterparts. It is important for institutional and professional organizational leaders to understand the interconnectedness of the environmental influences of the campus racial climate and the professional developmental factors that affect Black faculty's tenure and promotion.

The professional environment within and outside an institution has the potential to either encourage or discourage Black faculty as they pursue their careers. Institutions play a major role, and unfortunately, many institutions utilize hidden rules and processes that can potentially undermine the tenure and promotion process for this faculty population. Using anti-Blackness theory as an epistemological lens, this book underscores how White hegemony operates in ways that undervalue Black scholarship so that it is not weighted equally to White scholarship in terms of its ability to add value to the academic discourse. Too often the contributions of Black faculty members are overlooked and undervalued as indicators of institutional growth and development. Robinson-Armstrong (2010, p. 36) notes seven factors that faculty of color, particularly Black faculty, contributed to institutions:

1. Helped an institution achieve its mission of excellence in research and teaching
2. Increased benefits for European American students
3. Increased student retention and persistence
4. Added multiple perspectives, theories, and approaches to scholarship
5. Reduced isolation for faculty and students of color
6. Alleviated negative stereotypes held by White faculty
7. Positively impacted the campus climate for all constituencies

Regrettably, university structures, policies, and procedures do not account for the positive impacts that Black faculty have on campus. While institutions of higher education continue to grapple with antiracist sentiment both administratively and within the dissemination of scholarship, Black faculty's scholarship remains a crucial lever of change.

Many of the chapters in this book address the systematic relegation of Black scholarship in the academy, particularly as it relates to how scholarship is valued within the tenure and promotion process. In this current era of antiracism discussions, institutions of higher education are negotiating how to promote racial equity and inclusion while simultaneously holding on to their traditional institutional values. Within a broader context, it is often difficult for institutions, particularly PWIs, to acknowledge their own complicity in racial oppression, especially as tenure and promotion processes remain systemically designed to benefit White faculty. Thus, this book has presented ways Black faculty can navigate and help to challenge racism within PWIs by offering a validating space for Black faculty to share their respective experiences. This work also invites readers to engage in critical reflection and dialogue about strategies for surviving and resisting the various systems of oppression within the academy. Drawing on the predominant themes of the book, this final chapter will offer recommendations to stakeholders on ways to better support Black faculty members and discuss possibilities for future research.

Utilizing an anti-Blackness framework, this book centers the counternarratives of Black faculty to unearth the systemic hegemonic structures within PWIs that often devalue and marginalize Black scholars and their work. The themes presented throughout the book contextualize the lived experiences of Black faculty navigating the tenure and promotion process at PWIs. Throughout the book, four critical themes emerged as salient factors affecting Black faculty experiences: (1) anti-Blackness in higher education; (2) the lack of and need for more Black spaces in the academy; (3) the need to decenter Whiteness and to adopt a BlackCrit lens or Black epistemologies; and (4) the value of critical reflection for growth, awareness, and perseverance. Regrettably, in higher education anti-Blackness has long been an integral part of the value structure. In PWIs the blatant disregard for Blackness stems from the systemic racism that breeds oppressive policies and a dogged commitment to maintain the status quo (Wingfield & Feagin, 2012). American higher education is a mirror of dominant society in the United States, and, as such, the aim of anti-Blackness in higher education is to "uphold White racial privilege, positing Whiteness as more virtuous, intelligent, moral, and honest" (Wingfield & Feagin, 2012, p. 144). Dumas and ross (2016) further note that anti-Blackness within higher education encapsulates the continuous dehumanization and marginalization of Black people in our country. As such, countering anti-Blackness requires that Black faculty mount a collective defense in which they respond to institutionalized racism in higher education as a systematic attack on their intellectual and academic freedom to exist in the academy. Throughout the chapters of this book, the authors address how anti-Black sentiments remain interwoven in the fabric of higher education. Many of the contributing authors wrote about how their experiences with racism affect how they connect to the institutional culture and how they navigate their tenure and promotion processes, as well as causing them to feel out of *place and space* within their departments, schools, colleges, and universities.

Barajas and Ronnkvist (2007) emphasize that race is inextricably connected to how institutional processes, policies, and procedures are structured. They further assert that "White space was created and re-produced through an organizational logic, a mechanism of informal practice and formal policy that rendered 'difference' to disappear for the institution to appear race-neutral" (p. 1522). As the focus on diversity, equity, and inclusion in White institutions becomes more prominent, it is essential for more spaces in the academy to support the professional trajectories of Black faculty. Based on the literature, Black space-making depends on how institutions of higher education begin to reevaluate the ways their policies and procedures affect the Black faculty experience (Barajas & Ronnkvist, 2007; Dancy et al., 2018). Institutions must be willing to recognize that patterns of White supremacy that exist within all elements of their systemic structures stem from a racist and exclusionary historical context. Once institutions can be transparent about how they have been sys-temically unjust to Black faculty, then and only then can the institutions move forward to enact change that is equitable for all faculty.

This process also includes how critical theories are embraced and embedded within the scope of the evaluation of research at PWIs. Too often, critical theories such as a BlackCrit lens or Black episte-mologies are seen as disconnected ideological frameworks when compared with those of noncritical theorists. However, Dumas and ross (2016, p. 417) assert that "advancing BlackCrit helps us to more incisively analyze these 'more detailed ways' that Blackness contin-ues to matter, and in relation to CRT, how Blackness matters in our understanding of key tenets related to, for example, the permanence of racism and whiteness as property." Aligned with the theoretical foundations of a BlackCrit lens or Black epistemologies, tenured

Black faculty can leverage their protected status to push for changing systemic norms within their institutions, including how tenure and promotion are situated and evaluated. Wynter (1989) notes that BlackCrit and other Black epistemologies become necessary precisely because CRT, as a general theory of racism, is limited in its ability to adequately interrogate all aspects of the systemic structures that are affecting the experiences of Black faculty. For Black faculty, having the space to unpack their experience in the academy can be beneficial to their well-being and retention as well as the retention of other faculty of color. The use of critical reflection for Black faculty can influence how they internalize their experiences navigating the tenure and promotion process and the identification of problematic practices that contribute to a toxic work culture for all. It is vital to understand that Black faculty's reflection on their experiences includes understanding that their identities are not fixed and that they operate with invisible identities as opposed to a more central institutionalized identity that is reflective of majority culture. Arguably, the heart of this book is the candor with which the authors provide honest and transparent insight into how they have experienced the White academy. Having a more robust discussion of how Black scholarship is treated in the White academy allows for a deeper and more critical discernment of the nuances related to the development of Black scholarship and the marginalization of Black scholars. By intentionally focusing on how Black faculty experience the White academy, this book's mission has been twofold: (1) to heighten awareness about excluded viewpoints regarding Black scholarship and (2) to provide recommendations to mitigate this problem, which may help to promote the empowerment and advancement of Black faculty.

The recommendations to stakeholders offered here suggest ways to better support Black faculty members. These recommendations are intended to push institutional stakeholders to work toward an equitable and socially just campus climate that provides space for professional growth and career advancement for Black faculty.

- Institutional stakeholders should recognize the unique position-ality and contributions of Black faculty at PWIs. Expectations for promotion and tenure should be adjusted to account for their lived experiences of more diverse epistemologies, dispropor-tionate service expectations, lack of support, and disproportion-ately negative evaluation by students when teaching subject matter related to social justice and race.
- Institutional stakeholders must acknowledge the pervasiveness of anti-Blackness as a systemic issue within higher education and seek to rectify and equalize institutional policies and procedures that veil, complicate, and narrow the pathway to tenure and promotion for Black faculty.
- Institutional stakeholders need to make an explicit and strate-gic commitment to celebrate and take pride in Black scholar-ship, critical ideologies, and Black epistemologies as central theoretical frameworks for developing research.

Finally, we wish to highlight possibilities for future research in this area. The publication and dissemination of this book is merely the continuation of an ongoing essential conversation in the academy. Ad-ditional research is needed that centers the lived experiences and voices of Black scholars. Such research would provide best practices for institutions of all types (including minority-serving institutions [MSIs]) to actively work toward equitable antiracist practices and af-firm the persistence of anti-Blackness within the walls of the ivory tower. Toward this end, we recommend more research in the follow-ing areas:

- Understanding how Black faculty at PWIs define and iden-tify anti-Blackness within the context of their professional roles
- Understanding how Black faculty at MSIs define and identify anti-Blackness within the context of their professional roles
- Examining how Black faculty have successfully navigated their tenure and promotion processes at PWIs and MSIs

- Exploring the nature of anti-Black systemic structures within PWIs and how these structures have created barriers for Black faculty to successfully navigated their tenure and promotion processes
- Identifying the failures and successes of institutions of higher education of all types as they attempt to put into action diversity, equity, and inclusion policies, with the hope of informing other institutions embarking on the process

Closing Remarks

Currently, equity is at the top of the national higher education agenda. Unfortunately, this can be both a blessing and a curse. Equity, as it is currently framed, is often an abstract ideal. It can describe anything and everything and, worse still, nothing at all. Many times, this is by design. It is a lot easier to recommend and push policy when the language and methods are vague and can be broadly applied. It removes the political and scary conflict that comes when we talk about what is really going on. Until we start discussing systemic oppression, White hegemony, and White supremacy and its goals, language, actors, histories, and practices, we will fail to dismantle it and really advance toward equity. Audre Lorde said that the master's tools will never dismantle the master's house. We must start calling out oppression, racism, White supremacy, and colonization if we are going to begin to chip away at this project called White hegemony that continues to define what oppression and racism means and how it gets addressed. Until we do that, we will continue to chase an abstract goal and engage in business as usual. We recognize that a single book cannot alone tip the scales toward equity or highlight all anti-Blackness, but it is our hope that by amplifying the experiences of Black scholars, it will push the academy and institutions of higher education to acknowledge systemic racism and take steps to dismantle it so that all faculty can thrive and equity can become more than just an empty virtue.

REFERENCES

Arnold, N. W., Crawford, E. R., & Khalifa, M. (2016). Psychological heuristics and faculty of color: Racial battle fatigue and tenure/promotion. *Journal of Higher Education, 87*(6), 890–919.

Arnold, N., Osanloo, A. F., & Sherman Newcomb, W. (2021). Paying professional taxes for promotion and tenure: The costs of justice work for Black faculty. *Journal of Research on Leadership Education, 16*(2), 122–139.

Barajas, H. L., & Ronnkvist, A. (2007). Racialized space: Framing Latino and Latina experience in public schools. *Teachers College Record, 109*(6), 1517–1538.

Blackburn, R., Wenzel, S., & Bieber, J. P. (1994). Minority vs. majority faculty publication performance: A research note. *Review of Higher Education, 17,* 217–282.

Bonner, F. A., II. (2006). The temple of my unfamiliar. In C. A. Stanley (Ed.), *Faculty of color: Teaching in predominantly White colleges and universities* (pp. 80–99). Anker.

Campos, J. S., Wherry, E. J., Shin, S., & Ortiz-Carpena, J. F. (2021). Challenging systemic barriers to promote the inclusion, recruitment, and retention of URM faculty in STEM. *Cell Host & Microbe, 29*(6), 862–866.

Carey, J. M., Carman, K. R., Clayton, K. P., Horiuchi, Y., Htun, M., & Ortiz, B. (2018). Who wants to hire a more diverse faculty? A conjoint analysis of faculty and student preferences for gender and racial/ethnic diversity. *Politics, Groups, and Identities.* Advance online publication. https://doi.org/10.1080/21565503.2018.1491866.

Carter, T. J., & Craig, M. O. (2022). It could be us: Black faculty as "threats" on the path to tenure. *Race and Justice.* Advance online publication. https://doi.org/10.1177/21533687221087366.

Dancy, T. E., Edwards, K. T., & Earl Davis, J. (2018). Historically White universities and plantation politics: Anti-Blackness and higher education in the Black Lives Matter era. *Urban Education, 53*(2), 176–195.

Dumas, M. J., & ross, k. m. (2016). "Be real Black for me": Imagining BlackCrit in education. *Urban Education, 51*(4), 415–442.

Edwards, W. J., & Ross, H. H. (2018). What are they saying? Black faculty at predominantly White institutions of higher education. *Journal of Human Behavior in the Social Environment, 28*(2), 142–161.

Griffin, K. A., Bennett, J. C., & Harris, J. (2013). Marginalizing merit? Gender differences in Black faculty D/discourses on tenure, advancement, and professional success. *The Review of Higher Education, 36*(4), 489–512.

Haynes, C., Taylor, L., Mobley, S. D., Jr., & Haywood, J. (2020). Existing and resisting: The pedagogical realities of Black, critical men and women faculty. *Journal of Higher Education, 91*(5), 698–721.

Jayakumar, U. M., Howard, T. C., Allen, W. R., & Han, J. C. (2009). Racial privilege in the professoriate: An exploration of campus climate, retention, and satisfaction. *Journal of Higher Education, 80*(5), 538–563.

Lee, J. A. (2010). Students' perceptions of and satisfaction with faculty diversity. *College Student Journal, 44*(2), 400–413.

Orey, B. D. (2006). Teaching and researching "the politics of race" in a majority White institution. In C. A. Stanley (Ed.), *Faculty of color: Teaching in predominantly White colleges and universities* (pp. 234–246). Anker.

Robinson-Armstrong, A. (2010). Benefits of a diverse faculty: A review of the literature. In *A collection of papers on self-study and institutional improvement* (Vol. 26, pp. 34–43). Higher Learning Commission.

Ross, A. D. (2006). Learning to play the game. In C. A. Stanley (Ed.), *Faculty of color: Teaching in predominantly White colleges and universities* (pp. 263–282). Anker.

Sensoy, Ö., & DiAngelo, R. (2017). "We are all for diversity, but . . .": How faculty hiring committees reproduce Whiteness and practical suggestions for how they can change. *Harvard Educational Review, 87*(4), 557–580.

Subbaraman, N. (2020). How #BlackInTheIvory put a spotlight on racism in academia. *Nature, 582*(7812), 327–328.

Turner, C. S. V., González, J. C., & Wood, J. L. (2008). Faculty of color in academe: What 20 years of literature tells us. *Journal of Diversity in Higher Education, 1*(3), 139–168.

Urrieta, L., Jr., & Méndez Benavídez, L. R. (2007). Community commitment and activist scholarship: Chicana/o professors and the practice of consciousness. *Journal of Hispanic Higher Education, 6*, 222–236.

US Department of Education, National Center for Education Statistics. (2017). Characteristics of postsecondary faculty. In *The condition of education 2017*, NCES 2017-144. National Center for Education Statistics.

Valdez, R. B. (2017). Blatant, subtle, and insidious: URM faculty perceptions of discriminatory practices in predominantly White institutions. *Sociological Inquiry, 87*(2), 207–232.

Williams, B. N., & Williams, S. M. (2006). Perceptions of African American male junior faculty on promotion and tenure: Implications for community building and social capital. *Teachers College Record, 108*(2), 287–315. https://doi.org/10.1111/j.1467-9620.2006.00649.x.

Wingfield, A. H., & Feagin, J. R. (2012). The racial dialectic: President Barack Obama and the White racial frame. *Qualitative Sociology, 35*(2), 143–162.

Wynter, S. (1989). The ceremony must be found: After humanism. *Boundary 2, 16*(3), 19–70.

Zambrana, R. E., Harvey Wingfield, A., Lapeyrouse, L. M., Dávila, B. A., Hoagland, T. L., & Valdez, R. B. (2017). Blatant, subtle, and insidious: URM faculty perceptions of discriminatory practices in predominantly White institutions. *Sociological Inquiry, 87*(2), 207–232.

Zambrana, R. E., Ray, R., Espino, M. M., Castro, C., Douthirt Cohen, B., & Eliason, J. (2015). "Don't leave us behind": The importance of mentoring for underrepresented minority faculty. *American Educational Research Journal, 52*(1), 40–72.

CONTRIBUTORS

EDITORS
Robert T. Palmer is chair and professor in the Department of Educational Leadership and Policy Studies in the School of Education at Howard University. He is also a faculty affiliate of the Center for Minority Serving Institutions at Rutgers University. His research examines issues of access, equity, retention, persistence, and the college experience of racial and ethnic minorities, particularly within the context of historically Black colleges and universities. Dr. Palmer's work has been published in leading journals in higher education, such as the *Journal of College Student Development*, *Teachers College Record*, the *Journal of Diversity in Higher Education*, the *Journal of Negro Education*, the *College Student Affairs Journal*, the *Journal of College Student Retention*, the *Negro Educational Review*, and the *Journal of Black Studies*. Since earning his PhD in 2007, Dr. Palmer has authored or coauthored over 130 academic publications. Some of his books include *Racial and Ethnic Minority Students' Success in STEM Education*; *Black Men in College: Implications for HBCUs and Beyond*; *Black Graduate Education at Historically Black Colleges and Universities: Trends, Experiences, and Outcomes*; *Fostering Success of Ethnic and Racial Minorities in STEM: The Role of Minority Serving Institutions*; *Community Colleges and STEM: Examining Underrepresented Racial and Ethnic Minorities*; *Black Men in Higher Education: A Guide to Ensuring Success*; *Exploring Diversity at Historically Black Colleges and Universities: Implications for Policy and Practice*; *The African American Student's Guide to STEM Careers*; and *Black Men in the Academy: Stories of Resiliency, Inspiration, and Success*. Dr. Palmer has been the recipient of the Standing Committee for Men's Outstanding Research Award of the American College Personnel Association (ACPA); ACPA's Emerging Scholar Award; the Carlos J. Vallejo Award of Emerging Scholarship from the American Educational Research Association; the Association for the Study of Higher Education's Mildred García Junior Exemplary Scholarship Award; an Emerging Scholar Recognition from *Diverse Issues in Higher Education*; and the State University of

New York chancellor's award for Excellence in Scholarship and Creative Activities.

Alonzo M. Flowers III is an associate professor and chair of the Department of Educational Leadership and Policy Studies at the University of Texas at San Antonio. Dr. Flowers joined the department after serving as the inaugural associate dean of Diversity, Equity, Inclusion, and Justice in the Graduate College at Drexel University. Dr. Flowers's research focuses on educational issues including academic identity formation for men of color in engineering programs. In addition, his research focuses on issues of diversity and justice in STEM education across the PK–20 continuum, college teaching and learning, college student development, and qualitative research. His research continues to address the needs of underrepresented students in education; he has authored or coauthored several book chapters and articles that focus on students of color and their academic experiences. He is a coauthor of *The African American Student's Guide to STEM Careers*, which focuses on practical educational tools for African American students to navigate the STEM pipeline. To date, Dr. Flowers has completed fifty peer-reviewed national conference presentations, including several presentations at the Association for the Study of Higher Education and the American Educational Research Association. He is also a member of the *Journal of Race and Policy*'s editorial board. Dr. Flowers is currently one of the editors in chief of the *Journal of African American Males in Education*. He was the recipient of the 2021 School of Education at Drexel University Teaching Excellence Award for Tenured Faculty.

Sosanya Jones is an associate professor of higher educational leadership and policy studies in the Department of Educational Leadership and Policy Studies in the Howard University School of Education. Her research focuses on the nexus between policy and practice for diversity, equity, and inclusion. In particular, her work draws on the practical knowledge and voices of policy makers and institutional practitioners in order to glean insight about policy formation, adoption, and implementation and their connection to equity, diversity, and inclusion practices in higher education.

AUTHORS
Fred A. Bonner II is professor and endowed chair in Educational Leadership and Counseling and founding executive director of the Minority Achievement, Creativity and High-Ability Center at Prairie View A&M University. He was formerly the Samuel DeWitt Proctor Endowed Chair in Education in

the Graduate School of Education at Rutgers University and is an esteemed expert in the field of diversity in education. Before joining Rutgers, he was professor of higher education administration and dean of Faculties at Texas A&M University–College Station. He earned a BA in chemistry from the University of North Texas, an MS Ed in curriculum and instruction from Baylor University, and an EdD in higher education administration and college teaching from the University of Arkansas. Throughout his career, his work has centered on microcultural populations' developing attitudes, motivations, and strategies to survive in macrocultural settings. This social justice philosophy has led him to publish numerous articles, books, and book chapters on academically gifted African American male college students in varying postsecondary contexts (historically Black colleges and universities, predominantly White institutions, and community colleges); teaching in the multicultural college classroom; diversity issues in student affairs; diverse millennial students in college; success factors influencing the retention of students of color in higher education and in the STEM fields in particular; and faculty of color in predominantly White institutions.

NiCole T. Buchanan is a professor of psychology at Michigan State University. Dr. Buchanan researches the interplay of race, gender, and victimization and how they affect the nature of harassment, its impact, and organizational best practices. She also studies faculty of color and ways that their research is marginalized (i.e., epistemic exclusion). She has been highlighted in hundreds of media outlets, is a featured speaker on TEDx and National Public Radio, and provides bias and diversity-related training and consultation (e.g., for medical professionals, faculty, clinicians, human resource managers, and police). Dr. Buchanan is a fellow of the Association for Psychological Science and four divisions of the American Psychological Association (the Society of Clinical Psychology, the Society for the Psychological Study of Social Issues, the Society for the Psychological Study of Ethnic Minority Issues, and the Society for the Psychology of Women) and has received national and international awards for her research, teaching, and professional service.

Beverly-Jean M. Daniel is an associate professor at Ryerson University and holds a PhD in sociology and equity studies in education, a master's in counseling, a BA (Honors) in psychology, and a graduate certificate in women and gender studies. Her research, publications, and community work focus on the education sector and the factors that promote academic, personal, and career success among Black community members. She has been a strong proponent for addressing and eliminating anti-Black racism and its impact on Black communities. Her work investigates conceptions of race and racialization in relation to education, conceptions of Whiteness, discourses of White privilege, and education. The central component of her critical engagement concerns the production and treatment of difference as a way of investigating questions about power relations. She has published widely in the areas of race, racism, and equity in the education and justice systems in the Canadian context. She has an edited collection titled *Diversity, Justice and Community: The Canadian Context*. She has also published articles that highlight the outcomes of the Bridge program, a groundbreaking, strengths-based student intervention program—the first of its kind in any Canadian college or university—that identifies, develops, and implements programming and strategies that foster and enhance postsecondary academic success among students who self-identify as African, Black, or Caribbean.

Kristie Dotson is a University Diversity and Social Transformation Professor of Philosophy and Afroamerican and African Studies at the University of Michigan–Ann Arbor. She specializes in political epistemology, metaphilosophy, and Black feminist philosophy. Dr. Dotson has published and co-published numerous journal articles on epistemic oppression, diversity in philosophy, and intersectionality. She is currently working on a monograph aimed at what she calls Black girl world building, entitled *Love Politic*.

Antonio L. Ellis is an assistant professor of special education at the Radford University School of Teacher Education and Leadership. He received his doctoral degree in educational leadership and policy studies from Howard University. Dr. Ellis holds additional academic degrees in educational administration, theological studies, and special education and human development. He has served as an inclusion teacher, central office administrator, and school building administrator with the District of Columbia Public Schools. His passion is advocating on behalf of people with disabilities, with a special emphasis on African American males who are speech impaired. Dr. Ellis's research interests include social equity, pastoral care, pastoral ethics, educational leadership, multicultural education, critical race theory, and special education.

Edward C. Fletcher Jr. is an Education and Human Ecology Distinguished Professor in the Workforce Development and Education program at the Ohio State University. He serves as a faculty associate for the Center on Education and Training for Employment, coeditor for the *Journal of Career and Tech-*

nical Education, and associate editor for the *Career and Technical Education Research* journal. Dr. Fletcher also serves as director for research and grants for the Department of Educational Studies. He was an assistant professor at Illinois State University in 2009 and an assistant professor at the University of South Florida from 2010 to 2019.

Donna Y. Ford is a distinguished professor of education and human ecology and Kirwan Institute Faculty Affiliate at the Ohio State University. She is in the Department of Educational Studies, Special Education Program. She earned all her degrees from Cleveland State University. Dr. Ford focuses primarily on the underrepresentation of Black and Hispanic students in gifted education and advanced classes. She is well known as a leader in urban education. Dr. Ford has authored more than three hundred publications, including fourteen books. She presents extensively in school districts and organizations nationally on opportunity gaps, equity, multicultural curriculum, antiracism, and culturally competent educators.

Sheron Fraser-Burgess is a professor of social foundations and multicultural education at Ball State University in Muncie, Indiana. Her research interests cluster around moral, political, and epistemological questions raised by positing K–12 schools ideally as deliberative and inclusive spaces. Since a democratic society rightly gives pride of place to diversity, critical thinking, and equality of opportunity, she also explores the moral implications of teachers' social identity and social positionality. Most recently, her scholarship has turned toward John Dewey in consideration of his transactional politics for a creative democracy confronting racial activism. The neopragmatics of Cornel West's prophetic philosophy and womanism also offer Afro-centric worldviews through which to consider the morality of public policies. Dr. Fraser-Burgess teaches undergraduate courses in the teacher licensure and professional education program and graduate courses in philosophy of education and ethics and education. She is also director of the PhD program in educational studies. She has published papers in the *Journal of Thought*, *Educational Philosophy and Theory*, *Educational Studies*, and *Philosophical Studies in Education*. She has also authored conference papers for the American Educational Research Association, the Philosophy of Education Society, and the American Educational Studies Association.

H. Bernard Hall is assistant professor of urban teacher education at Drexel University. Dr. Hall's teaching and research interests include social justice approaches to teacher education and development, secondary English methods, and critical hip-hop pedagogy. His scholarship on hip-hop pedagogy was featured in *Schooling Hip-Hop: Expanding Hip-hop Based Education across the Curriculum*, the first edited volume devoted to hip-hop based education. His work has also been published in peer-reviewed academic journals such as *Urban Education*, the *International Journal of Multicultural Education*, *English Teaching Practice and Critique*, and *Research in the Teaching of English*.

Erik M. Hines is a professor in the Counseling program within the College of Education and Human Development at George Mason University. Dr. Hines prepares graduate students to be professional school counselors. His research agenda focuses on college and career readiness for Black males, parental involvement and its impact on academic achievement for students of color, and improving and increasing postsecondary opportunities for first-generation students, low-income students, and students of color, particularly Black males. Additionally, his research agenda includes topics related to career exploration in the STEM fields for students of color.

Nicole Johnson is a third-year PhD student in the Higher Education Leadership and Policy Studies program at Howard University. Her research includes issues of access to postsecondary education, with specific emphasis on college costs and student loan debt. She has been trained in social science research, including quantitative, qualitative, and experimental methods. Nicole currently serves as the chair of the American Educational Research Association's graduate student council. Additionally, she serves as a managing editor for the *Journal of African American Males in Education*. Her professional experience includes several collegiate student affairs departments and policy organizations that provide technical assistance to educational entities. Nicole earned her bachelor's degree in literature from Eastern Michigan University and her master's degree in education policy from Harvard University.

Martinque K. Jones is an assistant professor in the Department of Psychology at the University of North Texas. She received her BA in psychology from the University of Texas at Austin and her PhD in counseling psychology from the University of Houston. Her research applies an intersectional lens to the understanding of Black women's race and gender, mental health, and counseling processes. Dr. Jones has received several awards for her scholarship, including the Carolyn Payton Early Career Award for her research on Black women. Her research and community efforts have also been supported by the National Science Foundation, the American Psychological Association Office for Early Career Psychologists, and the American Psychological Foundation. Dr. Jones is an emerging leader and has held leadership positions in the American Psychological Association and the Association of Black Psychologists.

Chad E. Kee is currently an assistant professor of higher education and student affairs in the School of Education and Urban Studies at Morgan State University. Before Morgan State University, he worked in K–12 and student affairs administration for over fifteen years. His research interests are centered on opportunities to advance diversity, equity, and inclusion initiatives within college environments. Specifically, his research objective is to understand and interpret the experiences of marginalized undergraduate students. An additional branch of his research agenda is focused on specific positions and roles that support equity work, such as the chief diversity officer, diversity educators, director of admissions, and chief financial officers who are responsible for supporting programs that affect undergraduate student programs. In addition, Dr. Kee has conducted multiple diversity, equity, and inclusion assessments for colleges and universities throughout the nation. The assessments have yielded specific and actionable recommendations to center minoritized community members. He completed the Leaders in Equitable Evaluation and Diversity (LEEAD) Scholar program sponsored by the Annie E. Casey Foundation. As a result, Dr. Kee has developed advanced skills in culturally responsive research and evaluation design.

aretha f. marbley is a professor, clinical director, and coordinator of clinical mental health counseling in Counselor Education at Texas Tech University. She is an academic counselor and a critical humanist, womanist educator, storyteller, activist, servant, morally engaged researcher, and transdisciplinary scholar with a commitment to helping people and communities. Her scholarship focuses on critical global multicultural social justice activism, organic connections, and literacy advocacy across cultures, social structures, and social identities in mental health and communities. She has received numerous awards, including national human rights, social justice, anti-oppression, and multicultural research awards.

James L. Moore III is the vice provost for diversity and inclusion and chief diversity officer at the Ohio State University and serves as the first executive director of the Todd Anthony Bell National Resource Center on the African American Male. He is also the inaugural Education and Human Ecology Distinguished Professor of Urban Education in the College of Education and Human Ecology. Dr. Moore is internationally recognized for his work on

African American males. He has published more than 140 works; obtained more than $25 million in grants, contracts, and gifts; and given more than two hundred scholarly presentations and lectures throughout the United States and other parts of the world. In both 2018 and 2019, *Education Week* named him one of the two hundred most influential scholars and researchers in the United States who inform educational policy, practice, and reform.

Isis H. Settles is a professor of psychology, Afro-American and African studies, and women's and gender studies (by courtesy) at the University of Michigan. She received her BA from Harvard College and her PhD in psychology from the University of Michigan. Using an interdisciplinary, intersectional framework, her research focuses on the experiences, perceptions, and consequences of unfair treatment directed at devalued social group members, especially Black people and women, and protective factors that counteract the effects of those experiences. Dr. Settles is a fellow of the Society for the Psychology of Women, the Society for the Psychological Study of Social Issues, and the Society for the Psychological Study of Culture, Ethnicity, and Race. She has received several awards for her research, including the Committee on Women in Psychology Leadership Award and the Carolyn Payton Early Career Award. Her research has been funded by the National Institute of Mental Health and the National Science Foundation.

Stella L. Smith is an experienced qualitative and quantitative researcher with a focus on mentoring and leadership development of underrepresented populations in higher education, particularly African American women, access to higher education for underserved populations, community-university partnerships, and strategies for P–20 educational pipeline alignment. The associate director of the MACH III Center at Prairie View A&M University, Smith also served as a postdoctoral fellow and associate director of the Longhorn Link Program at the University of Texas at Austin. Smith is also an adjunct faculty member in the Department of Educational Leadership and Counseling at Prairie View, where she teaches a variety of classes including School Principalship and Community and School Relations. She has authored and coauthored several peer-reviewed articles and is a frequent presenter at local, state, national, and international conferences.

Terrell L. Strayhorn is professor of higher education and women's, gender, and sexuality studies at Illinois State University. He also serves as visiting scholar in the Evelyn Reid Syphax School of Education at Virginia Union University, where he lectures in psychology and directs the Center for the

Study of HBCUs. A leading authority on racial equity, student development, and social psychological determinants of student success in diverse learning contexts, Dr. Strayhorn is author of eleven books and over one hundred refereed journal articles and book chapters, including *College Students' Sense of Belonging: A Key to Educational Success for All Students, Living at the Intersections,* and *Theoretical Frameworks for College Student Research,* to name a few. Past chair of the Research Focus on Black Education Special Interest Group of the American Educational Research Association and past chair of the Council on Ethnic Participation of the Association for the Study of Higher Education, Dr. Strayhorn serves as associate editor of *Social Science and Humanities* for education and psychology, chief editor of the *Frontiers in Education* higher education specialty area, and editorial board member of several other journals. He is an expert advisory board member for several government agencies and foundations, including Freedom Schools National Research Advisory Board, the Children's Defense Fund, Minds Beyond Measure, the Thurgood Marshall College Fund, and various National Science Foundation projects.

Katrina Struloeff is a PhD candidate at Drexel University and the director of growth and impact, Catalyst @ Penn GSE. Before joining Catalyst @ Penn GSE, Katrina worked as an education researcher within higher education, school districts, and industry, including the School District of Philadelphia, Perkins Eastman architecture firm, and the Drexel University School of Education. She spent seven years in the New Orleans public charter school landscape as a middle school and high school administrator. Working across the United States, Katrina has facilitated national training for organizations that serve youth and families in vulnerable positions; facilitated out-of-school arts, STEM, and entrepreneurship programming for youth; engaged with community activism and social enterprise incubation; and led partnerships with numerous national and regional organizations for information-sharing and innovative evidence-based programming. She earned a master's degree from Carnegie Mellon University Heinz College in public policy.

Blanca Elizabeth Vega is the daughter of Ecuadorian immigrants. Dr. Vega earned a doctorate (EdD) from the Higher and Postsecondary Education program at Teachers College, Columbia University, and is currently an assistant professor of higher education at Montclair State University. She has worked in various administrative positions within higher education spanning over sixteen years. Some of these roles include providing financial aid counseling and coordinating and directing New York State opportunity programs such as the Liberty Partnerships Program and the Higher Education

Opportunity Program. Dr. Vega earned a bachelor of arts degree in anthropology from Brandeis University and a master of arts degree in Higher Education at New York University. Dr. Vega's scholarship broadly focuses on exploring the role of higher education and student affairs administrators and leaders in building just and equitable postsecondary environments. Her primary area of research situates racism and anti-immigrant sentiments as barriers that can affect higher education experiences and organizational learning. Dr. Vega's research specifically focuses on the following three themes: race-based organizational conflict in higher education, policies affecting undocumented students and postsecondary leadership, and racialization of Hispanic-serving institutions.

Larry J. Walker is an assistant professor and EdD program liaison in the Department of Educational Leadership and Higher Education at the University of Central Florida. Previously, he held faculty appointments at Howard University and Loyola University Maryland. Dr. Walker's research focuses on the impact that racism, leadership, and policy have on education and society. Dr. Walker has authored, coauthored, or coedited more than thirty journal articles, book chapters, and books. Additionally, he has discussed a variety of important societal issues on platforms including Fox Business, Fox Soul, and Roland Martin Unfiltered. Further, Dr. Walker served as the legislative director for former congressman Major R. Owens. His responsibilities included supervising the legislative staff and advising the congressman on an array of issues including education, appropriations, transportation, and foreign affairs. Before beginning his work in Congressman Owens's office, Dr. Walker was selected as a Congressional Fellow with the Congressional Black Caucus Foundation. During this time, he wrote policy briefs and met with congressional staff and researchers to examine complex issues.

Brian L. Wright is an associate professor and program coordinator of early childhood education in the Department of Instruction and Curriculum Leadership in the College of Education and coordinator of the Middle School Cohort of the African American Male Academy at the University of Memphis. His research examines high-achieving African American males in urban schools (PreK–12), racial and ethnic identity development of boys and young men of color, STEM and African American males, African American males as early childhood teachers, and teacher identity development. Dr. Wright is the author of the award-winning (2018 National Association for Multicultural Education Philip C. Chinn Book Award) and best-selling book *The Brilliance of Black Boys: Cultivating School Success in the Early Grades* (2018).

INDEX

Abbott, Greg, 200
affirmative action, 24–25, 150, 178
African identity, students' connection
   with, 60
Afro-descendant scholars, 98, 99
Afro-pessimism, 4–5, 117, 118–19, 136–37
American Association of University
   Professors, 2
American Educational Research Associa-
   tion, Hip-Hop Theories, Praxis, and
   Pedagogies Special Interest Group, 63
American Indian/Alaska Native faculty, 39
American Psychological Association,
   Publication Manual, 52, 53–54
Anaya, Rudolfo, "Take the Tortillas Out of
   Your Poetry," 65
Anderson, Eric, 191–92
anti-Blackness ideologies, in higher
   education, 4–9, 16, 18, 19–33, 20–22, 22–23,
   26, 39–41, 117, 202–4, 205, 235, 239; in
   academic publishing, 34–44, 37, 40–41,
   201–2; corrective policies and practices,
   26–27, 160–64, 166–67; definition, 18, 109,
   146; as educational inequity, 101–2; history,
   impact, intervention, and maintenance
   response, 161–64, 166–67; implications for
   Black scholarship, 27–29; institutional
   failure to address, 235; internalized, 62;
   intersection with disabilities, 213–33;
   name, own, frame, and sustain response,
   160–61; overview, 17–18; racist history of,
   20–21, 26, 27, 240; in teacher education, 6,
   7, 61, 62–63, 66–73. *See also* bias, anti-Black
Asian communities, 147, 151, 164
Asian faculty, 236
Asian/Pacific Islander faculty, 39
autoethnography, 205–8, 214, 221–26. *See also*
   counterstories; personal narratives

Bell, Derrick, 199, 204; "The Space
   Traders," 102–3, 107
Bell-Scott, Patricia, 184
bias, anti-Black, 5, 18, 27, 182; academic
   discipline-based, 24, 81, 82, 83–85, 87, 91,
   92–93, 100; epistemic exclusion-related,
   24, 79, 81, 82–83, 87, 91, 92–93, 94, 100;
   political, 201; social identity-based,
   24, 82–83, 92, 93, 100, 163; in student
   evaluations, 185–88; toward Black
   faculty with stuttering disability, 215–18,
   222–23, 224, 226; toward Black female
   faculty, 185–88; toward Black women,
   183; in White spaces, 101
Biden, Joseph, 70
Black Arts movement, 64
Black bodies: brutalization, 141–42, 150–51;
   objectification and devaluation, 6, 17–18,
   19, 103, 136, 145, 147, 155, 162–63, 202–3
Black Canadian faculty, anti-Black racism
   toward, 8–9, 141–72; historical context,
   143–49, 162–63, 165, 166; history, impact,
   intervention, and maintenance
   response, 161–64, 166–67; institutional
   policies against, 157–60, 163, 166–67;
   from White faculty, 150–52
Black codes, 202. *See also* Jim Crow laws
Black college graduates, PWI and HBCU
   longitudinal study, 45–48, 53
Black college students, 98; awareness
   of African history and heritage, 60;
   Black faculty support for, 150; college
   enrollment, 38, 109–10, 112; comparison
   with White students, 46, 53, 54, 55;
   dehumanization, 101–2; devaluation
   of Black faculty by, 155; enrollment
   patterns, 38, 215; hostile racial climate of,
   101–2; involvement in organizational

Black college students (*continued*)
conflict, 105-10; longitudinal outcomes
study, 45-48; male, 205; racial microaggressions toward, 101; retention, 38
BlackCrit theory, 8, 100, 108-10, 111, 113,
240-41
Black/cultural tax, 34, 42, 182
Black diaspora, 121, 195
Black faculty: lack of institutional support,
2, 3, 42, 235; underrepresentation, 2, 24,
38-39, 42, 79, 149, 199-200
Black female faculty, 39; biased student
evaluations, 185-88; CRT-based personal
narrative, 176-77, 179-82; discriminatory
tenure and promotion practices toward,
35-36, 203; epistemic exclusion, 83, 84,
85, 86, 87, 88, 89, 90; experiences of
intersectionality, 177, 183-89, 190-91; as
heads of offices of equity and inclusion,
159; lack of support from White
colleagues, 150-51, 159; leadership roles
in PWIs, 176-77; positive impacts on
students, 215-16; racial microaggressions
toward, 8, 117-40, 154; underrepresentation, 39, 199-200; White students'
attitudes toward, 155, 185-88
Black feminist theory/scholarship, 24;
Africana, 183-84; applied to intersectionality, 177, 183-84; perspective on
Black masculinity, 192, 195
Black History Month, 151
Black identity, 18, 60, 241; attacks on, 28; of
Black female faculty/scholars, 184, 185;
of Black male faculty/scholars, 177,
189-95; of Black women, 176, 177, 183-89,
190-91, 213; hip-hop culture and, 54;
ultra-Black, 61-62, 63, 72-73. *See also*
intersectionality
Black identity scholarship, 36-41, 61, 91-92
Black junior faculty, 2, 34, 94, 222-23, 225
Black Lives Matter (BLM) movement, 19,
163-64, 184, 201
Black male faculty: experiences of
liminality, 176, 177, 189-95; intersectionality of identity (mascu'sectionality), 177,
189-95; mistreatment of, 205; retention,
200-201; with stuttering disability as
tenure obstacle, 213-33; underrepresentation, 39, 199-200

Black masculinity, Black feminist
perspective, 192, 195
Black men: intersectionality of identity
(mascu'sectionality), 177, 189-95; role
models, 190; with stuttering disability,
213-28
Black nationalist movements, 223
Blackness, concept of, 17-18
Black Panther Party, 225
Black Power movement, 184
Black scholars: conservative harassment
of, 203, 207; cooperative research with
White scholars, 26, 40; lack of recognition, 88
Black scholarship: benefits of, 28, 238;
definition, 21, 98; development and
purpose, 21-22; institutional support for,
242; intellectual tradition of, 103-4;
literature review on, 6; White scholars'
examinations of, 195. *See also* research
Black scholarship, undermining and
devaluation of, 1-2, 3, 5-6, 21-22, 24, 25,
28-29, 103-4; in academic publishing,
34-44, 45-48, 50-58; as barrier to tenure
and promotion, 227-28; in Canada,
152; by White faculty, 235-36; White
hegemony and, 2, 3, 15-16, 19-22, 25, 37,
237-38; by White students, 153-54,
165-66. *See also* epistemic exclusion;
research devaluation
Black spaces, 8, 26, 27, 98-116, 99-100;
administrative closure, 105-8, 109, 110,
113; BlackCrit perspective on, 100,
108-10, 111, 113; as organizational conflict
source, 105-10, 111; recommendations
for, 111-13, 209, 240, 241
Black student centers, 109-10
Black student organizations, 8, 100, 105, 107
Black studies and departments, 8, 100, 107,
109-10, 112
"Black voices," 49, 55, 56
Black-White binary, 53, 55, 146, 195
Black womanist theory: applied to
intersectionaity, 183-84; applied to racial
microaggressions, 8, 117-40; influence
on intersectionality, 177; narrative
inquiry, 122-38; narrative self-reflection,
119-22; theological ethics, 121-22, 137;
Walker's definition, 120-21

diversity, equity, and inclusion: in academic publishing, 93–94; as attack on Whiteness, 153–54; Black faculty service work in, 2, 237; of Black faculty with disabilities, 214–17, 226–27; Canadian university equity policies, 157–60; committees, 66, 132–33, 237; epistemological inclusion, 111–12; of faculty, 235; institutional promotion of, 180, 237, 238, 240, 243; neoliberalism and, 109; in recruitment of faculty, 216; superficial, 63, 64–65, 150; White students' perceptions of, 106, 108; woke as critique of, 153–54

doctoral advisors, 40–41, 50

Dunbar-Nelson, Alice Moore, 183, 184, 188–89

educational resource distribution inequities, 100, 101–2, 106–7, 108, 111, 113

Education Full Text, 16

Emdin, Christopher, 60–61, 72

emotional and psychological trauma, experienced by Black faculty, 22–24, 25, 39–40, 155–56; effect on faculty retention, 23–24, 27–28; epistemic exclusion-related, 89–92; as racial battle fatigue, 2, 22–23, 39; racial microaggressions-related, 123–38; self-care and healing resources for, 27, 94–95

epistemic exclusion, 7–8, 21, 24–25, 27, 28, 79–97, 112; academic rank-related, 83–85, 86, 88, 89; Black feminist theoretical framework, 79–81, 92; CRT framework, 79–80, 81, 92; definition, 24, 79, 100; disciplinary bias in, 81, 82, 83–85, 87, 89, 91, 93; economic costs, 90–91; educational resource scarcity-related, 100, 113; in evaluation processes, 84–87; formal processes, 84–87; in hiring process, 24–25, 28, 79, 91–92; impact, 89–92; informal processes, 87–89; phenomenology, 83–92; social identity bias in, 82–83, 92, 93, 100; strategies to address, 90, 92–95, 100; theory of, 82–83

epistemic injustice, 24. See also epistemic exclusion, 24

epistemic practices, 21

epistemological inclusion, Black spaces for, 98–116

evaluation processes: epistemic exclusion in, 84–87; faculty assessments, 27. See also student evaluations; tenure and promotion process

expertise, scholarly, 2, 87, 91–92, 126, 228

faculty: demographics, 2, 38–39, 199–200, 215; stress index, 40. See also Black faculty; Black female faculty; Black male faculty; White faculty

Family Educational Rights and Privacy Act, 186

Felder, Cain Hope, 223

feminist movement: Black women's identity within, 184; White feminists, 150–51. See also Black feminist theory/scholarship

"fitting in" concept, 37, 40, 176, 194

Flavor Flav, 61

Florida, conservative politics of, 200, 201–2, 206–7, 209

Floyd, George, 37, 69, 104, 141, 147, 151–52, 163, 201

Ford, Donna Y., 36, 42–43

Forman, M., ed., *That's the Joint! The Hip-Hop Studies Reader*, 59

Fox News, 70, 206

Furious Five, "The Message," 70

Google Scholar, 16

Gramsci, Antonio, 20

Grandmaster Flash, 70

grants, 26, 43, 65–66, 85–86, 88

Graves, Daren, 63

Gravey, Marcus, 223

Grillo, Lisa Maria, 225

Gutiérrez y Muhs, K., *Presumed Incompetent: The Intersections of Race and Class for Women in Academia*, 42

Hall, Arsenio, 193

Hamer, Fannie Lou, 223

Hannah-Jones, Nikole, 237; 1619 Project, 3–4

Harris, Paul, 1–2, 3, 4, 237

Hartlep, Nicholas D., 225

Harvard University, 63, 66

hegemony, 20. See also White hegemony

Henfield, Malik S., 42–43
higher education and student affairs
(HESAs) professionals: attitudes toward
Black spaces, 100–101, 105, 110–12, 113;
Black, 112; responses to racism, 106–7,
108–9, 110
Hill, Marc Lamont, 59; *Beats, Rhymes, and
Classroom Life . . .*, 60
Hill-Collins, Patricia, 184
hip-hop, 206
hip-hop based education (HHBE), 60, 69,
72. *See also* hip-hop pedagogy
hip-hop cultural practices, 60, 67
hip-hop cultural studies, 59–60
Hip-Hop Nation, 61
hip-hop pedagogy, 7, 59–76; cross-cultural
value, 63–64; CRT-based perspective, 67,
68–73; English language arts, 62, 67, 71;
higher education's interest in, 63–66;
ultra-Black, 61–62
hiring process: Black faculty's participation, 152; in Canadian higher education,
152, 157–58; epistemic exclusion in, 24–25,
28, 79, 91–92; equity hires, 149, 152; for
faculty diversity, 215; "play it safe"
agenda, 65. *See also* interviews
Hispanic communities, 147
Hispanic faculty, 39
Hispanic-serving institutions (HSIs), Black
spaces in, 101, 105, 106, 107, 108, 109, 110,
111
historically Black colleges and universities
(HBCUs), 35, 149, 181, 182, 190; graduates'
outcomes, 45–48
historically White institutions. *See* predominantly White institutions (PWIs)
hooks, bell, 184; *Black Looks*, 136–37
Howard University, 4
Hudson-Weems, Clenora, 184
Hull, Akasha Gloria, 184
human rights codes, 157, 158, 159, 163
Hurtado, Sylvia, 50–51

identity: Canadian, 143–44; discrimination
based on, 143–44, 157, 158, 163; effects of
stuttering disability on, 219; gender, 158;
professional, 40–41, 136, 175–76. *See also*
Black identity; intersectionalty; social
identity

immigrant communities, anti-Blackness
among, 147–48
immigration policies, 145–46, 161–62
imposter syndrome, 37
incivility, racial: in Canadian higher
education, 8–9, 141–42, 149–53; student
codes of conduct and, 142, 157–60; of
White students, 8–9, 142–43, 152–60, 164,
165–66, 185–88
Indigenous people, 18, 23, 36–37, 147, 161;
First Nations, 143, 157
individualism, 79–80, 99
Individuals with Disabilities Act, 217–18
integration, 38, 145
interest convergence, 69, 81, 102–3
intersectionality, 150, 176, 227; of Black
Canadian faculty, 167; of Black female
faculty, 177, 183–89, 190–91; of Black male
faculty, 177, 189–95; definition, 183, 213
interviews, 65, 66, 215; bias toward persons
with stuttering disability, 216–18, 222–23,
224, 226
invisibility, of Black faculty and scholars,
2, 54, 81, 88, 92, 109, 187, 188–89, 228
isolation, of Black faculty and scholars, 26,
40, 185, 203, 228

Jackson, David, 192
Jay Z, 70
Jim Crow laws, 21, 54, 63, 66, 71, 203–4
Johnson, Georgia Douglas, 183–84
Jordan, June, 183–84
Journal for Multicultural Education, 43
*Journal for Women and Minorities in Science
and Engineering*, 43
*Journal of African American Males in
Education (JAAME)*, 1, 43, 192
Journal of Black Psychology, 43
Journal of Family Strengths, 43
*Journal of Minority Achievement, Creativity,
and Leadership*, 43
*Journal of Multicultural Counseling and
Development*, 43
Journal of Negro Education, 43
journals, scholarly/peer-reviewed: anti-
Blackness of peer-review process, 7,
45–48, 50–57, 65; of Black, Brown, and
Latinx scholarship, 1–2, 6–7; coauthored
versus single-author manuscripts, 40–41;

journals (*continued*)
databases, 16; hip-hop scholarship in, 59–60; impact factors, 35, 65; minoritized, 43; policies to address epistemic exclusion, 93–94; scholarly legitimacy, 1–2. *See also titles of individual journals*
Joyce, P.A., et al., "Honoring Liminality . . . ," 189
JSTOR, 16
Jung, Carl, 188

Kelly, Lauren Leigh, 63
Kimmel, Michael S., 191–92
King, Martin Luther, Jr., 223
KRS-One (the Teacha), 61

Ladson-Billings, Gloria, 67, 178, 225
LatCrit, 204
Latinx students, 108
LBGTQA+ community, 84
legitimacy, scholarly, 1, 24–25, 87–88, 91–92
Lerner, Gerda, 183–84
liberalism, 49, 68, 81, 203
Lil Baby, 71
liminality, 176, 177, 193–95
Lorde, Audre, 183–84, 213, 229, 243
Love, Bettina L., 60–61
luxocracy, 137

macroaggressions, racial, 235–36
marbley, arethra, "Protecting Black Women Faculty from the Unchecked Abuse of Power of Student Evaluations That Publicly Blame and Shame," 177, 183–89
marginalization, of Black faculty and scholars, 6, 23, 47, 103, 228; Black Canadian faculty, 167; Black female faculty, 124, 184–85; Black male faculty with stuttering disability, 217–18; institutional failure to address, 235; remedial institutional policies for, 27, 94. *See also* Black scholarship, undermining and devaluation of; epistemic exclusion
marginalized communities, 67; advocacy for, 223; anti-Black racism of, 147–49; Black, 239; in Canada, 143; narrative of, 22; as research focus, 94; women of color, 184

Marshall, Thurgood, 204
Martin, Trayvon, 19
McCarthyism, 207
media: attacks on Black scholars, 203; conservative, 70, 199, 206. *See also* social media
mentoring, 50–51, 65–66, 158, 194–95, 215; as Black/cultural tax, 34; of Black faculty with stuttering disability, 225; by department chairs, 208, 209; disproportionate caseloads, 236–37; for epistemic exclusion, 94–95; for faculty retention, 27; inadequate, 25–26, 42; R.A.C.E. (research, advocacy, collaboration, and empowerment) Mentoring, 42–43
meritocracy, 39, 42, 49, 79–80, 81
microaggressions, racial, 2, 5, 42, 47, 65, 70, 117–40, 164, 208; Black womanist perspective, 8, 117–40; definition, 118; devaluation of Black scholarship as, 228, 235–36; toward Black female faculty, 8, 117–40, 154, 187; toward Black students, 101. *See also* incivility, racial
Milner, Rich, 225
minority-serving institutions (MSIs), 105, 106–7, 109, 110, 111, 242
mission statements, 69, 94
Morris, Monique, *The Criminalization of Black Girls in School,* 119
multiculturalism, 49, 109

NAACP, Legal Defense Fund, 204
Nas, 61, 71
National Institutes of Health Research Project Grant, 88
National Student Clearinghouse Research Center, 38
Neal, M. A., ed., *That's the Joint! The Hip-Hop Studies Reader,* 59
neoliberalism, 70, 81, 108, 109
Niebuhr, Reinhold, 223
Nkomo, Stella, 22
No Child Left Behind, 66, 67

Obama, Barack, 122–23
onto-ethics, 121, 136
organizational conflict, racial, 113; resource scarcity-related, 106–7, 108, 111

Palmer, Robert T., 225
peer pedagogies, 102
peer-review process, anti-Blackness
  perspective, 7, 45–48, 50–57, 65
peer teaching evaluations, 40
Pelzer, Dante, 192
Pennsylvania State University, 2
personal narratives, of Black faculty in
  PWIs, 9, 175–98, 241; CRT framework,
  176–77; intersectionality framework, 176,
  177, 183–89; liminality framework, 176,
  177, 189–96; as womanist self-reflection,
  119–40
predominantly White institutions (PWIs):
  Black graduates' postcollege outcomes,
  45–48; Black student enrollment, 38; as
  White spaces, 101. See also White spaces;
  names of individual colleges and
  universities
professional development, 70, 237
property: Black people as, 17, 19, 27, 117, 162,
  202; Whiteness as, 68–69, 70, 71, 81, 240
Public Enemy: "Brothers Gonna Work It
  Out," 206, 209; Fears of a Black Planet
  (album), 206; "Fight the Power," 61, 70;
  "Power to the People," 206, 208, 209
publishing, academic: anti-Blackness
  policies and practices, 34–44, 37, 40–41,
  201–2; antiracist policies and practices,
  56–57; diversity, equity, and inclusion in,
  93–94. See also journals, scholarly/
  peer-reviewed

race, as social construct, 17–18, 27–28, 55, 56,
  178–79
race consciousness, 48–49
R.A.C.E. (research, advocacy, collaboration,
  and empowerment) Mentoring, 42–43
race neutrality, 49, 52–53
racial battle fatigue, 2, 22–23, 39
racial equality, power dynamics of, 178–79
racial hierarchy, 55, 117, 148, 203
racial homogeneity, 46
racial justice, 19–20, 104
racial myths, 178
racial profiling, 200
racial toxicity, 2, 4
racism: internalized, 50, 62; new/cultural,
  54–55; post-civil rights era, 103–4

racism, institutional, 235, 236–37, 239–40;
  in academic work environment, 2–3;
  administrators' versus students'
  perceptions of, 106–7; transdisciplinary
  approach to, 49–50. See also anti-
  Blackness ideologies, in higher
  education
racism, structural and systemic, 2, 27, 239,
  242, 243; in academic publishing, 47;
  anti-Blackness framework, 18; in
  education, 71; history of, 17; racialized
  violence of, 22–23
rap music, 60, 61, 64, 70
recognition, lack of, 4, 87, 88, 89, 90
recruitment: of Black/minority faculty,
  24, 28, 42, 209, 215, 227, 236; of Black
  students, 38
research: about Black faculty in PWIs and
  MSIs, 242–43; benefits of researchers'
  diversity, 216; on Black males with
  stuttering disability, 228–29; counterstories, 49; cross-racial comparisons, 46, 53,
  54, 55; deficit perspectives, 104; equitable
  focus, 26; as grant source, 26, 43, 65–66,
  85–86, 88; required for tenure and
  promotion, 236
research devaluation, 1–2, 3, 6–7, 19, 22,
  25–26, 37; CRT-based response, 50–58;
  institutional response, 209; methodology issues, 28, 46, 51, 53, 80, 82–83, 85, 93;
  as occupational stress cause, 39–40;
  respectability issue, 46, 51–53, 54, 61;
  through epistemic exclusion, 82–88, 89,
  91–92
respectability politics, 46, 51–53, 54, 61
retention, of Black faculty, 7, 23–24, 27–28,
  37, 42, 79, 90–91, 94, 208–9, 227, 236–37
retention, of Black students, 38
role models, 180, 190, 223–24, 225
Rose, Tricia, Black Noise, 59
Ryerson University (Toronto Metropolitan
  University), 158–59

salaries, 35, 87–88, 91, 92, 127, 149, 202
Sandler, et al, Chilly Classroom Climate: A
  Guide to Improve the Education of Women, 42
Scarborough Charter on Anti-Black Racism
  and Black Inclusion in Canadian Higher
  Education . . . , 160

van Gennep, Arnold, 189
Vega, Blanca Elizabeth, "Lessons from an Administrative Closure . . . ," 105
victim blaming, 42
violence, anti-Black, 5, 8, 19, 22–23, 27, 141–42; in higher education, 117, 202–3; media-based, 203; White responses, 141–42
virtue signaling, 158, 166
voting rights, 201
Voting Rights Act, 204

Walker, Alice, 184; *In Search of Our Mothers' Gardens*, 120–21, 122
Walker, Larry J., 4
Web of Knowledge, 16
West, Cornel, 63, 64, 66, 70, 71; "The Dilemma of the Black Intellectual," 226
White faculty: devaluation of Black colleagues, 150–52, 228, 235–36; predominance, 2, 199–200, 215; retention and tenure, 236
White female faculty, 150–51; gatekeeper role, 150, 152; lack of support for Black colleagues, 150–51, 159; racial microaggressions toward Black colleagues, 122–38
White females, fragility trope, 127–28
White hegemony, 19, 243; anti-Blackness theory of, 19–20; definition, 20; devaluating effect on Black scholarship, 2, 3, 5, 15–16, 19–22, 25, 37, 237–38; implications for Black women, 184; in teacher education, 66–67, 68–69, 72

White male faculty, gatekeeper role, 151–52
White men, 153, 154, 201
White nationalism, 153–54
Whiteness, as property, 68–69, 240
White privilege, 36, 81, 239. *See also* critical race theory; White hegemony
White scholars, cooperative research with Black scholars, 26, 40
White spaces, 66, 98, 101–2, 103–5, 112, 240
White students, benefits of Black faculty for, 215–16, 238
White students, racial incivility toward Black faculty, 142–43, 144–45, 153–56, 165–66, 228; biased evaluations, 185–88, 241–42; institutional equity policies and, 157–60, 163, 164; non-reporting of, 158–59, 163, 164; penalties for, 164, 166
White supremacy, 17, 19, 71, 103, 136–37, 203, 227, 240, 243; CRT-based disruption, 4, 204–5; diversity and inclusion as attack on, 152–53; immigrant communities' alignment with, 147–49; internalized, 62; racist violence of, 202; White students' role, 152, 156
Whiting, Gilman, 192
Wiggins, Carmen, 184
Wilfrid Laurier University, 159–60
Williams, Marsha, 184
woke, 153–54; Stop WOKE act, 200
Women's Rights Convention (1851), 175, 183
Wood, J. Luke, 192
work-life balance, 182
Wu-Tang, 64